MW00575896

Cacaphonies

Cacaphonies

THE EXCREMENTAL CANON OF FRENCH LITERATURE

*****

Annabel L. Kim

University of Minnesota Press
Minneapolis
London

The University of Minnesota Press gratefully acknowledges the financial assistance provided for the publication of this book by the Faculty of Arts and Sciences' Tenure-Track Faculty Publication Fund at Harvard University and by the Murray Anthony Potter Fund of the Department of Romance Languages and Literatures at Harvard University.

A different version of chapter 5 was previously published as "Dans l'béton, dans la merde: Anne Garréta's Intractable Materiality," *Critical Review of Contemporary French Fixxion* 21 (2020): 121–30. A different version of chapter 6 was previously published as "The Excremental Poetics of Daniel Pennac's *Journal d'un corps*," *French Studies* 73, no. 3 (2019): 416–33; Oxford University Press.

Copyright 2022 by the Regents of the University of Minnesota

All rights reserved. No part of this publication may be reproduced, stored in a retrieval system, or transmitted, in any form or by any means, electronic, mechanical, photocopying, recording, or otherwise, without the prior written permission of the publisher.

Published by the University of Minnesota Press
111 Third Avenue South, Suite 290
Minneapolis, MN 55401–2520
http://www.upress.umn.edu

ISBN 978-1-5179-1087-7 (hc)
ISBN 978-1-5179-1088-4 (pb)

A Cataloging-in-Publication record for this book is available from the Library of Congress.

Printed in the United States of America on acid-free paper

The University of Minnesota is an equal-opportunity educator and employer.

UMP BmB 2022

CONTENTS

WE HAVE ALWAYS BEEN FECAL

***

The Frenchman . . . is an animal of Latin race; he has no objection to ordure in his domicile, and in literature he is scatophagous. He delights in excrement.

—Baudelaire, "My Heart Laid Bare"

French literature is full of shit. The medieval and early modern canon is replete with examples: medieval fabliaux such as *Audigier,* which features a coprophilic knight who falls in love with women in proportion to how shit-covered their bottoms are; François Rabelais's *Pantagruel* and *Gargantua,* excremental masterpieces, which feature scatological episodes such as the famous *torche-cul* episode (Gargantua, as part of his princely education, with Edisonian persistence, works through a vast array of bottom-wiping materials— satin, sage, fennel, hay, a cat, a hat, a rug—before settling on a gosling as the best) and the digestive episode wherein the narrator defecates in Pantagruel's giant mouth; and the Marquis de Sade's *Cent vingt journées de Sodome* (*The 120 Days of Sodom*), which regales its readers with coprophagy. This briefest of scatological enumerations does not elicit surprise, and those familiar with French literature will recognize these earlier stagings of the excremental. The lack of surprise seems to map onto contemporary expectations that a literature that predates modern plumbing, when waste management was a much more embodied and direct confrontation with fecal matter than nowadays,

1

would of course pay more attention and give more space to such material matters. But with the advent of modern sanitation systems, literature, it would seem, reflects the more sanitary conditions in which we moderns live—the excremental Rabelaisian body giving way to the modern body that brushes its teeth and bathes regularly.

Bruno Latour, in declaring that "we have never been modern,"[1] deflates this modern fantasy of distinguishing between nature and society. While we dig our heels into this fictive dualism, refusing to let go of the illusion of progress as something that cuts us off from our past, French literature from the last century, despite the advent of the flush toilet, has shed none of the fecality that characterizes its earlier counterparts. The literature produced under modernity recognizes, in ways that society more broadly does not, that we have never been modern, by expressing how we have always been fecal, and will continue to be fecal.[2] This unsheddable fecality, as distasteful a truth as it is to many, needs to be examined, and it is in literature that we can find one of the most productive means of doing so.

The time is ripe for a fecal awakening in French studies. The growing interest we have seen in recent years in mainstream culture—for example, interest in fecal transplants and probiotics aimed at optimizing the microbiome, a book like Giulia Enders's *Gut: The Inside Story of Our Body's Most Underrated Organ* making the bestseller charts internationally, products like Poo-Pourri and the Squatty Potty selling in big-box stores all across the United States—has been matched in scholarship by the emergence of waste studies.[3] An interdisciplinary field, waste studies responds to the urgent ecological, planetary crisis posed by the Anthropocene, a period of planetary change brought about by the production of more and more waste as a species—the result of our excessive consumption. While shit differs from the trash with which it makes up waste studies[4] in that shit is waste produced by bodies whereas trash is waste produced outside our bodies, both fall under the larger umbrella of waste as an imperative to think about production and consumption, about expenditure and excess, and the impact these have on our interconnected world.

Waste studies is deeply attuned to the contemporary stakes of

waste as a question of planetary survival, animated as it is by an
ethical drive to confront our waste and respond to it rather than
continue to disavow it despite the disastrous consequences. While
dominated by work in the social sciences that attends to the political, environmental, economic, and ethical consequences of our waste
management practices[5] (many of waste studies' most important theorists, such as Mary Douglas, Zygmunt Bauman, Gay Hawkins, and
Michael Thompson, come from social science backgrounds),[6] the
literary branch of waste studies is rapidly growing and provides an
important complement to social scientific narratives of waste by attending to its representation, to its presence not just in our physical
world but in our imaginaries as a crucial site of knowledge—aesthetic,
social, and political. Literary waste studies also, importantly, insists
on the connection between the medieval and early modern and
the modern and contemporary. Through its fortuitous intersection
with waste studies, literary studies is beginning to take shit seriously
as a modern question, expanding beyond the important work devoted to the medieval and early modern literary expressions of shit
that have dominated literary studies of excrement to take up modern waste more broadly as one of the most pressing concerns for
our epoch.[7]

Cacaphonies joins this current of literary waste studies to make
sense of the modern French canon's profound excrementality. It attends to shit's presence in this prized, foundational element of French
identity, treating it as a continually uttered desire to manifest the universality that France aspires to but continually fails to realize in its
stubborn refusal to acknowledge difference. *Liberté, égalité, fraternité*—
this slogan that captures France's universalist ambitions? Its best expression is shit—this humble, ubiquitous material that binds all bodies in a shared and inescapable fecality. It is in shit that we find a
concrete universalism that rectifies the violence and shortcomings of
a universalism conceived as abstraction, a crucial point I will return
to later. The universality of shit, which traverses all bodies with complete disregard for the usual embodied forms of difference (e.g., race,
sex, age), has implications for the canon: it brings to the surface the

tension that inheres between the democratic impetus of universality and the logic of singularity that animates the canon.

My desire to extend French literature's fecal through-line through the modern canon takes me to some of France's most celebrated authors: Louis-Ferdinand Céline with his unforgettably fecal narrator, Ferdinand, in *Mort à crédit* (*Death on the Installment Plan*); Samuel Beckett with his flatulent homage to Céline's Ferdinand in *Molloy*; Jean-Paul Sartre's staging of bad and willful defecation in *L'Enfance d'un chef* (*The Childhood of a Leader*); the excremental reverie of Jean Genet's *Notre-Dame-des-Fleurs* (*Our Lady of the Flowers*), where shit and farts provide us with the noblest, truest experience of humanity; Romain Gary's *La Vie devant soi* (*The Life before Us*), which gives us the angry defecator Momo's transformation into the person who wipes the obese Madame Rosa's bottom; Marguerite Duras's haunting description in *La Douleur* (*War*) of Robert Antelme's unhuman shit following his return to Paris from Dachau. And from the ranks of well-respected contemporary French writers, I turn to Anne Garréta's virtuosic word play and cowshit play in *Dans l'béton* (*In Concrete*), and the explosive diarrhea around which Daniel Pennac's *Journal d'un corps* (*Diary of a Body*) is structured.

Cacaphonies poses the question of what all this shit is doing in the works we have canonized or might canonize, which are handed down to every generation of new readers as exemplars of French culture and identity. This book asks us to see the fecal matter that constitutes French literature despite our strong socialization against the fecal. If there is so much fecal matter in these works by writers that matter, it is not there incidentally, as a transgressive garnish that we can brush aside, but as a fundamental component of this literature in its modernity. Why, I ask throughout *Cacaphonies,* is shit essential to the modern French literary enterprise? How does it articulate and elaborate its own necessity? And—a question that we've posed as long as we've been fecal—what are we to do with this shit?

In working on and speaking about this book with others, there have been a few different types of responses that arose repeatedly. Some people were skeptical of the project, wondering if there was a there there, if French literature were really as excremental as I was making it out to be; others responded enthusiastically, imagining that of course this meant I was working on Georges Bataille; yet others assumed I would be engaging psychoanalytically with excrement via Sigmund Freud and Julia Kristeva. The first reaction denotes an incapacity to see all the fecal matter I was seeing everywhere—fecal blindness; the second reaction is the opposite, seeing shit where there actually isn't any (more on Bataille's non-fecality later)—fecal illusion; and the last reaction, which presumes psychoanalysis to be the authoritative interpreter of shit, assumed I would be reading fecal matter *through* something else—fecal filtration. *Cacaphonies* responds to all three types of reactions with, as its title implies, an attentive listening to the plural and varied forms of fecality in modern French literature I feature here, in order to hear what they have to say to us. Rejecting fecal blindness, fecal illusion, and fecal filtration, I attempt in this book to take shit on its own terms.

Unlike our sanitation practices, which would minimize the contact we have with our feces, to the detriment of our environment, my reading practice in *Cacaphonies* is to maximize the contact we have with my corpus's excrement in order to see what it means and does, both actually and potentially. As Susan Signe Morrison puts it, "Excrement, once it is voided from the body, cannot *be* avoided. Excrement's ubiquitous materiality demands attention."[8] This, I realize, is not the most savory enterprise, and to those more sensitive readers, whose socialized aversion to the fecal is deeply ingrained and strong, I apologize in advance: I believe, however, that what this literature's fecality offers is far richer than and outweighs whatever unpleasantness feces elicit.

On a similar note, I believe it is important to employ the term *shit* over the less profane alternatives language offers. I use *shit* as often as I do because the writers I examine here write about *merde* (shit) and use the verb *chier* (to shit) rather than their more polite counterparts. To sanitize my language and evacuate it of shit, leaving only excrement, fecal matter, feces, or waste behind, would be to present a distorted textual experience, one that makes my writers' language cleaner and more assimilable than it is. It is precisely because of the unease or sense of distastefulness that the language of *shit* may provoke that I feel compelled to use it. This is not simply to be provocative but rather, to reproduce, in its apparent vulgarity, the same kind of force and shock that obtain in these texts' confrontations with and productions of fecality. We cannot understand the full force of these texts' staging of shit if we cloak discussion in decorous, felicitous language that smooths over shit's indecorousness and infelicity.[9]

Before providing some context for this project and laying out its critical investments and parameters, I want to first address the fecal blindness, illusion, and filtration that my interlocutors have expressed, as doing so will help sharpen the outlines of my project.

Bataille's Fecal Illusions

Fecal blindness and fecal illusion, while operating in seemingly antipodal ways—the one can't see shit, the other sees shit where it isn't—both constitute a refusal to engage with shit as a material experience. Fecal blindness, in its denial of excrementality, deals with the distasteful matter of fecal matter by refusing to admit its presence and would make modern French literature to be cleaner than it is. Fecal illusion, on the other hand, claims to see shit but, by projecting fecality onto something that lacks it, dematerializes the idea of the fecal by seeing shit only in its less material evocations.

Fecal illusion leads to centering Georges Bataille as the exemplar of an excremental French literature when, in fact, Bataille's corpus is notably non-fecal. Falling for this sleight of fecal hand is understandable: Bataille, after all, produced deeply transgressive literary works that feature the body in extreme situations, as well as critical work theorizing scatology. But scratch the surface of Bataille's writing and while you get plenty of other bodily excretions—saliva, sperm, blood, vomit, and copious amounts of urine—feces are surprisingly absent.

Take *Histoire de l'oeil* (*Story of the Eye*) for instance, which is the text that people most often referred to in assuming my engagement with Bataille. This text has plenty of anality—fingers up anuses, buttocks cracking open eggs, and prolific mentions of *cul* (ass), but all of this without a mention of shit. There's plenty of soiling from literal mud and soil, but no shit. Where shit is evoked is in its preface, "W.C.," and in the curious postface-like "Réminiscences" ("Coincidences") that follows the narrative of the narrator's erotic encounter with Simone. In "W.C.," Bataille explains the meaning of Lord Auch (the pseudonym the novel was published under): "The name Lord Auch [pronounced *osh*] refers to a habit of a friend of mine; when vexed, instead of saying 'aux chiottes!' [to the shithouse], he would shorten it to 'aux ch.' *Lord* is English for God (in the scriptures): Lord Auch is God relieving himself."[10] Bataille goes on to describe helping his blind syphilitic father down from his bed so that he could defecate into a chamber pot. And in "Coincidences," the father makes an appearance again, described as giving off a foul odor because "he sometimes left shit on his pants" (107). Yes, there's shit here, but it's of a different order than the shit we find in the corpus I examine of Céline, Beckett, Sartre, Genet, Duras, Gary, Garréta, and Pennac. Where all these writers align the writerly, narrative position with a direct, physical contact with shit, Bataille always puts distance between himself and shit. In "W.C.," he describes "seeing my father shit a great number of times" (115)—without giving a description of said shit, without giving the reader some kind of engagement with this fecal matter as matter, without himself having a close fecal encounter. He describes smelling shit, but without looking at or touching it. Even the claim that Lord Auch is God in the toilets places the text at a remove from fecality: God, in relieving himself, fills the *chiottes* not with shit but with urine, sperm, blood—the bodily fluids of *Histoire de l'oeil*.

We can find this same distancing from fecality in Bataille's other works. *Le Bleu du ciel* (*Blue of Noon*) implies fecality indirectly when the narrator describes his lover, Dirty, as having a "sour smell of armpit and ass"[11] without indicating explicitly what would account for such a smell. Contrast this to Céline, for example, whose narrator in *Mort à crédit* avows his malodorous bottom and explicitly chalks it up to the layer of shit that is always on it. Just as with Lord Auch's swerve away from the fecality promised by his name, we get a similar swerve in *Le Bleu du ciel* when Xénie, another of the narrator's lovers, describes having seen "a chamber pot in the bathroom full of some whitish liquid, and in the midst of it a drowning fly" (50). Rather than fill the chamber pot with excrement, Bataille here has filled it with a whitish liquid that is most likely sperm. The excremental is gestured to by the naming of an excremental object—the chamber pot—but it is present only allusively, in its absence.

In the same passage, the narrator opens "an avant-garde magazine" and reads a sentence "in which a country priest retrieves a heart with a pitchfork from a pile of manure" (50). There's distance folded in between the reader and shit here. Shit is not materially present in the narrative space—the narrator reads aloud from a magazine about shit that's not there with him. The description of the magazine as being avant-garde, read surrealist,[12] creates a certain aesthetic distance from shit via the scene's oneiric nature, which we expect from surrealism.

The shit gestured to here does not have the same kind of fecal impact as a writing of shit that attends to its materiality. This sort of writing is to shit what indirect speech is to direct speech. The same strategy of evoking an indirect contact-free shit is repeated later when the narrator rants about fans of Sade, shouting out "Did any of them eat shit? Yes or no?" (68). Here again, Bataille takes a distance from shit that the writers I treat in *Cacaphonies* do not, that Sade himself does not. Where Sade gives us coprophagy, Bataille gives us speculation about coprophagy. Bataille's shit is intertextual and rendered immaterial: what is present is the gesture of pointing to rather than the object being pointed at.[13] In Bataille, shit is never proper to the narrative, never necessary to the narrative in the same way as with my corpus here.

And yet, fecal illusion works to propagate a narrative wherein Bataille is cast as *the* scatological figure par excellence. In the case of *Le Bleu du ciel,* readers noted "his marked interest for toilets [*cabinets*] (the word occurs seven times in the novel)," which resulted in his being attacked by the surrealist André Thirion as a "theorist of shit."[14] Besides the fact that seven times in the course of a novel does not seem like a particularly high number as to warrant being described as a sign of marked interest, the toilets are mentioned those seven times not in a defecatory context but in an emetic one—the narrator spends much of his time in the novel vomiting in the *cabinets*. Then, as now, fecal illusion tied Bataille much more strongly to fecality than he ever warranted.

Bataille is not the scatological center of modern French literature, but rather a *mouche à merde* (shit fly)[15] that circles around the shit that other authors produce and that he cannot bring himself to produce. As his narrator puts it nicely, "I was sorry my bedpan wasn't full—I would have chucked the shit in her face" (94). In short, Bataille has shit envy but that desire does not translate to narrating a present, material fecality: Bataille's shit is truly obscene in the etymological sense of being offstage. Even in his evocation of scatology in his critical work, there is no scat, save through whatever horizon of fecal expectation the use of that particular word establishes. Instead, Bataille shifts immediately to heterology, where scatology is cast as the science or study of the other.[16] Certainly, it's not difficult to see how this could be applied toward scatology in its usual sense to think through the way feces map onto alterity, but what is important to me here is the way Bataille still shies away from admitting the material dimension of scat in his treatment of scatology, immediately transforming shit into an abstraction. We can see this same abstracting tendency in Bataille's *La Part maudite* (*The Accursed Share*) where, in a work on waste and expenditure, his theorization of a purportedly general economy neatly ignores the digestive economy as a source for thinking about consumption and excess. The concrete example to which Bataille turns is not digestion, which is precisely the process by which we consume and produce/expel an excessive, non-recuperable element, but rather, the solar abundance of sunlight as a notably immaterial form of unquenchable energy.[17] Bataille, if he can be said to produce shit, produces shit without substance. Bataille's shit, like Plato's, is ideal, which makes it not shit at all and excludes it from excrementality.

Excretion is not excrement, despite the shared etymological root in *excernere,* "to sift out." Excretion diverges from excrement along material lines: excrement carries with it material, solid connotations that excretion does not. So it is that when you look at the definition of *excrement,* the *Oxford English Dictionary* indicates that it refers primarily to "waste matter discharged from the bowels" whereas the older definitions that encompassed liquid waste products such as urine are all qualified as being either rare or obsolete. *Merriam-Webster's* puts things much more bluntly, defining excrement as "waste matter discharged from the body *especially:* FECES," providing as *excrement's* synonyms the notably fecal constellation of "dirt, doo-doo, dropping, dung, excreta, feces, ordure, poop, scat, slops, soil, waste."

What does it mean that so many people would point me toward Bataille as a kind of excremental center or touchstone for my project when Bataille, while filled with excreting bodies, lacks excremental ones? What Bataille—and the way he has been taken up and read as excremental despite a lack of excrementality—points to is the way his work is perceived as having excremental form even as it lacks excremental substance and matter. But, and this is one of the central points in *Cacaphonies,* excrement is matter—hence the matter in fecal matter, which evinces a materiality not attributed to urine, which we do not call urinary matter, or to saliva, which we do not call salivary matter, or to sperm, which we do not call seminal matter. This materiality is key because it allows shit's universality to resist abstraction: to stay, stubbornly, in the realm of the concrete.

Bataille's bodies are certainly very wet and leaky, but they do not produce matter the way the bodies in *Cacaphonies'* corpus do. Bataille, for all that he's associated with literature's transgressive potential,[18] does not transgress the fecal taboo. He tiptoes around shit, assuming adjacency without ever actually handling it. Despite wanting to force art to counter the sublime, to force it to acknowledge its base materialism—a move that would abolish the hierarchy inhering in other forms of materialism by placing so-called base, or low, matter on the same level as high, idealized matter[19]—and despite understanding the way the high depends on the low, the way the ideal is built on the base, Bataille never really confronted the base materialism of fecality. In

aesthetic accounts of base materialism, such materialism is associated
with the formless (*l'informe*), which he sees as a "term that serves to
bring things down [*déclasser*] in the world." Formlessness thwarts the
categorizing, classifying will to form that characterizes philosophy for
Bataille: "All of philosophy has no other goal: it is a matter of giving
a frock coat to what is, a mathematical frock coat."[20] Such widespread
formlessness, which would transform the universe into "something
like a spider or spit,"[21] is at the heart of Bataille's anti-hierarchical
project, which explains perhaps why he would swerve away from shit,
which, in its usual manifestations, takes on the form of the turd. Even
as diarrhea, which might appear to be less material and more formless than the turd, shit still holds out the promise of being matter, as
the turd is simply liquid feces that have been properly processed by
the colon, which absorbs water. Fecal matter's destiny, if you will, is
matter and form.

Fecal illusion—the desire to see shit where it isn't, the desire to
allow allusion/illusion to pass as presence—is an indicator of just how
disruptive, unnerving, and disquieting fecal matter is. For being one
of the most banal and unrelenting sites of an encounter with materiality that we as embodied creatures have, shit is also one that triggers
the strongest disavowal. But it is this very disavowal that is itself disavowed by Céline, Beckett, Sartre, Genet, Gary, Duras, Garréta, and
Pennac, who put shit to various literary, ethical, and political uses.
Rather than perform fecal sleights-of-hand, these writers confront us
with a shit that is anything but illusive/allusive/elusive.

Selfless Shit: Theorizing Fecality Otherwise
Attending to my corpus's fecality requires shedding fecal blindness
and illusion, and it also requires suspending the will to fecal filtration—
the will to read shit through something else. Again, in fecal filtration,
we find the desire to attenuate the consequences of confronting shit
as a material, embodied experience. The predominant filter for fecality that we have currently is psychoanalysis, which has a monopoly
on accounting for what shit signifies. But psychoanalysis effectively
dematerializes shit by mapping psychical structures onto it.

In "Character and Anal Erotism," Freud famously formalizes an equivalence between gold and feces, drawing on folklore to do so.[22] This feces–gold equation is doubly dematerializing, first transforming fecal matter not so much into another substance—gold—but what that substance signifies—wealth—which enables Freud to tie miserliness to fecal retentiveness as a child, which constitutes a second act of dematerialization, turning feces into a stand-in for personality or psychology. Freud elsewhere ties feces tightly to the self, positing that "feces are the child's first *gift,* the first sacrifice on behalf of his affection, a portion of his own body which he is ready to part with, but only for the sake of someone he loves."[23] Finally, Freud attends to the physical sensations of defecation to link feces to libido, where pleasurable sensations obtain around controlling defecation, which becomes an erotogenic activity.[24] While here, feces might seem to be attended to in their material dimension, as attention is paid to physical sensation, this still constitutes a swerving away from the matter of fecal matter: feces, while engaged with physically, are turned into the abstract notion of sexuality, so that the focus is not on the fecal matter in itself but on the response to feces—pleasure, gratification—which again ends up shoring up a focus on the self as a psychical entity.

This same focus on our psychical structures applies to Julia Kristeva's post-Freudian theory of abjection. In *Pouvoirs de l'horreur* (*Powers of Horror*), Kristeva attends to the way certain objects—corpses, open wounds, shit, the skin that forms on warm milk—cause a reaction of horror and disgust that signals a breakdown in meaning following from a breakdown in the distinction between self and other. These material objects, which remind us of our own materiality, send us into a psychical crisis that, according to Kristeva, can be resolved through religion or art, which serve to regulate and purify the abject, providing the threatened subject with a cathartic, mediated experience of abjection. Unlike Freud, Kristeva ties abjection (and by extension, fecality) to language, and more specifically, to literature, where it is avant-garde, disruptive, innovative literature (like that of Céline, whose *Voyage au bout de la nuit* [*Journey to the End of the Night*] occupies a central position in *Pouvoirs de l'horreur*) that serves to protect the secular subject from abjection by regulating it, taking over that function from religion, which was the social structure we had in place to deal with abjection through purity codes and rituals.[25] As with Freud, Kristevan readings of fecality through abjection take the self and its psychic structures as the beginning and end of any reading.

I am not saying that psychoanalytic readings of shit are invalid or uninteresting, but rather, that their dominance in the realm of shit exegesis has cut off other possibilities that we should consider, and that readily present themselves if we set aside fecal filtration as our hermeneutical instinct when it comes to dealing with shit.[26] Psychoanalytic fecal filtration forecloses other possibilities for reading fecality and flattens feces into a rather narrow identitarian frame, where thinking shit begins and ends with the self, the psyche. Where Freud and Kristeva tell us what shit stands for within narrowly defined strictures of the self, *Cacaphonies,* by trying to take shit on its own terms, demonstrates instead what shit *does,* how it crosses any number of boundaries, proving itself to be a material marked by its many potentialities—for narrative, for ethics, for politics, for art.

Psychoanalysis sublimates shit, turns it into concept, into symbol. Shit is never itself, it always stands for something else. Literature, rather than turn shit into a concept, demonstrates how shit itself conceptualizes within the narrative framework of a text. Rather than creating shit in our own image, *Cacaphonies* attempts to discern the way shit is its own figuration. Attending to my corpus's cacaphonies makes clear that shit is not a psychological material whose telos is subjectivity but rather, a conceptual and creative material that builds something other than the self, something other than what the self would embed in or assimilate to itself.

Shit purges literature of the self in ways that resonate with the physical experience of defecation, which is also an emptying out of self. The readerly encounter with literature has so often been cast as one that is anchored in the self, as when people claim literature as an object that produces empathy, allowing the reader to inhabit someone else's skin, to identify with someone different. This celebration of literature as a site of identification is one I hear regularly from my students when I ask them why they read, and it can also be found in scholarship, as with Lynn Hunt's *Inventing Human Rights,* which argues that reading practices, and the empathy they engendered, enabled the conception of human rights that emerged in the eighteenth century.[27]

For me, literature has never been such a self-centered experience (while the acquisition of empathy and the promotion of acceptance of difference are certainly not selfish experiences, they are deeply self-centered in that there is a self required to acquire such qualities). I recognize that this kind of subjective reading is rewarding and offers up pleasures to the reader, but I would argue that this kind of reading only serves to reinforce hierarchy—the kind of hierarchy against which shit, as a leveling material, works—for where there is identity, there is a subject, and where there is a subject, there is subjugation and the unequal exercise of power.[28]

I read literature because it is a form of thought, which enables me to understand and experience not the self but the world that exists outside the self and makes it possible. Literature theorizes, and the shit in literature theorizes, too. *Cacaphonies'* literary theorization of fecality cuts across literary, ethical, and political lines, positing shit as a universal material that operates as a sign and vector of radical equality and contains transformative potential in its fertilizing capacity, by which inassimilable waste becomes a growth medium. Examined in its fecality, literature turns into something other than the endless confirmation of identitarian desire, in which the world is reproduced in fiction only to reflect back to the reader who they are, enabling the reader to shore up their sense of self, to feel secure within their psychical structures. Instead, this literary theorization turns its conceptual crosshairs on itself, on literature, by pointing to the ways literature itself needs to undergo this egalitarian leveling as a precondition for growth and renewal.

When we follow this anti-identitarian logic to its conclusion, the excremental canon calls for freedom from the canon (or, more precisely, as I discuss in the conclusion, freedom *within* the canon), from these structures that have been used to shore up national identities in their classed, raced, and gendered dimensions. Bataille wasn't incorrect in associating scatology with alterity, but that alterity doesn't inhere in shit. Shit is very much not other, as it comes from the very deepest, most visceral part of ourselves: it is what pushes us to turn toward what we deem other only to negate that assignation of alterity through shit's leveling action. We do not assimilate shit but shit assimilates us.

"The Frenchman . . . Delights in Excrement"

By taking French literature as my object, my aim isn't to claim some kind of scatological exceptionalism for France, doing with shit what France has done with concepts such as human rights and democracy, claiming them as universal values while touting itself as their original and most perfect exemplar and practitioner.[29] What I can posit, however, is a specificity to the French language's (and hence its literature's) entanglement with shit that is lacking in Anglophone literature, for instance, because English, as a language, is not as fecally invested as French.

I first became attuned to this fecal specificity when thinking about what gets lost in translation between French and English. The French language, in its most quotidian manifestations, is replete with excrementally tinged words. Where, in French, it is commonplace to exclaim "Ça me fait chier!," in English, we would never cry out, "That makes me shit!" in response to a frustrating situation. "Fuck you" can be rendered in French as "Je t'emmerde" and the urinary connotation of "to piss off" is replaced with the excremental in *emmerder*. Profane language aside, we can find the imbrication of everyday language with the excremental in such non-profane utterances as "Ça va?," popularly described as originating from the French monarchic practice of defecating in public, where the *Ça* in "Ça va" would refer then to the act of defecation.[30] Metonymically, we find *cul*, from which shit emerges, embedded in everyday, non-profane words such as *reculer*: where, in English, we would talk about backing up, French draws our attention to the ass that's below the back. The same goes for *acculer,* "to corner": in English, the emphasis is on the space in which one finds oneself stuck, whereas in French, the emphasis is on where your ass is. *Cul* serves as a kind of point of reference in French and has a phenomenological status that is missing in English.

If we trace the etymological trajectory of *merde* in French, we can see notable divergences from the English case that point to the French lexical field around shit being richer and more complex than its English counterpart. Where *shit* enters English first as a verb in the fourteenth century (around 1335, according to the *OED*), it does not come to mean excrement nominatively until the 1580s, even though it was used to refer to an offensive or obnoxious person earlier, in 1508. English thus features a phased-in process by which shit begins first as an action before coming to function as a noun, assuming its figurative sense well before its literal sense, and it would not be until the nineteenth century (1865) that it would be recorded being used as an interjection. Lexically speaking, in English, shit was kind of diaphanous or amorphous before, fairly recently, in the nineteenth century, coming to assume all of the meanings and uses we ascribe to shit today.

French is precocious when it comes to shit. *Merde,* according to the *Trésor de la langue française,* emerged around 1179, over 150 years before *shit* did in English, and from its earliest instance, it was used as an interjection and had both literal and figurative connotations. Interestingly, in French, shit didn't exist as a verb until the advent of *chier* (*merder* exists, but dates considerably later to 1596), which emerged in 1202. Despite the split between the nominative and verbal forms of shit in French, the fact remains that even with the later *chier,* French was still a century ahead of English in having a language for shit. French, as a language, records thus a certain intuition or sensibility that perceived the multivalence and polysemy of shit, speaking both to its formal, material capacity and to its conceptual, abstract one.

What strikes me as being particularly noteworthy is that *merde* and *chier,* which are now considered to be profane and vulgar language, actually predate all the more polite words we have to refer to excrement. *Chier* (ca. 1202), for instance, predates *défequer* by over six centuries: *défequer* would only come to mean *defecate* in 1886 whereas it was used from the sixteenth century (1583) on to refer to the process of clarification—of removing impurities from a liquid. *Excréter* would have to wait until the nineteenth century as well (1836) and the regal and litotic *faire* wasn't used to refer to defecation until the eighteenth century. For the nominative forms of shit, *déchet* doesn't emerge until toward the end of the thirteenth century (1270s), a century after *merde*; *matière* becomes corporeal around 1256; *ordure* doesn't take on an excremental connotation until the beginning of the fourteenth century (1316) and it's around 1372 that *diarrhée* comes into existence as a word; *selles* takes on its metonymical excremental meaning toward the end of the fourteenth century; *excrément, caca, déjection,* and *fèces* don't emerge until the sixteenth century. (While correlation isn't causation, this relative proliferation of excremental terms maps onto the period when Rabelais lived and wrote.)

The linguistic history of and around fecality aligns with Norbert Elias's theory of the civilizing process, which tracks the way medieval and early modern European culture progressively began conditioning bodies, producing a culture of shame, which, as we have seen, had linguistic consequences.[31] We started out in shit and it was only as we became "civilized" across the centuries that we started to have terms like excrement and feces—the terms we use now. Our language cleaned up just as our bodies did. Elias has been criticized for a teleological bent to his work, which would map civilization and progress onto each other, but the narrative of civilization is a telling one, as it shows us to what extent we want to disavow our shit roots. But French literature, in its modern iteration in the last century, takes shit as its ground, refusing the cultured veneer that is applied by our supposed modernity and the benefits of modernization. The excremental French literature I examine gives lie to the myth of modernity and progress. It confronts and reclaims the fundamental truth of our inescapable fecality and posits a continuity between modern literature and its earlier counterparts.

French literature is able to see what a civilizational narrative would deny—the fecality that has always marked human experience and the formal and conceptual potential of a fecal matter that has, in the French context, always joined the figurative and the literal, the abstract and the concrete. This particularly French fecal intuition is borne out, again, in the history of its language, if we look to what other terms for shit emerged at the same time as *merde* and *chier*. As we've seen, all the polite terms took their sweet time to emerge, but *fiente* (liquid excrement—used most often to refer to bird shit, but not only), *crotte* (solid excrement), and *étron* (turd) all come into use at around the same time as *merde* and *chier*. While French took a while to clean up its language, its history evinces an interest in shit's formal capacities from the very beginning, from its entrance into the French language. This French fecal word mapping reveals that users of language were interested in what shit looked and felt like: Is it liquid? Is it solid? What kind of solid?[32]

From the lexical beginning, French has been invested in shit as a formal matter in addition to the simultaneous polysemic investment that we see in the French use of shit language. This etymological investment in shit's formal capacities is shared by the writers I examine in *Cacaphonies*. Each writer I include here demonstrates an interest in and awareness of shit as a material, formal, and conceptual object that they work on and with. My writers, in writing the excremental, strip away French literature's cachet—they lay bare this object that has been touted as a fundamental part of the French civilizing mission and of French national identity, and return us to that foundational fecal state that socialization has papered over. In reading shit, we are returned to that felicitous lexical nexus, which is where we can have a visceral experience of language and literature as a formal, material, and conceptual affair—malleable, transformative, abundant.

A Twentieth-Century Affair

While you may consent to the Frenchness of *Cacaphonies*' corpus, you may wonder why I begin in the twentieth century and not in the nineteenth,[33] which is arguably the beginning of the period we call the modern. The long nineteenth century, after all, is an important period of transition from the grotesque Rabelaisian body to the current regime of cleanliness we live under, with all the political consequences that shift entails.[34] Literarily speaking, however, the nineteenth century is where shit, understood as a deeply embodied experience, disappears from literature. A caveat: this absence I am remarking on is observed in *canonical* nineteenth-century literature—such established figures as Honoré de Balzac, Émile Zola, Gustave Flaubert. It is possible that there are extracanonical nineteenth-century texts featuring the kind of strong fecality we find in *Cacaphonies'* corpus, but what is significant is the way the nineteenth-century texts we have retained as important purge shit, departing from the literature that comes before and after it.[35]

This is not to say that the nineteenth-century canon is devoid of fecality. Victor Hugo describes the sewers in *Les Misérables* in the chapter titled "L'Intestin de Léviathan" ("The Intestine of Leviathan") and mourns the throwing away of so much human waste that could be turned into fertilizer, Gustave Flaubert memorably places Rodolphe's seduction of Emma in *Madame Bovary* at the agricultural fair as they're walking on and around manure, and Émile Zola famously compares Nana to a plant growing out of fertilizer and a "mouche d'or" (golden blowfly)—a fly feeding on excrement and cadavers. These examples of nineteenth-century fecality, however, depart from both their early modern and twentieth-century counterparts insofar as they move away from the quotidian, banal, visceral, and embodied experience of fecality that we find in literature before and after it to turn it into a way of thinking not about the individual body as a fecal one but about the social body as one that seeks, over the course of the century, to distance itself from the corporeality that its early modern predecessors had centered in their cultural production. The nineteenth-century French bourgeoisie renounced the physical body.[36]

Early modern shit, though it had powerful symbolic effects (e.g., Rabelais's carnivalesque subversion of power structures, as theorized by Mikhail Bakhtin; Sadean destruction of social norms), was always written as a deeply material substance, of which the reader was assumed to have an intimate, visceral understanding.[37] Corporeality was a given, and this corporeality, which is a fecal one, becomes unmoored from literature in the nineteenth century as the corporeal is transformed into metaphor. It's in the nineteenth century, with the advent of a new kind of project of modernity—urbanization, Napoleonic conquest and expansive settler colonialism, industrial capitalism—that shit is deployed as a metaphor for all the social entities that the bourgeoisie would like to purge from its social body.

The examples of Hugo, Flaubert, and Zola given above have as their backdrop the discursive transformation of prostitutes, poor people / the underworld (*les bas fonds*), the colonies, all manner of "corruption" into excrement as a rhetorically potent symbol of all the undesirable elements that must be continually expelled by the bourgeois body politic.[38] The body that matters is the social body. Zola is not interested in Nana as an individual body but as a sign of the degeneration he tracks in his epic *Rougon-Macquart* cycle as a hereditary phenomenon and threat to the health of the French body politic. Hugo, in his description of the sewers, wages a critique of the social body, not, as is the case of Zola, in tracking the physical and psychological effects of degeneration, but by pointing to the excesses and wastefulness of a mercilessly acquisitive bourgeoisie that lead to the oppression of *les misérables*. Flaubert's deployment of manure is a deft literary maneuver that allows the whole culture of *Madame Bovary*—from the pharmacist Homais's social climbing pretensions to Emma's pop culture–informed romantic delusions, from Rodolphe's investment in an increasingly impotent aristocracy to Charles's dumb credulity—to be skewered parodically as being a whole lot of shit. All these examples of shit use it as an illustration for something else rather than as the site of a material encounter with embodiment and the convergence of body with text. And beyond this mobilization of shit as metaphor, as befits the century of miasma theory (wherein noxious odors were considered a major threat to public health), shit also becomes dematerialized, transformed into a kind of atmospheric presence—as seen, for example, in Balzac's novels that describe characters tromping through the mud of city streets, which the nineteenth-century reader would have known was not just mud but also shit.

Even as nineteenth-century literature was severing shit from the corporeality in which it had been anchored in previous centuries, it was an issue of considerable importance. Christophe Bonneuil and Jean-Baptiste Fressoz, in their history of the Anthropocene, describe the nineteenth century as a period where expanding urbanization placed increased pressure on the food supply chain to be more productive, such that the question of human waste became central to pressing agricultural concerns.[39] Indeed, excrement transcended agricultural concerns to have profound economic, political, and social implications: "The fate of excrement is at the heart of essential debates. It is linked to the social insofar as an impoverished soil leads to famines, poverty, and revolutions; to the fate of civilizations (Rome, according to Liebig, fell because it didn't know how to manage its excrement); to geopolitics as seen in Britain's monopoly over guano from Peru; to health and hence the degeneration of populations."[40] Shit was everywhere, on everyone's minds, but in literature as in the sociopolitical debates of the day, the shit was transposed from the plane of individual, embodied experience to the plane of collective social ordering. French literature would have to wait until the twentieth century to take back up the continuous thread of an embodied, material fecality that the nineteenth century had tried to cut.

Fecal Ethics

Why does the twentieth century mark a return to the excrementality of excrement, to excrement as excrement? Perhaps it has something to do with the kind of war and technologies of violence that emerge in the twentieth century in contrast to the much more traditional, limited warfare of the nineteenth century. The twentieth century's wars made it impossible not to be attentive to the corporeal in the ways they mutilated millions of soldiers: the First World War, for instance, gave rise to the rumor of the basket case—a term denoting a soldier having lost all four limbs, thus needing to be carried around in a basket. This is the kind of traumatic embodiment that Céline writes from and after in *Voyage au bout de la nuit,* where the reader is regaled with guts and blood galore. I would argue that the fecality of the twentieth century is intimately bound up with the way the body becomes exposed and targeted in its vulnerability in this century of unprecedented violence and bloodshed. The twentieth-century body becomes a necropolitical one, to borrow Achille Mbembe's term, in which war, as Mbembe puts it, is "the sacrament of our times."[41]

With the convergence of the sacramentalization of war, of the so-called right to expose bodies to death, with the disembodying, de-materializing, disindividuating logic of capitalism and the difference-invested ideology of the straight mind (what Monique Wittig posits as the ontological mutilation of innumerable persons based on the naturalization of difference into hierarchy, a naturalization that takes the body as its target),[42] the twentieth-century body is a particularly ethically charged site.

The necropolitical comes to us from a political perspective. From a literary perspective, poet Joyelle McSweeney riffs off Mbembe to theorize the necropastoral as the recognition—exemplarily manifested in literature—that "the premier celebrity resident of Arcadia is Death."[43] For McSweeney, life in the Anthropocene, in this necropolitical, mass-extinctive moment, is death.[44] This imbrication of life with death, of life experienced as death, death experienced as life, captures the troubling multivalence of shit as a material that embodies this paradox: shit reminds us of decay, the decomposing, rotting death that awaits us, and yet it is, as fertilizer, a medium for life. This mutual contamination of life with death, death with life, is shit's nature.

Shit's double nature is felt especially keenly as an ethical issue in the context of the death-saturated twentieth century that produced the idea of the Anthropocene—this death sentence in which we live. How can excrementality possibly be an ethical figure for thinking twentieth-century culture when what we have seen over and over again in this past century is the wholesale massacre and destruction of peoples, posited on their reduction to shit, of which the Holocaust provides, in recent history, arguably the most horrific and catastrophic example.[45] In a post-Holocaust moment, can one possibly justify a humanistic project that would seek to take up culture—so closely tied to human identity—and treat it as shit? By reading a notorious anti-Semite like Céline as well as Holocaust narratives like those of Romain Gary and Marguerite Duras, don't I risk skirting too closely to an ethical edge that, if crossed over, would lend itself to a culture of escalating dehumanization that we ought to be combating, not inadvertently abetting?

This ethical question is an important one, but I see the excrementality of modern French literature as a remedy for the kind of dehumanization wrought by the identification of some persons with a subhumanness for which shit is the referent. Shit is a pharmakon, both poison and remedy. The shit of the poison is different, though, than the shit that is the remedy. The poisonous, unethical shit is shit that has been stripped of its universal, embodied context—the fact that we are all, every single one of us, fecal bodies—to serve, simply, as a signifier for what is base, abject, worthy of our disdain and disgust. Dehumanizing shit, in other words, is shit that refuses to recognize its shared, universal bodily provenance—that refuses to see that it finds an origin in every single body. The ethical shit that would remedy the dehumanizing potential of shit is, by contrast, shit that sends us back to a shared experience of the embodied vulnerability of which defecation is the quotidian reminder. Treating someone like shit is only dehumanizing if we refuse to recognize our fecality as something that levels whatever kinds of distinction humans would erect to partition humankind and binds us together in a universal embodiedness.

It's through disavowing the quotidian experience of fecality that shit is cast away from us as something that is not us, not of us. And yet it is us, and it is of us, as felt in its inseparability from our sense of embodied self when it is inside us, as seen in our confrontations with our bowel movements, knowing that it was our body and not someone else's that produced that matter. It is when we refuse shit as something of and from us that the distance created by such fecal disavowal allows for the likening of humans to shit to participate in a dehumanizing, necropolitical logic. If we all claim our fecality and acknowledge that we are shit (at least in part), then to identify someone—Jew, Palestinian, Uyghur, et cetera—with shit is to claim that they are part of us, is to recognize a shared humanity. It is when we refuse our fecal constitution that persons can be *reduced* to shit by placing shit in the position of baseness. When we accept our fecality as an intrinsic and necessary dimension of our humanity, the likening of persons to shit loses its toxic meaning. Shit, when taken and accepted in its smearing solidity—rather than an abject, repulsive object to be expelled and disavowed—is a vector for solidarity, for a concrete universalism that rectifies the failures of the abstract universalism that has passed itself off as the one and only universalism.

Fecal Universalism

Ever since the French revolutionaries articulated an abstract universalism to serve as the foundation for the new republic they were attempting to create,[46] that universalism has been subject to vociferous critique, both by its believers and its detractors. As Maurice Samuels has shown in *The Right to Difference: French Universalism and the Jews,* which historicizes a concept that has proven remarkably resistant to historicization, universalism has been the object of both internal and external critique: its believers disagree on whether universalism should be assimilationist or pluralist—whether universalism requires the abolition of difference or whether it can accommodate it[47]—and its detractors point to how universalism has always been used as an alibi for domination of those subjects who are excluded from the universalist compact, with the rhetoric of equality papering over the power differentials it would seek to conceal.[48]

The issue is not with the ideal of radical equality that universalism represents, but with the attempts at realizing it, which have always left out groups marked by difference. False universalism—where a particular identity appropriates the status of the universal for itself so that men get to be purportedly neutral, universal subjects in contrast to gendered women in their particularity; whites the centered, generic, unmarked subject in contrast to racialized individuals; and all other configurations where *universal* becomes synonymous with *majoritarian* and *particular* becomes synonymous with *minoritarian*—is the only sort of universalism that the world has known. The political failure, both French and otherwise, to realize true universalism, or what Naomi Schor calls "utopian universalism," has led Schor, among others, to question whether universalism is doomed to failure by *requiring* exclusion "as though by definition."[49]

If universalism has always failed, the fault lies in its having been conceived (in both French and American contexts) as an inherently abstract concept. Universalism, the much-touted brainchild of the Enlightenment, was devised, in Cartesian fashion, as a concept cut off from a suspect and incompatible corporeality. As Joan Scott argues, in the French case, "both the nation and the individual are abstractions, not reflections of social groups or persons," and it is this abstraction that would be "the foundation of a successful politics."[50] Scott explains why this abstract universalism would have to exclude women: "Embodiment, after all, was the opposite of abstraction; hence women could not be abstract individuals."[51] (Even though men have bodies, those bodies were figured as neutral, the reference in relation to which leaking and parturient bodies, in their femaleness, were marked as different, animalistic, in contrast to cogitating man.) Replace *women* in Scott's formulation with any other kind of marked or minoritized form of embodied subject—for example, *Jews, homosexuals, poor people* (these examples demonstrate the tendency to attribute bodily difference to any kind of minoritarian identity, be it the caricatural hook nose, the elusive gay gene, or a set of rotted teeth)—and you can see how universalism's originary abstraction sets the stage for all the exclusions that would be made in its name following that first radical revolutionary Declaration of the Rights of Man and the Citizen.

This inegalitarian loophole that abstraction built into universalism extends beyond the French case, as Saidiya Hartman shows, writing about American slavery and its wake: "Citizenship presupposed the equality of abstract and disembodied persons, and this abstraction disguised the privileges of white men. The presumed whiteness and maleness of the citizen transposed the particular into the universal, thus enabling white men to enjoy the privileges of abstraction and a noncorporeal universality."[52] The privileges of abstraction and a noncorporeal universality were, in effect, human rights. The foundational lie of Enlightenment universalism was its claiming human rights as universal, when, as seen in its exclusion of women and Black people—the two parties most visibly excluded from the universalist Declaration—rights were anything but. Not everyone is born with rights, not everyone is born free. But it is the abstract, conceptual nature of rights that would lead to, as Schor puts it, "one of the foundational paradoxes of post-Revolutionary France that those left out of the universalist compact readily enlisted the very principles of the Declaration to press their own claims: for example, feminists (from Olympe de Gouges to Simone de Beauvoir) and the 'Black Jacobins' of Haiti."[53] White men, as the model for the abstract citizen, were able to exercise the privileges of being endowed with human rights for themselves alone, while those without rights were able to desire and aspire to those privileges because of their promise of universality, where universality was, in effect, a promissory note that was never honored.

If the problem with universalism is its abstraction and noncorporeality, then, it would stand to reason, the solution would be a concrete and corporeal universalism. A concrete universalism that is not also explicitly corporeal, however, cannot fully realize its promise. Aimé Césaire, in his universalist aspirations, envisioned "a universal enriched by all that is particular, a universal enriched by every particular: the deepening and coexistence of all particulars."[54] Césaire's utopian universalism is grounded in the concreteness and situatedness of lived experience, but this lived experience is already somewhat abstracted in its distance from the bodies that are our point of contact and interface with the world we live in. Not to acknowledge the condition of embodiment that grounds particular experience is to have but a partial view of universality, and a universality not fully seen, is, I would argue, not truly universal.

Fecality provides the opportunity to ground the universal in something that is concrete and corporeal, even to the point of revulsion. But as distasteful as fecality is for most, I would argue that it is the only form of corporeal universality and of universality tout court that we can accede to. Unlike human rights, fecality is truly universal. Everyone defecates. Even if the sanitary conditions in which one def-

ecates are not universal, with unequal access to sanitation constituting a major global health crisis, the fact of defecating is. The means of
defecating are also not universal—those with colostomy bags bypass
the rectum to defecate through a stoma—but the fact of defecating is.

In order to show how a true universalism must be concrete
through being corporeal, I want to discuss two previous proposals
for correcting abstract universalism, neither of which is able to reach
the level of immediate, visceral embodiment and concreteness that
fecality entails: (1) the French feminist *parité* movement, which, in the
1990s, sought to redefine the abstract citizen as a sexed one so that
women would be represented in equal numbers as men in government; and (2) Judith Butler's proposal of precarity as the basis for a
kind of universalism in *Frames of War: When Is Life Grievable?*

The *parité* movement tried to formulate their argument as being
purely abstract, redefining the abstract individual as characterized
by an anatomical dualism that was itself also abstract—that is, free
from the concrete trappings of the meanings imputed onto this dualism via social, cultural, as well as biological discourses. This was
a project that could not but fail: as Joan Scott writes, "The problem
was that it was hard to detach bodies from the meanings attributed
to them, especially since the meanings usually offered nature as their
justification. . . . The arguments slid easily from the register of abstraction to the register of embodiment."[55] A larger problem of *parité*,
however, was that it attempted to redefine the abstract individual to
make it accommodate sex but no other form of difference, like race.
The *paritaristes* were driven by the desire to include only one group
of excluded humans in the universalist compact—women. A goal so
partial could not but be doomed to failure in attaining the universal.[56]

There is nothing partial about Butler's universal argument for
precarity as the condition that binds all humans. Precarity, she writes,
"cuts across identity categories as well as multicultural maps" and
would thus be a superior political foundation to the identity subtend-
ing a fracturing identity politics.[57] Butler moves away from a rights-
based discourse that asserts the equality of different identity groups
and instead focuses on a universalism of precariousness. All lives, she

says, are precarious, requiring certain basic things like food, water, and shelter in order to be sustained. Having more of the available resources obscures the precariousness of privileged lives, but does not change the fact of the precarity of all life: "No amount of will or wealth can eliminate the possibilities of illness or accident for a living body, although both can be mobilized in the service of such an illusion."[58] Our precarity is clearly tied to our corporeality as a condition of vulnerability and mortality, and this universal fact is seen as opening a new kind of politics focusing on the basic needs of all people, on their equality in the face of precariousness's inescapability.

The primary difference between a universalism of precarity and a fecal universalism is that precarity can be denied or forestalled, even if only illusorily. Put another way, precarity hovers over all humanity as a possibility that is realized to differing degrees: because of the inegalitarian nature of political and economic structures, some people—that is to say, some bodies—are decidedly more or less precarious, even if the risk of vulnerability is universal. But fecality isn't something we're at risk for: fecality is a present and undeniable condition of life. While will and wealth can be mobilized into outfitting one's bathrooms with golden toilets or paying others to clean our shit rather than dealing with it ourselves, the fact remains that you can't buy your way out of shitting or outsource your shitting to someone else. Fecality as a basic human condition cannot be unevenly distributed or reallocated the way precarity can. And this is why shit is a stronger foundation for a concrete universalism than the precarity that is undeniably our shared, universal condition. Shit levels difference unendingly, cutting efficaciously with each bowel movement through whatever differences we use to partition humanity into categories, letting no distinction stand in the way. Young or old, fat or thin, man or woman, straight or queer, poor or rich, disabled or nondisabled, mansion-owner or homeless, sick or well—every body shits.

Here, I would like to make the case for the fecal specificity of this concrete, embodied universalism. Shitting, more than our other bodily functions, is the site of the strongest, most difference-leveling universalism. While there are other bodily functions that are universal, such as urination, say, or bleeding, neither urine nor blood provoke the same kind of disgust and disavowal that feces do, because neither of them has the same kind of materiality that feces have. Fecal matter, more than these fluids, impresses onto us the materiality and heavy concreteness of human existence: its materiality reminds us of our mortality—itself a consequence of our materiality—and is best able to shatter the illusion that we are clean abstractions.

Mortality is the one other universal human condition—just as everyone shits, everyone also dies—and it is a manifestation of the temporal situation of our bodies: because we are bodies in time, we are bodies that will run out of time. Defecating, more so than urinating or bleeding, is able to relate to time as the condition of our mortality. We associate fecality with regularity—with the passage and repetition of time—in a way that we don't with urine. And if one were a non-menstrual body that lived in a protective suit, it is possible that one could go throughout all of life without ever seeing one's own blood. Shit, however, makes itself known day after day, punctuating our quotidian and setting itself up as a measure of the time we have, the time we are in.

This fecal universalism—a concrete, embodied, and temporal universalism—is what is articulated throughout the excremental works that make up *Cacaphonies'* corpus. I would argue that French literature's seemingly irrepressible fecality is the dark underbelly of the Enlightenment: it is a reminder that these concepts were produced by *bodies,* that ideas cannot be so easily separated from the corporeal envelope that contains them. Excremental literature reunites the severed head with its body and provides to abstract universalism the corporeality and concreteness it requires if it is ever to be, truly, universal.

Genet, in his essay "Ce qui est resté d'un Rembrandt déchiré en petits carrés bien réguliers, et foutu aux chiottes" ("What Remains of a Rembrandt Torn into Little Squares All the Same Size and Stuffed into the Shitter"), understands the connection between fecality and universality.[59] This essay, consisting of two separate texts running in separate columns down the same page (a format that Derrida would emulate in *Glas,* his homage to Genet and Hegel), posits the interchangeability of human existences—a radical universality—in an excremental context. The left-hand column has Genet staring at an ugly man sitting across from him on the train hocking loogies onto the floor, which leads to the realization of "a sort of universal identity with all men," while the right-hand column has Genet discussing Rembrandt's portraits of Hendrickje Stoffels and of the Syndics of the Drapers' Guild, imagining their bodies as defecating ones: "*Under Hendrijke's skirts, under the fur-lined cloaks, under the frock coats, under the painter's extravagant robe, the bodies dutifully carry out their functions: they digest, they are hot, they are heavy, they smell, they shit.*"[60]

Genet's universality is fecal. Genet is compelled to pair the more abstract epiphany about our shared identity, which is itself grounded in the dirty, mustached concrete body of the fellow passenger,[61] with the addition of an extra layer of fecal corporeality onto the bodies painted by Rembrandt in sober portraits that minimize their figures' corporeality. *Cacaphonies,* like Genet's fecal musing, points to the clean, respectable body of a canonized literature that is a vital vector for the dissemination of Frenchness, and reminds us that under its extravagant, canonical robes, we will find a body that digests, that is hot, that is heavy, that smells, that shits.

A Fecal Constellation

I want to turn now to these writers that I've brought together in my cacaphonic corpus as the case studies for a literary presentation of shit as shit. *Cacaphonies* is not an exhaustive catalog of all twentieth-century canonical writers who could be deemed excremental. To name just a few examples of left-out writers: André Gide is not included, despite his fascinating dossier on the shit-covered *Sequestrée de Poitiers* (*The Confined Woman of Poitiers*); Jean Giono is absent as well, despite the abundance of shit in his cholera epic, *Le Hussard sur le toit* (*The Horseman on the Roof*); Albert Cohen also does not figure, despite the tremendous excremental scene we find in *Mangeclous* (*Nailcruncher*) that reimagines a scene from *Anna Karenina* but with diarrhea expelled into a bowler hat, in an explosive bringing together of shit with literature. In deciding on the corpus for *Cacaphonies,* I performed my own excrementality, in the etymological sense of sifting, and sifted out, from the larger body of French literature, Céline, Beckett, Sartre, Genet, Duras, Gary, Garréta, and Pennac because of the way their works cohere to constitute a strong fecal through-line in twentieth-century literature.[62] I have chosen to limit my corpus to the set of texts and authors that enable me to most forcefully argue for taking seriously the fecal matter with which canonical literature is constructed: it is this particular fecal literary constellation that elucidates the centrality of fecality to the construction of a literary edifice that, in its canonicity, claims a position of paramount importance in the construction of French culture as the expression of a French identity and sensibility.

Part I takes up Céline and Beckett as avatars of French modernism that explode open French literature onto the fragmented, traumatized subject and body of modernity, wielding language with an unprecedented violence that enables it to move beyond the literary horizons of the nineteenth century. In Céline's *Mort à crédit* and Beckett's *Molloy,* we get the elaboration of a literary vision that posits shit as a fundamental part of any modern literary enterprise. Part I is thus the articulation of fecal necessity, of excrement as a structural rather than ornamental element of French literature.

Part II examines two pairs of authors—Sartre with Genet, Duras with Gary—in order to show how, in addition to being a material that does formal, structural work, shit does conceptual work. Reading Sartre's *L'Enfance d'un chef* together with Genet's *Notre-Dame-des-Fleurs* shows shit to be the phenomenological material through which freedom, that idea so central to both writers' work and thought, can be conceived and articulated. Bringing together the Holocaust narratives of Duras's *La Douleur* and Gary's *La Vie devant soi* situates shit as the exposition of a radical care ethics—transcending the way care has been gendered as feminine—that would remedy the Nazi reduction of certain humans to shit by calling on all of us to enter into and remain in intimate relation with shit as the expression of a shared embodiment that cuts across all differences to point to a universal fecality that must not go ignored.

Part III leaves behind the solid canon of Céline, Beckett, Sartre, Genet, Duras, and Gary to enter the twenty-first century. Where these previous authors demonstrate the formal, aesthetic, and conceptual dimensions of shit—how shit makes, how shit thinks—I take up Garréta and Pennac as authors writing with the question of their canonicity an open one, as contemporary authors—authors with whom we share time, whose political landscape is ours. Here, the difference-leveling, radically egalitarian force of shit is most explicitly presented, and in Garréta's *Dans l'béton* and Pennac's *Journal d'un corps,* we get demonstrations of the political uses for shit—shit as an anti-racist, anti-patriarchal material, in Garréta, and shit as the democratization of literature and culture, in Pennac. This last part of the book thus follows on the previous ones, which show how shit makes and thinks, to point to how shit can be used: how we as readers can take shit out of its literary containers and put it to use as well.

Hearing Shit

Where does the *-phonies* in *Cacaphonies* come from? How can we hear shit? What does it mean to *listen* to it? I would like to conclude by turning to the French philosopher Louis Marin's digestive musings in *La Parole mangée* (*Food for Thought*) on the encounter between reader and text as an embodied one as a useful way of thinking through these questions. Marin, in his chapter on Rabelais's *Gargantua* and its depiction of the utopia Thélème, posits the literary encounter as an embodied one but stops short of considering the fecal implications of a statement like the following:

> The representation becomes equivocal and this ambivalence is globally produced by the formal structure of the text; yet the most important point is that an effect of displacement is produced, a diversion or difference that allows a space of play to emerge, a space that absorbs the reader who is ingested in and through the text. I shall call this difference the mouth of the text, the orifice that is its point of entry. We shall eat-read the text and we shall be

consumed-read by it. As a result of having read the text as a body, we shall be constituted as an other-body, as a body of pleasurable sensations.[63]

This image of eating the text and being eaten by it triggers a set of fecal images that Marin never articulates: the text shitting out a transformed reader, the reader shitting out a transformed text, that digestive transformation into shit the process by which we turn into an *other-body*. Marin, in developing the idea of a reader's encounter with a text as one where we enter a text through its mouth, veers away from the obvious anal route—the usual egress for food that has been consumed and processed—when it comes to exiting said text:

> How are we going to be expelled from the Thélème text? How is this text going to give birth to us, how will it engender or regenerate us? In my opinion, these questions are one and the same. First of all, they both play on the ambivalence of the double orifice of the vagina and anus. Second, the poem that we read at the end of the discourse of Thelema is at the foundations, at the basis of Thélème. In short, the peroration of the discourse, its noble part, its end, understood as its completion and perfection, is also its base, its anal foundation.[64]

Marin readily acknowledges the generative capacity of the anal site, the anal foundation, but displaces it onto the vaginal site, making birth the operative metaphor for generation, rather than turning to the generative capacity of shit that agriculture is a continual reminder of. In opting for parturition and positing the vagina as an orifice that is more or less the same as the anus, Marin severs a specifically digestive line of thought. Why must we be birthed to be generated by the text? Why not follow the digestive tract to its logical conclusion and choose to see ourselves as being shit out by the text, having been processed by it into generative matter?

Marin, in his description of literature as a digestive, intimate, incorporating event, comes so close to the fecal and yet never quite reaches it. Shit is Marin's conceptual asymptote. In approaching it but never quite reaching it, Marin remains close to the figure of the orifice throughout his essay, and, in concluding, shifts from the anal orifice to the buccal one, thinking about the text as buccal, vocal product:

> The product is at once identified with its place of production
> and replaced by it. In other words, the story is no longer a repre-
> sentation produced by an internal narrative activity that assumes
> an external, historical referent during the act of enunciation: the
> referent, history, is the exploration of the site where the narrative
> activity takes place. It is the exploration of the mouth, of the inte-
> rior of a body-world that has been reduced to a prodigious orifice,
> to an immense and resounding cavity. Without distance, the story
> becomes its own site of narration. In this way, the text becomes the
> story of the body, and the body, a text.[65]

For Marin, the orifice is profoundly important as a sound chamber that allows the text to resound in a lyrical articulation of a textual architecture that would also be a corporeal architecture. And the story of the body being told here, for all its anality, is one that is firmly oriented around the buccal. The example of the narrator shitting in Pantagruel's mouth that Marin comments on here proves the point: the narrator's shit is firmly contained within the larger narrative buccal orifice of Pantagruel, who is being narrated. The container (the narrator who produces the story that would contain Pantagruel) is itself contained (by Pantagruel's mouth)—the narrating is subsumed and swallowed up, literally, by the narrated. Voice—represented by the buccal—trumps the fecal, the anal.

Where the non-excremental canon, which is admittedly much of the French canon, produces texts that can be identified with the voice, and hence with the mouth as the place of production, and by extension, the head, as the part of the body that houses the mouth, *Cacaphonies'* writers produce texts that can be identified with shit, with the anus as the place of production. Like the mouth, the anus is also a resonant sounding chamber, but one containing fecal matter that fills the cavity and blunts its resonance, making us forget this orifice's acoustic capacities, despite the melodic farts that escape daily.

The empty orifice of the mouth is filled with the voice, the gaseous, atmospheric voice that articulates words, and through them, narratives. But what following the fecal through-line of the last century in French literature reveals is that the mouth is also paired with the anus—the other end of the tube. Fecal matter is the positive substance that acts as the counterweight to the negative, empty orifice that produces voice. Marin, like so many of us, assumes that the mouth is where the voice is found. But shit is a kind of voice. French literature, as a combination of excremental and non-excremental writing, is built as much from the rectum full of shit as it is from the empty mouth producing voice.

If Marin had followed the digestive tract from the "prodigious orifice" of the mouth through to the anus on the other side, without making that vaginal detour, he would have been able to cast literature's generative quality not in terms of reproduction—a modality of life anchored in sameness—but in terms of growth and transformation—a modality of life anchored in heterogeneity, in, to put it in Césairien terms, an enriching coexistence of all particulars. No matter the origins and nature of the various comestibles that are eaten, they all wind up transformed into the uniform (but also varied, from bowel movement to bowel movement) consistency of shit.[66]

Marin's desire to frame the literary encounter as an embodied one makes of literature a visceral affair, one that speaks to its vital importance, but the swerve away from the fecal destiny of our passage through the text to privilege the mouth and voice only serves to uphold the primacy that has been accorded to speech over writing and fetishizes the voice that dominates our conception of literature: the written word—the text—has been subjugated to the voice as a "simple supplement to the spoken word," as Derrida puts it in his critique of the hierarchy founded by this relation of subordination.[67] Derrida's anti-hierarchical project has an ally in French literature's cacaphonic canon, which points to the way fecal matter, in its multivalence, paradoxicality, and democratizing nature, is the material through which we can thwart difference and distinction, exemplified by binary thought.

What I am proposing in *Cacaphonies* is to, like Marin, embrace an embodied encounter with literature, consuming and being consumed by it, but by listening to the cacaphonic chorus that becomes audible if we allow our reading to take its natural, digestive, fecal course. Shit has been there from the beginning as a constant utterance and it is time to hear what it is saying: the unending refrain of a universalism that awaits the bodies that can inhabit it. Shit is the material through which we can best understand literature's own intuitive understanding of its transgressive work: a transgression that transcends the text, imbedding itself into our readerly other-bodies that might become the site of the ultimate transgression that would be radical equality—being (in) shit together.

Part I

NECESSARY SHIT

) 1 (

CÉLINE
Shit on the Installment Plan

***

It is impossible to tell the story of French modernism in literature without touching on Céline. The bugaboo of modern French literature, he bears the distinction of being both one of the most important authors of the twentieth century and one of the most odious, given his virulently anti-Semitic writing in his infamous (and long-censored) pamphlets and his fascist sensibilities. While my project here is to explore the literary politics of the abundant excrementality of Céline's work, rather than his extraliterary politics, or his political politics, it is necessary to remark on what a controversial figure Céline remains, as the anathema around his politics informs his ambivalent relation to and status in canonical French literature. In other words, to be able to get to Céline's shit, it is necessary first to acknowledge his shitty politics.

Louis-Ferdinand Céline (1894–1961) was born Louis Ferdinand Auguste Destouches in the Parisian suburb of Courbevoie. This son of petit bourgeois parents would grow up to become a physician, le docteur Destouches, but he is far better known to posterity for having modernized French literature than for his contributions to medicine. A literary and political monster, Céline has posed to readers of French literature the prickly question of how far art for art's sake can go, and what limits, if any, ought to be placed on our consumption of cultural products. Simply put, does genius, and significant contribution to what we often assume to be the inherently humanistic project of art, outweigh the anti-humanism of anti-Semitism and fascism? Does the aesthetic matter more than the political? Is there a literary statute of limitations? (Here, I'm thinking of how the French government tried, in 2011, to include Céline alongside authors like Blaise Cendrars, Jean-Jacques Rousseau, and Théophile Gautier in its yearly commemoration of French cultural figures, Le Recueil des Célébrations nationales, only to face vocal opposition from critics who were outraged at what they saw as the rehabilitation and pardon of Céline's anti-Semitism.)

The strategies for responding to the literary monster[1] that is Céline can be boiled down essentially to three different types. One is to blacklist him altogether and refuse to read the work of someone with such poisonous political views. Another is to split Céline the brilliant novelist from Céline the pamphleteer and celebrate the one while condemning the other, which is effectively to cordon off and privilege "literary" writing over "political" writing.[2] And the third is to take a holistic, global view of Céline's oeuvre and identify a continuity between the two forms of writing and assert the coherence and cohesiveness of his entire corpus, as seen in attempts to identify the germs of his degraded political writing in the pages of his novels and track the transformation of the writer into the propagandist, for instance.[3] What each approach has in common, however, is an acknowledgment of Céline as a figure unavoidably tied up with the political. For any besides the most naïve reader, someone who might pick up a novel by Céline and avoid learning anything about the man, the political question is one that must be dealt with, and the kind of politics that that question is tied to is almost always the politics of anti-Semitic, nationalist, fascist populism that would result in Céline's being condemned as a Nazi collaborator. The politics that interests me here, however, is not so much the question of Céline's anti-Semitism, which has been widely and intelligently discussed, but the politics of the poetics animating his unprecedented reworking of language, of his desire for literature and his vision of what literature ought to be.

Many scholars and critics have offered sensitive and acute accounts of Céline's literary importance, and it has become something of a truism to affirm that Céline revolutionized French literature: His first novel, *Voyage au bout de la nuit* (*Journey to the End of the Night*) (1932), was like an atomic bomb blowing French literature up and radiating the field for years to come. After the polished *tournure* of genteel, well-bred authors like Proust (an aesthete par excellence), or Gide, for instance, the sentence by which Céline started *Voyage* and entered literature, "Ça a débuté comme ça" (It started like this), with its casual *ça,* was like flipping the bird at the entire literary establishment.[4] Henri Godard, one of Céline's most enthusiastic readers, the editor of the prestigious Pléiade edition of his published works (minus the pamphlets), and the author of several works of Céline criticism as well as a biography, has even claimed that Céline is as important to French literature as Proust, that eminently respectable and continually memorialized literary monument. For Godard, it is Céline, not Proust, to whom we can look to see how French literature enters modernity.[5] In general, the extant work on Céline fails to consider, in its consideration of his political and poetic importance, the significance of the deeply excremental quality to be found throughout his entire oeuvre, both fictional and propagandist, but especially in the earlier, pre-pamphlet years, before Céline's anti-Semitism would become explicitly and virulently articulated.[6]

Take the example of Julia Kristeva. She is a major figure in Céline criticism because of her use of his corpus to anchor her examination of abjection in the landmark text, *Pouvoirs de l'horreur* (*Powers of Horror*). Kristeva, in this work, while gesturing to the sorts of manifestations of physical and psychical abjection we see throughout Céline's corpus (with an emphasis on his first novel, *Voyage au bout de la nuit*), immediately instrumentalizes these immanently material experiences and positions, using them to channel her reading of Céline—predictably, given Kristeva's psychoanalytic angle—into a maternal framework that places Céline's writing under the sign of a fraught, boundary-blurring (hence the abjection) identification with the mother. The need to read the moments of physical abjection and horror through a psychoanalytic lens sweeps us out of the realm of the physical and the material into the psychical.[7] The guts, pus, blood, vomit, and shit of Céline's writing lose their sharp odor, seeming to prove Barthes right when he claims that "when written, shit does not have an odor."[8]

While Kristeva has played a large role in rehabilitating Céline as a writer worthy of our sustained consideration,[9] her examination of Céline's writing's excrement curiously erases and sanitizes it—the critical equivalent, say, of turning foul-smelling and disgust-inspiring feces into an eminently usable and productive biosolid. This has had the effect of modeling a way of dealing with his shit without having to actually deal with the shit-ness of it. Kristeva's rehabilitation of Céline involves taking a *torche-cul* to his shit-smeared work when his most memorable characters remain covered in shit.

In Alice Kaplan's much more critical reading of Céline, which refuses Céline the psychoanalytic alibi that Kristeva provides, she offers an acute account of the entrails and viscera that take center stage in Céline's work: the "loss" that elimination of the excremental sort produces is key to Céline's working of language, where "the separation of words from the mouth [is] reminiscent of the body's daily losses" and loss is "the real 'raw material' for storytelling."[10] Kaplan coins the phrase "tripe-talk" to refer to Céline's turn to viscera and excrement as vectors by which he might be able to get at the truth of death, the one real authentic thing there is to say. In Céline's literary universe, that which is hidden or contained—our guts, our shit—is revealed, and their revelation brings us as close as we can get without actually dying to the truth of death, to the continual loss that the tripes are an organ of. But here too, the excremental is elided in a metonymic gesture that would have us recall the organ that produces and holds the shit rather than the actual fecal matter that is contained by it. Tripe-talk, after all, is just another way of saying "shit": what do the tripes "utter" if not the fecal?

Returning to Barthes, I want to cite the full sentence from which the assertion of shit's odorlessness is taken. Describing Sade's excremental libertinism, Barthes writes, "Language has this property of denying, ignoring, dissociating reality: when written, shit does not have an odor; Sade can inundate his partners in it, we receive not the slightest whiff, only the abstract sign of something unpleasant."[11] Céline's poetics could not be further from what Barthes sees as an abstracted excremental Sadism: language, in Céline's hands, becomes the means through which he plunges us ever deeper into the reality that is our mortality, the truth that is death—the ultimate object of Céline's literary project. As we will see, it is difficult to read Céline and come away with anything but the impression that this is someone who wants his shit, even the written stuff, to smell. Indeed, he will insist that his work's shit smells. This chapter thus responds to treatments of Céline that either dematerialize and deodorize his shit or turn away from it to focus on what is adjacent it, by centering fecal matter as the matter that it is for Céline—something that hits our sensorium; the opposite of abstraction.

In working through Céline's masterwork, *Mort à crédit,* a novel that is excremental through and through, it becomes clear that Céline's poetics are fundamentally excremental: for Céline, any poetics that would be able to take on the task of writing death must do so through shit, which for him is deeply tied to the questions of temporality, mortality, and abject materiality that are caught up with and in death. Through *Mort à crédit,* which features a narrator, Ferdinand, whose bottom is constantly covered in shit, Céline articulates a specifically excremental poetics that, in privileging fecality as the vehicle for his narrative, rejects an optimistic, Zolaesque realism and seeks instead to anchor French literature's continued existence and future not in the realism that has come to dominate modern models of literature, but rather in the kind of bawdy, scatological Rabelaisian corporeality of French literature's earlier productions. French literature is thus cast as a fundamentally excremental enterprise.

This reframing requires that we rethink how we've come to conceive of French literature—in particular, the sanitized accounts of modernist, modern, and contemporary French literature that tacitly tie its modernity to being cleaner, less fecal than the literature of its premodern and early modern predecessors, literary progress thus tracking neatly onto developments in sanitation and waste management.[12]

If we accept Céline's status as a literary innovator and indispensable literary figure despite his politics—an account I agree with—then we cannot continue to reject the fecality that was so central to his conception of literature. Instead, like Céline, we must attend to his fecal sensibility, which itself responds to the fecality of French literature writ large. Céline's work is effectively a call to fecalize the modern French canon, rather than dismiss its fecality as incidental or unimportant. This is a radical kind of literary politics, one that turns the logic of the canon on its head and throws a wrench into the processes by which literary and cultural capital are determined, accrued, and reproduced. Fecal matter, in the context of the French tradition, turns out to be a literary matter, one that would rework our very definition of literature and sense of literariness: French literature is literary not despite but *because* of its fecality.

Mort à crédit

If I examine Céline's second novel, *Mort à crédit* (*Death on the Installment Plan*) (1936), in order to work through his excremental poetics, it is because, in addition to being, arguably, his most important novel literarily, as well as his most excremental one, it is also the inflection point that tethers Céline the brilliant author to Céline the delusional anti-Semite. It is after *Mort à crédit* did not receive the literary recognition Céline desired that the aspiring author took a hard turn toward right-wing politics. Indeed, it was following *Mort à crédit*'s flop that Céline wrote and published the first of his virulently anti-Semitic political pamphlets, *Bagatelles pour un massacre* (*Trifles for a Massacre*), in 1937, signaling the novel's importance for its author.[13]

    Mort à crédit could be described as an anti-bildungsroman where what is mapped out over the course of the very long narrative is not the development and the education of its narrator, Ferdinand, but rather, his incapacity to do anything but fail, and this spectacularly. Ferdinand has the opposite of the Midas touch. Everything he touches turns not to gold but to shit (although in psychoanalytic readings that liken shit to gold this would mean that Ferdinand has exactly the Midas touch): he fails in his studies, he fails in his multiple apprenticeships with shopkeepers, he fails by proxy as an assistant to the enterprising but incompetent inventor Courtial des Pereires, who, like Ferdinand, is unable to bring anything to fruition (his attempt at creating super-potatoes results in a terrible maggot infestation, and his attempt at creating a utopian school and community for youth winds up as a center for juvenile delinquency)—and through it all, he fails most of all at being a son to his parents, who abuse him and are abused by him.

It is perhaps for the omnipresence of the structure of the nuclear family (and its variations, as when Ferdinand winds up living at a British boarding school, Meanwell, with the schoolmaster and his young wife, or when he lives with des Pereires and his wife) that *Mort à crédit* has been endlessly described and analyzed as a kind of poster child for the psychoanalytic theory of the Oedipus complex. The novel, in all its heft—it is a brick at more than six hundred pages long in the Folio version and its small type—has been more often than not reduced to Ferdinand's attempt to kill his father (which ends the first part of the novel, which recounts the endless string of failures that Ferdinand produces in his inability to follow through with the projects laid out for him by his father), and the subsequent attempts to replace his father by turning to another failed father, Courtial des Pereires (Pereires playing off *père,* father), joining des Pereires in his string of catastrophic failures.

Also remarked on has been the literary mise en abyme, where the novel opens with a febrile oneiric sequence that reveals the narrator's failed project of writing *La Légende du Roi Krogold* (*The Legend of King Krogold*), which serves as a partial or broken frame narrative for the principal, and drawn-out, story of Ferdinand's childhood—partial or broken because it does not close the novel, which ends, somewhat anticlimactically, with Ferdinand at his uncle's home, intending to enlist in the army, and his uncle telling him where the toilets are should he have diarrhea or need to vomit.

The question I ask here, however, is about the importance and the function of the excrement that permeates the novel from start to finish. Rather than quickly gloss it as a simple scatological device, in line with Céline's general disregard for *mœurs* or *bienséance* (decorum)—something meant simply to incite a reaction, to shock—I want to follow and examine it for the poetic vision it reveals, without which we cannot understand Céline, nor, for that matter, French literature's entry into modernism. This exploration is a dialectical one that examines the interplay between two excremental polarities: one is that of the excrement that surrounds Ferdinand, which is produced by others but that he winds up being in contact with—in short, other people's shit and vomit, the contents of other people's bodies; the other is that of the narrator, Ferdinand, and the way the narrator's behind is revealed to the reader to always be covered in shit, which serves as a stable point of reference that, at seemingly arbitrary but crucial intervals, returns us to the familiar excremental situation of Ferdinand's shitty bottom as a way to orient ourselves in an otherwise disorienting and chaotic narrative, by always pointing the reader back toward the excrementality that is a central, rather than ancillary, operation of the novel. I would like to take this scatological North Star, which guides us through the narrative, as our point of entry into the excremental universe of *Mort à crédit*.

A Shitty Narrator

Mort à crédit, despite being a kind of bildungsroman, begins, not in childhood or youth, but with Ferdinand as a jaded older man who feels closer to death than not—a point I will return to later. The prologue's fever-dream sequence jumps abruptly from Ferdinand hallucinating in bed about *La Légende du Roi Krogold* to the story of Ferdinand's childhood, which begins with a nostalgic evocation of the nineteenth century: "The last century—I can talk about it, I saw it end . . ."[14] Céline, who was born in 1894, would have been only six years old at the end of the century. The nostalgia and awareness of ending he attributes to Ferdinand, who is meant to be an approximatively autobiographical figure or at least to have an ambiguous relation to Céline (Ferdinand shares one of Céline's names, is a medical doctor the way Céline was, and grew up in the Parisian covered passages, as did Céline), is a fabricated one—what can a six-year-old remember or know of his epoch?

And yet, it is important for Céline to cast Ferdinand as a fundamentally nostalgic figure,[15] turned always toward a past and a history that are irrecuperable, as a kind of consolation for the terrible present in which he lives—in Ferdinand's case, this present is one of war, of World War I, its aftermath, and the degradation that led to it. Despite the awfulness of his childhood, that past, in its proximity to a bygone time, is preferable to whatever future the new century has to offer. Ferdinand deplores the costliness of modernity, the flattening wrought by a twentieth century that would bring about standardization, Taylorization, and the dehumanizing transformation of worker into machine, of human into capital. In this world characterized by *mass*—mass production, mass media, mass consumption, mass death, with the human the consistent loser in all these forms of massification—Ferdinand looks to the nineteenth century as an epoch where life and death were still on a human scale. The nineteenth century, unlike the industrialized, modernized twentieth century, was a time where existence still had flavor, color, character, unlike the banal, dull, and flattened reality that took its place.[16]

The childhood narrative portion of the novel—which, for all intents and purposes, *is* the novel—turns back to the nineteenth century via a description of a yearly autumnal trip to visit an old aunt, the oldest living member of the family, in Rungis, a suburb of Paris. This stubbornly and astonishingly alive aunt, called repeatedly *l'aïeule,* or ancestor, is described as an outmoded relic: "My aunt conversed only in the imperfect subjunctive. Old-fashioned" (49; 545).[17] It is in the context of this yearly pilgrimage to a living dinosaur of a woman that we have the first evocation of what will be Ferdinand's constantly shit-covered bottom: "We were in such a hurry to get there that I went in my pants . . . To tell the truth I was in such a hurry all through my childhood that I had shit on my ass until the army" (48; 545).[18]

At this narrative beginning, we have our narrator telling us bluntly that he is literally a shitty narrator—that shit, and his proximity to and familiarity with it, is a constant for the Ferdinand we will encounter for the lengthy remainder of the novel. From the beginning, Céline ties this excrementality to time.[19] If Ferdinand is constantly shit-covered, it is because he has no time. His parents rush him as they're en route to see the ancestor and as a consequence he shits himself. While this already seems like an absurd situation, it isn't beyond the pale—when one has to go, one has to go, and one's will sometimes loses out to one's sphincter. What is odd is the way the army is set up as a context where Ferdinand would finally have time, when, for all intents and purposes, the army is where time would be highly regimented. And, as we would presume, Ferdinand's decision to enlist in the army at the end of the novel would lead to his being deployed as a soldier, as Céline himself was, in World War I, when he would certainly not have had much leisure in the trenches. The obvious question that Ferdinand's temporal framing of his shittiness raises, then, is that of the relation between shit and time: Why doesn't Ferdinand have the time to defecate properly? What is the particular nature of his being always pressed for time?

After this first mention of Ferdinand's shit-covered ass, the next twenty-one pages[20] are spent engaging in a more or less normal narration, describing his mother's work selling fine lace, his father's work as a secretary at an insurance firm, and his childhood spent working for the family business (an occupation that will lead to Ferdinand's being sexually molested and abused by his mother's client) and being the regular object of parental, especially paternal, ire. Regaled with a dense, fast-moving narration of the unfortunate events that are Ferdinand's childhood, that first mention of Ferdinand's shit-covered ass seems like a one-off, a peculiar interjection, not particularly significant against the backdrop of one absurd happening and misadventure after another. To give an example of the absurdity of Ferdinand's picaresque tale, Ferdinand's grandmother, Caroline, who hates the abusive patriarch, Auguste, buys a little dog to keep Ferdinand company. Ferdinand kicks and abuses the dog, whom he has named Tom, acting as his father does, only to see that the dog "acted [*faisait*] exactly like me" (68; 565),[21] at which point he turns to caressing the dog instead, who reacts by having an erection. What, in another novel, could have been the moving and pathos-stirring representation of an abused child, is turned in Céline's text into a farcical one, where something as serious as the trauma of child abuse is interrupted by the ludic obscenity of a canine erection, the two narrated in the exact same tone.

It thus comes as a surprise when, on the very next page following the recounting of Ferdinand's canine abuse, we have a reprise of Ferdinand's claim to a shitty ass for lack of time:

> Foreseeing that I'd be a thief, my father blared like a trombone. One afternoon Tom and I had emptied the sugar bowl. It was never forgotten. But that wasn't my only fault. In addition my behind was always dirty, I didn't wipe myself, I didn't have time, that was my justification, we were always in too much of a hurry . . . I never wiped myself properly, I always had a sock coming to me . . . and hurried to avoid it . . . I left the can door open so as to hear them coming . . . I shat like a bird between two storms . . .
>
> I bounded upstairs and they couldn't find me . . . I'd go around for weeks with shit on my ass. I was conscious of the smell, I'd be careful not to get too close to people.
>
> "He's as filthy as thirty-six pigs! He has no self-respect! He'll never make a living. Every boss in the world will fire him! . . ." He saw a shitty future in store for me.
>
> "He stinks! . . . We'll always have him on our hands . . ."
>
> My father looked far ahead and all he saw was gloom. He put it in Latin for emphasis: "*Sana . . . corpore sano.*" My mother didn't know what to say. (69; 566)

This scene has been invoked as an illustration of what a terrible home life and set of parents Ferdinand had, which is then mobilized to produce a psychologizing reading of *Mort à crédit* as an extended Oedipal drama where Céline is diagnosed as a writer unable to transcend his murderous hatred for the paternal or to come to terms with his ambivalence toward the maternal.[22] This reading does not account for the role Ferdinand's shitty bottom plays in the construction of the text nor is it able to account for the sort of bizarre non-transitions that precede and awkwardly tie these irruptions of the fecal to the text around them: the link between suffering from the character flaw of being a thief and having a constantly soiled bottom is hardly a clear one.

The timing of this second irruption of the fecal is, I would submit, hardly arbitrary or non-motivated, and neither is the first fecal instance. Céline is not randomly placing these shit scenes here and there. Instead, his insertions of the fecal orient the reader. As Céline writes further on, to describe the role that the dog plays in leading the way when Ferdinand, his parents, and his uncle Édouard go for a Sunday outing in Édouard's car (a modern contraption that falls apart), "Tom ambled along ahead of our expedition, we took our bearings by his asshole. He had time to piss wherever he pleased" (72; 569). Just as the car followed the dog's anus, so too are we, as Céline's readers, to follow Ferdinand's anus. The question then is what Ferdinand's fecality leads us toward: in the context of Céline's project of writing death as a way to resist it, how does the excremental get us there, and what does time have to do with it?

Time is crucial to the answer, but not the sort of time that is being narrated on the surface of these passages. To take at face value Ferdinand's claims that he is too pressed for time to defecate and wipe properly is to see his parents as terrible, ready with a slap if he spends too much time on the toilet, imposing a distorted, untenable rhythm on him in their desire for economic success. In this case, defecation is an inconvenience—an obstacle to the kind of maximum productivity that is the asymptote of capitalist striving. Certainly, life under capitalism provides no shortage of examples of this kind of intersection of temporality and excrementality: we can find contemporary news stories of poultry workers who must wear diapers because they are not allowed bathroom breaks, or of slanted toilets designed to increase productivity by being painful to sit on for more than five minutes.[23] The notion that one might not have enough time to defecate under capitalism doesn't seem particularly far-fetched. Perhaps Ferdinand's ludic descriptions of his constantly shit-covered ass are simply a satirical way for Céline, who was keenly aware of economic inequality, having come from a not particularly privileged economic class and having experienced firsthand the devastations of the global economic depression of the 1920s, to condemn capitalism.[24]

Such an economic reading of Céline, while convincing, is ultimately incomplete because it does not treat shit in the novel as a literary question when Céline, as an author, worked and reworked his texts, so attached to their global functioning as a whole that when his publisher, Denoël, censored a considerable portion of the text for its crude and vulgar representations of sex, he insisted on having the published version reproduce the blank spaces left behind by the censor's redactions. This was a writer, then, who was attached to the totality of his text, one which comprises these moments of fecality. Ferdinand states bluntly that his entire childhood is one marked by shit, where he smelled all the time of shit and where fresh excretions accreted onto his bottom—each day or each defecation marking an addition to the *crotte,* or fecal crust. This effectively places the entire novel under the sign of shit, the childhood that is the primary object of Céline's narrative synonymous with the constant presence of shit.

Let us consider Auguste's declaration of Ferdinand's "shitty future" (*l'avenir à la merde*), alongside the title of the novel, *Mort à crédit,* or *Death on the Installment Plan.* Given that the future or end result of the installment plan is the acquisition of what one is putting away for, Auguste and the title are effectively tying futurity to fecality and to mortality. Auguste gives us shit as the future, and the title gives us death as the future: shit and death converge on the plane of futurity, or destiny, if you will. Accordingly, the shit that is always on Ferdinand's ass, that he cannot wipe away, that accumulates and has a particular odor, is itself a figuration of death. Death on the installment plan amounts to shit on the installment plan. You can put away diligently, living life in the kinds of increments for which capitalism primes us, with indebtedness and payment schedules constituting a primary rhythm of life, but in the end, all it will buy is death, or shit. Céline, in short, reveals the incrementalism of life under capitalism to be, at its core, an excrementalism whose only product is death. Shit—as a sign of death, each bowel movement a reminder of the passage of time that leads to the putrefaction that awaits us—interrupts the narrative that is lived life with a regular reminder of its end. And what produces this sign of death is a body that is undeniably, unquestionably alive—in life, *en vie.*

This necropastoral conjoining of life and death, where life presents as death and death presents as life, becomes particularly clear in a scene later on in the novel where Ferdinand and his mother go to Père Lachaise to tend to his beloved grandmother Caroline's tomb:

> While we were cleaning up, she sobbed the whole time . . .
> Caroline was down there, not very far away . . . I always thought
> of Asnières . . . The way we'd knocked ourselves out for those
> tenants. I could see her, so to speak . . . The place was spic and
> span, we washed it every Sunday, but there was a funny little
> smell from down below . . . pungent, subtle, kind of sour, insinu-
> ating . . . once you'd caught it, you smelled it all over . . . in spite
> of the flowers . . . mixed in with the scent . . . clinging to you . . .
> It makes your head spin . . . it comes from the hole [trou] . . . you
> think you must have been mistaken. And there it is again! . . . It
> was I who went down to the end of the lane to fill the pitchers for
> the vases . . . When we'd finished I didn't say a word . . . And then
> the little smell came back at me . . . (110; 115)

While the passage describes the odor coming from the tomb, its description is laden with fecal connotations, given that Asnières, evoked here, is the place where Ferdinand's grandmother had to clean out her tenants' shit—a scene we'll get to shortly. The *trou* in question invites association with Ferdinand's *trou du cul* (asshole), the tomb and the anus serving as figurations of each other. Céline's response to the question posed by the title of Leo Bersani's essay "Is the Rectum a Grave?" could be "The Grave Is a Rectum." Céline thus has multiple strategies for tying together excrementality with mortality. What we have then in the passage where Ferdinand declares that he never had the time to wipe his ass is not so much a representation of time under capitalism—the sort of time that *is* represented in the novel when Ferdinand relates how his father, Auguste, was always looking at his watch (271; 635)[25]—but rather, an articulation of how mortality is the condition of never having enough time.

If he is so hurried it is because the shit that comes out of him is a quotidian and constant leaking out of death from his body, the odor he gives off from shit serving the same function as the odor that emanates from Caroline's tomb: sometimes you stop noticing it, but before too long, "there it is again!" to remind you that you are destined for death. This intermittence that Ferdinand experiences vis-à-vis the smell of his grandmother's decomposing body—of her deadness—is taken up by him structurally in the narration of his childhood as a series of misadventures that merely bring him closer to obtaining the death that all of us are laying away for: he reminds us from time to time that his ass is covered in shit, only to have the shit become submerged by and in the events that make up the majority of the narrative fabric. And just when the non-excremental narration has progressed for long enough to make the ever unsuspecting reader believe that perhaps it is gone, *there it is again!* Ferdinand comes back with a reminder that yes, reader, his ass is still covered in shit, and that that smell never fully went away, that, even when we thought the novel was shit-free, there was still plenty of shit on the narrator's ass, the narrator without whom there would be no novel. Just as there is no escaping death in our human condition, there is no escaping shit in the narrative, and Ferdinand exposes his shit-covered ass just frequently enough for it to serve as the text's continuity, its logic, in what seems otherwise like one endless stream of absurd and random events. Just as death is life's unassailable end and logic, so too is shit, in the life of the novel.

What Ferdinand suffers from—in addition to the abuses visited by his parents who are foolishly trying to make it in a capitalist system driven by the imperative to, in the name of modernization, produce more and ever more—is a visceral consciousness of his own mortality, and the feeling it engenders of our lives never being enough. Ferdinand does not have enough time because he will never have enough time, just as none of us will ever have enough time, if we are to judge from the mythologization and continual narration of attempts to defeat death that pervade our cultural narratives (e.g., zombies, vampires, science-fictional accounts of technological solutions to death, the myriad afterlives that different religions envision). As Céline writes, in his correspondence with the art historian Élie Faure, he has a keen "awareness of the brevity of our personal miracle, of our incredible fragility," where this sense of life as a brief, fragile miracle stems from a sense of the omnipresence of death in life: "Man is cursed [. . .] From the ovum, he is nothing but death's plaything."[26]

If Ferdinand resists wiping his bottom, preferring his filth even as he shies away from others, it is what it seems like: the giving up of human relationality in order to maintain a relation with mortality. Ferdinand would rather have his shit as a constant layer covering his fragile skin—a material reminder of the death that is always there as a possibility—than an artificially cleaned skin that would be the precondition for establishing a connection to another human being. There is a certain logic to this: human relation can only ever be a distraction from the truth of death, and Ferdinand refuses to sugarcoat existence, as evinced by the kind of macabre and sordid narrative he delivers to us, in which any love and tenderness he experiences is always brutally taken away from him.

But this refusal of human relation undoes itself, and Ferdinand's opting for alienation is precisely what brings him into solidarity with everyone else, who, like him, is subject to alienation. In Céline, shit is always both a thing and the thing's negation.[27] In the case of not wiping oneself, we have the evocation of the beginning of life—a very childish refusal or incapacity (the ability to wipe oneself properly being acquired well after the ability to control one's sphincter)—and we have the evocation of life's end, incontinence and the inability to wipe oneself being some of the indignities of old age. And in the case of the accumulation of Ferdinand's shit on his bottom, the time gained from not taking the time to wipe also produces the material sign—layers of shit accreting onto layers of shit—of not having enough time. What shit does, it undoes, in a kind of equilibrium, but the undoing always leaves behind the shit that is its agent.

In case there are any readers who might want to insist on a solely economic reading of Ferdinand's assertion about time and shit, where Ferdinand does not have time because his parents impose capitalist time on him, I would point out that Ferdinand rebels against everything else his parents stand for, by merely pretending to do what they want him to do (e.g., he is sent away to a British boarding school, Meanwell, to learn English, and refuses to do so; he is apprenticed out to various tradesmen and dutifully goes to work but never gains any real skills or knowledge in his apprenticeships), but on the shit front, there is no pretending: he cannot pretend he does not shit. Shit transcends economy. Shit demands the truth—it is the site of absolute veracity, incapable of being harnessed for deception.

Céline's truth, which he will reiterate over and over, is that we are all alone, but we are in shit together. This commonality, however, affirms not any human feeling but rather the constancy of the materiality and existence of shit, and affirms that if we are in shit together it is because we are essentially shit. Céline could be seen as expanding on St. Augustine's oft-cited dictum that we are all born between shit and piss—*inter faeces et urinam nascimur*—to declare that not only do we start life covered in shit (our mother's) but we end it returning to shit. And, to top it off, the interval between beginning and end is also shit—one endless (or, rather, only too end-full) set of repeated eliminations until we ourselves are eliminated, like a turd shit out by the world that bears us.

We Built This City (and Everything Else) on Shit

Céline, in addition to establishing the narrative as a fundamentally excremental one that reeks of the death we will all reach, constructs an architecture of shit, where the space in which our shit existence takes place is itself excremental. *Mort à crédit,* with its rich description of life in central Paris at the turn of the twentieth century, abounds with descriptions of the city itself and of the post-Hausmann environment in which Ferdinand, and Céline himself, grows up. As befits a writer who has been described as populist,[28] able to communicate and understand viscerally the people's misery, Ferdinand's Paris is a sordid, insalubrious place, the sort of place that can produce nothing good. As Céline describes it, "I have to admit that the Passage was an unbelievable pesthole. It was made to kill you off, slowly but surely, what with the little mongrels' urine, the shit, the sputum, the leaky gas pipes. The stink was worse than the inside of a prison" (70; 568).

Effectively, the Passage Choiseul which Ferdinand calls home serves as a receptacle for waste—for shit (produced by dogs, certainly, but possibly by humans as well), saliva, urine. Céline insists on the particularly fecal nature of the Passage, however, when he describes Ferdinand's father's hopeless battle against the dog turds that litter the Passage outside their home and boutique. In a parodic rendering of Auguste, and his aspirations toward bourgeois status, as Sisyphus, Céline describes the man's daily battle against the constant accretion of shit:

> His nightmare was cleaning the sidewalk outside our shop. He'd wash down the flags every morning before going to work.
> He'd come out with his pail, his broom, his rag, and the little trowel he'd slip under the turds, to pick them up and throw them in the sawdust. What a humiliation for a man with his education! The turds increased in number and there were many more in front of our shop, lengthwise and crosswise, than anywhere else. Obviously a conspiracy. (75; 573)

Ferdinand lives and is raised in a literal shithole. Under such conditions, what good could Ferdinand ever come to? Especially when he does not have the slight protection afforded to him by the kind of bourgeois aspirations (read, delusions, given the near impossibility of social mobility in a regime of industrial capitalism) his father has, which compel the latter to struggle to free himself of an excremental existence that is their immutable lot in life.

Céline does present us, in the figure of Ferdinand's grandmother, with a healthier and more positive familial model than what we get with either of Ferdinand's parents—with Auguste and his delusional quest for social mobility, with Clémence and her resigned forbearance and acceptance of the world as it is, her conciliatory nature and attempts at doing the best with what one has been given. In this novel, which is, among many things, a representation of life under crushing capitalism, Céline gives us Ferdinand's grandmother, who, like Proust's grandmother in the *Recherche*—an author and a work he abhorred, perhaps because of its closeness to Céline's own project[29]—is beloved. Against Clémence and Auguste, with their future-oriented gaze, Grandmother Caroline emerges as a decidedly nineteenth-century figure whose goodness maps onto her lack of regard for and suspicion toward the modernizing narratives of the twentieth century.[30] And yet she too is placed under an excremental sign, as seen in this passage recounting her endless efforts at clearing her suburban tenants' toilets that they stop up on purpose with their shit:

> We got to the rue de la Plaisance. That's when the work began. Collecting the rent was a headache . . . the tenants were in full revolt. They fought every inch of the way and they never paid in full . . . never . . . they tried every slimy trick . . . The pump was always out of order. The discussions were interminable . . . They started griping about everything under the sun before Grandma even opened her mouth . . . The shithouse [gogs] was stuffed up . . . They were very dissatisfied . . . they shouted their complaints from every window in the place . . . they wanted it fixed . . . and right away! . . . They were afraid we'd put one over on them . . . They hollered to prevent us from mentioning the rent . . . They wouldn't even look at the bills . . . Their shithouse [tinette] was really stopped up, it was overflowing into the street . . . In winter it froze and the bowl cracked under the slightest pressure . . . every time it cost 80 francs . . . The bastards [charognes] wrecked everything in sight . . . That was the tenants' way of getting even . . . [. . .] Grandma pinned up her skirts with safety pins and stripped to her shift on top. Then we went to work . . . We needed lots of hot water. We had to get it from a shoemaker across the street and bring it over in a pitcher. The tenants wouldn't give us a drop. Then Caroline started poking down into the drain. She worked her pole back and forth and dislodged the muck. The pole alone wouldn't do it. She plunged in with both arms, the tenants came out with all their brats to watch us cleaning out their shit . . . and the papers . . . and the rags . . . They'd wad them up on purpose . . . Caroline was undaunted . . . What a woman! Nothing could get her down . . . [. . .]

Nobody's bothered to try to keep them up . . . Grandma
knocked herself out, it didn't do her any good . . . when you come
right down to it, that's what killed her . . . messing around that day
in January even later than usual, first in cold water, then in boiling
water . . . always in the faucet, putting oakum in the pump and
thawing out the faucets. (96–98; 594–96)

Here, we have Céline condemning the working poor, clearing up any
confusion we may have had about any kind of explicit alignment with
a particular group of people. Céline is not a man of the people; he is
not a man to be tied to any party.[31] He may have a particularly keen
awareness of economic inequality, but in this passage, it is toward
Ferdinand's landlord grandmother that any sympathies are directed.
The working poor are cast as parasites sabotaging their own homes
for the purpose of making this old woman's life horrible, blocking up
their own toilets with wads of paper, cloth, and their own shit. And
yet Caroline, who could be described as Ferdinand's protector, more
of a mother to him than weak Clémence, rolls up her sleeves and
skirts and accepts the task of cleaning up other people's shit, literally.
The task of handling excrement produced by others, cast as the most
abject of tasks,[32] becomes instead, in Ferdinand's eyes, the manifestation of Caroline's goodness, and her superiority over others. And
this goodness, this dignity and responsibility, is cast as the reason that
Caroline dies from exposure to the elements in the middle of winter:
her handling of shit lands her in the shit that is death.

Shit, in Céline's hands, is thus a multivalent material that does not
appear to have any intrinsic valuation: it is not simply abjection, nor
is it conversely a good. Rather, it is a sign of conflict, where conflict is
quite simply the attestation of difference, of the fact that others exist
in the world, others who are not you, who do not share your perspective or your experience or your interests.[33] From the mere fact of this
alterity, conflict arises. Shit is thus, in the description of the Passage
Choiseul, a sign of the conflict between Auguste and his neighbors,
the accumulation of dogshit the sign of some kind of conspiracy. And
in the passage just discussed, the tenants' weaponization of shit is a
sign of the conflict between them and Caroline, a conflict that arises

not because of any real characteristic found in or action committed by Caroline, but simply because of the interval that exists between their respective classes: Caroline is a landowner, integrated in some measure into the bourgeoisie, whereas they are the working poor.

And yet, the shit that arises wherever there is difference is also there to immediately negate that difference. As seen earlier, shit undoes the very thing it does and ultimately works against distinction, as everything falls into shit's indistinction and indifference. Shit touches bad people, the *charognes* (bastards in Mannheim's translation, literally *carcasses*) Ferdinand rails against, as well as good people such as Caroline. Regardless of who you are or what you do, shit awaits you. You can use shit against others or have it used against you, but in the end, everyone is dealing and living with shit (the tenants, by blocking their toilets to target Caroline, have their homes overflowing with it into the street so that they too are caught up in it). In a social order marked by pettiness, constant betrayal, and discontent—marked by, in other words, division—shit is the tie that binds, the one thing that everyone shares, and is thus the source of an undesired solidarity, a commonality that will not disappear.[34]

Shit, as it would turn out, is the best solvent for the problem of human particularity. But where, in an earlier work like *Voyage au bout de la nuit*, Céline, in describing in fantastic detail a scene from New York's public toilets, evokes this defecatory space as a joyous one, "un communisme joyeux de caca" (a joyous caca communism),[35] the shit in *Mort à crédit* is joyless. In the years between Céline's first and second novels, years marked by bitterness and disappointment at his lack of literary recognition (Céline was shortlisted for the prestigious Prix Goncourt for *Voyage au bout de la nuit,* which ultimately went that year to a less-deserving work and author who are no longer read, having fallen out of French literary memory), and by a Europe heading steadily toward a second world war, the solidarity that inheres in shit loses the potential for joy. Joy is replaced instead by a perpetual sense of waste—not the wastefulness of abundance but rather the loss connoted by a euphemism for defecation like *elimination.* We thus move from a joyous communism to a communal catastrophe of caca, where the catastrophe and the loss that binds us all is that of mortality, of our own elimination from the shit heap that is the world.

Of Shit and Vomit: A Tale of Two Poetics

We can see this communal catastrophe and the shit that undergirds it in one of the most notorious passages of *Mort à crédit*: that of a maritime passage and the seasickness that takes over all the passengers, rendered in nauseating detail. The passage, which occurs while crossing the Channel during a vacation that Ferdinand takes with his parents to Dieppe, a Normand village, has been read by critics and scholars for the spectacular vomiting that animates it from beginning to end. It is a disgusting passage, filled with a seemingly endless stream of description of all the undigested things coming out of the passengers' guts, with Céline's trademark use of ellipses as punctuation mirroring the rhythmic nature of the contractions vomiting entails. To give an example of this revolting maritime scene, here is an excerpt describing Ferdinand and his mother vomiting together:

> My mother was down on her knees on the deck . . . she smiled with a sublime effort, she was drooling at the mouth . . .
> "You see," she says to me in the middle of the terrible plummeting . . . "You see, Ferdinand, you still have some of that tuna fish on your stomach too . . ." We try again in unison. Bouah! and another bouah! . . . She was mistaken, it was the crêpes . . . With a little more effort I think I could bring up French fries . . . if I emptied all my guts out on the deck . . . I try . . . I struggle . . . I push like mad . . . A fierce wave beats down on the rail, smacks against the deck, rises, gushes, rolls back, sweeps the deck . . . The foam stirs up the filth and spins it around between us . . . We swallow some of it . . . We spit it up again . . . At every plunge the soul flies away . . . at every rise you recapture it in a wave of mucus and stink . . . It comes dripping from your nose, all salty. This is too much! One passenger begs for mercy . . . He cries out to heaven that he's empty! . . . He tries again! . . . And a raspberry comes up after all! . . . He examines it, goggle-eyed with horror . . . Now he really has nothing left! . . . He wishes he could vomit out his two

eyes . . . He tries, he tries hard . . . He braces himself against the mast . . . He's trying to drive them out of their sockets . . . Mama collapses against the rail . . . She vomits herself up again, all she's got . . . A carrot comes up . . . a piece of fat . . . and the whole tail of a mullet . . . (123–24; 623)

The maritime-crossing passage, which other critics are too polite to quote from in any sustained manner, tests its readers' sensibilities (and stomachs).[36] This passage, which continues for several pages, has been treated as a staging of human corporeality and the abjection that is the fact of our embodiment, or as a sort of allegory of a language that is broken by the reality of war, so that the only thing or language that ought properly to come out of the mouths of a transformed humanity is vomit, with such embodiment taking over the task of expression for a language that can no longer properly function.[37]

On my end, however, I see this passage, between its vomit-like rhythms and onomatopoeia (*Bouah! Bouah!*), and its merciless inventory of stomach contents, narrated in an immediate present tense that produces an immersive, suspenseful experience—we expect tuna to come up from Ferdinand's stomach only to have a crêpe emerge, we expect the nameless passenger to be cleared out only to have a single raspberry come out, obscene in its singularity—as the manifestation of a kind of topsy-turvy realism and an allegory of writing that condemns the literary models that dominated Céline's contemporaries' sense of literary possibility.

What stands out in this vomit scene is the sheer legibility of the food items being expelled from all the passengers' guts. While our vomit certainly does retain a kind of legibility that our feces do not, when it comes to drawing conclusions about what a person has eaten, rarely do our vomited-up meals retain the kind integrity that we see here. What's being vomited up is narrated as being whole: an entire raspberry, a carrot as opposed to a chewed-up bit of carrot, an entire fishtail. And yet, it seems highly unlikely that everyone on board the ship would have neglected to chew their food to the point of being able to vomit it up in such an intact state. The food that is vomited up is thus hyperrealistic in its uncanny resemblance to food that has not yet been eaten.

Given the analogy that is easily established between vomit and language as products that are both expelled through the mouth, I submit that the vomit passage is actually staging the processes (or lack thereof, as Céline would have it) of a venerable French literary realism originating in the nineteenth century with Balzac and pushed toward a more extreme form by Zola with his creation of the naturalist literary movement.[38] Céline admired Zola, going so far as to give a speech in homage to his naturalist predecessor,[39] the only literary homage he would ever render, but embedded within his praise of Zola was a critique. Zola's naturalism was able to capture the horror of Zola's time, but his naturalist method, if attempted in the twentieth-century, post–World War I context in which Céline wrote, could only be doomed to fail: reality had become utterly indescribable, unrepresentable. Céline was posing the question of the impossibility of representation years before World War II would break out as the cataclysmic event of the twentieth century that irreparably broke the human subject, the haunting question of how to speak the unspeakable driving the work of a generation of writers and thinkers trying to account for the Shoah.

Céline critiques Zola's faith in virtue, his optimism that through the proper—read naturalist—use of language, man could be pushed to improve society.[40] At the heart of naturalism's optimism was the notion that literature, as a particular use of language, could, by conveying the knowledge or truth of how the world worked, then work to ameliorate said world. Céline, cynical and jaded from his experience on the front lines of the First World War, had no such optimism, and he wrote against any humanistic current of literature. For him, the desire to continue to write in the twentieth century as Zola had in the nineteenth was thus marred by two fundamental flaws: the optimistic project behind Zola's naturalist realism; and the utter incapacity of language to capture a reality that was beyond language's grasp.[41]

These two mistakes come together in the vomit scene to parody the kind of hyperrealism that would have been part of Zola's project.

The vomiting is described in painfully precise detail, and yet, if we as readers are as disgusted or nauseated as we are by the passage, it is because we imagine the stinky, messy reality of vomit in our minds and know it to exceed in grossness whatever reality is being described on the page. What language merely gestures to here, our bodies and our own lived experience of vomit—both outside the purview of language—remember and reenact. And as far as the social dynamic of the ship goes, there is no reason for optimism to be found in this environment marked by utter tribalism. In the paragraphs following the above passage, families help their own, but vomit violently on others and wind up in physical altercations with those who are strangers. There is no solidarity beyond familial boundaries, but everyone ends up covered in the same loathsome material.

Underneath the maritime-crossing passage's spectacular and absurd staging of vomit, which critiques the kind of literary realism practiced by Zola, is the articulation of a positive literary vision via the excrementality that subtends the passage. The way the passage is set up, the collective, riotous vomiting commands our attention as its roiling textual surface, but Céline anchors the passage in the fecal instead, which serves as its subtler and less spectacular foundation. Thrown in casually like an aside, Céline gives, at the beginning of the passage, a description of the boat's bathroom facilities: "There was only one toilet . . . in one corner of the deck . . . It was already occupied by four vomiters [vomitiques] in a state of collapse, wedged in tight . . ." (123; 622). This description of the boat's facilities is sandwiched between descriptions of people vomiting every which way, and of the sea's rocking motion, which results in so much vomiting that the horizon is replaced by one made of food being expelled forcefully from people's guts: "On the horizon were jams . . . the salad . . . the chicken . . . the coffee . . . the stew . . . everything was coming up! . . ." (123; 623).

The mention of the bathroom would at first appear to be placed under the sign of vomit, which is without a doubt the predominant matter at hand in the passage, but Céline effects an elegant displacement from vomit to feces when he ends the maritime-crossing passage by returning to the bathroom. Ferdinand gets caught up in the physical altercation that breaks out between Auguste and a big hulk of a man who is incensed that Ferdinand vomited all over his beloved wife—"I give his fair lady a complete hank of noodles . . . with tomato juice . . . a drink of cider three days old . . ." (125; 624)—and retaliates by charging at Ferdinand, striking him so hard he lands in the toilet, bringing the maritime-crossing passage to an end:

> He charges me . . . I skid . . . He flings me at the shithouse
> [gogs] . . . like a battering ram . . . I smash into it . . . I bash
> the door in . . . I fall on the poor sagging bastards . . . I turn
> around . . . I'm wedged in the middle of them . . . They've lost
> their underwear . . . I pull the chain. We're half drowned in the
> flood. We're squashed into the bowl [tinette]⁴² . . . But they never
> stop snoring . . . I don't even know if I'm dead or alive. (126; 625)

We come full circle, reencountering the four *vomitiques* who are so expended from their vomiting that they have somehow fallen asleep, but without their underwear—a detail that evokes their bare bottoms and thus a certain anality. Ferdinand finds himself catapulted into merging with these four men whose asses are hanging out for the world to see, and winds up falling into the *tinette,* the receptacle that holds all the waste. While the passage had up to this point been in the key of vomit, it modulates suddenly as Ferdinand falls into shit, his whole body covered in the waste that the *tinette* holds, in a spectacularly exaggerated reiteration of Ferdinand's confession of his having always had an ass covered in shit because he never wiped.

While this maritime crossing is discussed primarily for its remarkable vomit, Céline, as can be seen, attaches the passage's narrative fate to the excremental architecture of the ship's bathroom, which, through the evocation of the *tinette,* is a space that is inextricably tied up with the feces that are expelled there. The passage begins with the bathroom as a point of orientation, and the bathroom serves as a way out of this narrative interlude: without the deus ex machina of the toilets, the passage could have gone on interminably, vomit begetting vomit in an endless cycle of vomiting, one's being vomited upon triggering one's own vomiting upon, with the target of one's vomit then being impelled to vomit again—an exchange and reciprocity that keeps reproducing itself. Céline's excremental structure thus sandwiches and supersedes the vomitous allegory of a Zolaesque realism. He mobilizes this juxtaposition between vomit and feces, and the difference between the two kinds of matter, by which we can compare Zola's literary project, founded in a naïve (according to Céline) optimism in the power of representation, and his own. Céline's renunciation of the realist register—no one could describe Céline's delirious, dreamlike narrative and its picaresque stream of absurdities as realist in the usual sense of the term—trumps the nineteenth-century pretention to represent the world as it is and the particularly Zolaseque ambition to, above describing reality, explain *why* it is as it is and make sense of the reality recorded faithfully.

Vomit represents Zola's logic while feces represent Céline's, and these two bodily processes map onto each writer's poetics. Céline, in emphasizing the intactness of the passengers' stomach contents, points to how little their bodies did to process the food inside them. The passengers took the food in, but instead of digesting the food, extracting nutrients and water from it, transforming it into feces that no longer resemble what was taken in, they expel it back out whole, this unprocessed expulsion rendering the food completely useless, and beyond useless—revolting. Zola, for all his literary merits, is taken by Céline to be, for Céline's moment, a useless writer—useless because he founded his project on a humanist conviction in humanity's capacity to progress. Zola's literary project, which had been brilliant in the previous century, is a revolting response to the reality of the twentieth century. In the new age that is the twentieth century, with its monstrous new ways of making war, its monstrous new ways of manufacturing goods and capital, a naturalist–realist approach to writing cannot properly account for and digest the world.

Instead of vomiting out a text marked by resemblance, by "realness," we are to model textual production on defecation instead, which is the only way to properly respond to the new reality. Through the digestive process, we eat—we take in life—and then we expel matter that, through its odor and distastefulness, gets likened to *pourriture*—to rot and decomposition, to death. In a reality that takes human life and destroys it, as demonstrated by World War I and its shocking new technologies of death and rejection of all the kinds of ways of making war that had preceded it, the production of shit is the only honest response to the becoming-shit that Céline feels keenly is our lot in life. Over and against an outdated realism, Céline introduces a cosmology or universe of shit that, rather than realistically and precisely describe the world outside the text, captures instead the essence of what that world is. If we live in a shithole of a world where our miserable existences are but our passage through an existential gastrointestinal tract—Céline's description of the excremental passage where Ferdinand grows up establishes an analogy between that passage and our gastrointestinal tract—only to be expelled from life as a rotting corpse, then the most authentic literary position is to communicate the excremental mode in which humanity produces and reproduces until it passes away.

Vomit and excrement, in addition to concretizing two opposed approaches to reality, also constitute incompatible positions vis-à-vis the question of memory, which is key to the mode of the bildungsroman and its recounting of a past period of growth and development. In Céline's case, he ties shit to memory, as he places his entire childhood, the past that is the object of *Mort à crédit*'s remembrance, under the sign of shit—"I had shit on my ass until the army." Shit, unlike vomit, renders unrecognizable what the body takes in. Where the passengers on board the ship in the maritime-crossing passage vomit up their food intact, shit processes food beyond recognition: feces as matter do not themselves reveal what their origin is in the way that vomit visibly does.

Reading memory onto these bodily functions, where the act of expulsion and the material expelled stand in for the object of memory, we can derive a Célinian formalism in which the past is not an object to be recognized and conjured up again in the present, à la Proust, who abolishes the boundaries between past and present so that the past can be the present, as with his descriptions of having a magic lantern project mythical stories onto the walls of his bedroom, or of having an entire village reconstructed from a cup of tea. Proust's project of memory in *In Search of Lost Time* is about reliving the past moment, restoring to the past all the freshness of the present. Céline's project of memory in *Mort à crédit,* however, is about refusing the freshness of the present to the past. Via writing, he processes and works through the past, the way the digestive system processes food to transform it. Instead of the freshness of the present we have then a past that has been transformed and worked, with the end product of that transformation being shit.[43]

Memory is turned into shit, with all the redolence and viscous materiality of shit. Shit sticks to surfaces, and the odor it gives off is an olfactory signal that a transformation has been effected, that a process has occurred, that what we started out with—in this case, Ferdinand's childhood—is no longer what it was, and cannot be recuperated whole and intact the way Proust's narrator's childhood is, in all its fragrance, beauty, and emotive strength. We see this clearly with Céline, who transforms Ferdinand's childhood into shit: the memory he evokes is of his shitty childhood growing up in a shithole with shitty parents and living through shitty experiences. Unlike the porosity of boundaries that we get with Proust, where waking life melts into dreams, past into present, with Céline we have a reinforcement of boundaries, as shit's stickiness only reinforces the distinction between shit and the surface to which it adheres, be it Ferdinand's bottom or the tile floor of a Parisian passage.[44]

Rather than the aesthetically pleasant simultaneity of temporalities we get with Proust, Céline gives us the jarring collision between the past and the present: it is no pleasant thing—it is even dangerous—to call up the past. On the narrative side, we receive the story of Ferdinand's childhood only when a grown Ferdinand becomes gravely ill, a fever opening his mind to the project of recalling the past. And on the readerly side, the price Céline makes us pay for having access to Ferdinand's childhood and his memory is the shit that covers him constantly and permeates the whole narrative fabric. The past, Céline seems to say, is shit, and shit is difficult, effortful—

a problem.[45] And yet, to try to pass over shit or do without it is inconceivable. Shit, like life, like the writing of a text, must be seen through to the end.

No Time Not to Shit

Thus far, we have seen the way Céline uses excrement to construct *Mort à crédit*'s temporality, anchor its narrative structure, and critique modes of writing that offer up legible renderings of the world, in Zola's case, and aesthetically pleasing renderings of the world, in Proust's case. For Céline, to begin—life as well as a narrative—is to land in shit, and to end—life as well as a narrative—is to land in shit. The telos of Céline's novel, as for his oeuvre in general, is to get as close as possible to writing, while still alive, the truth of death, when the only truly authentic expression of death is to be dead. Shit is what enables Céline to get at something like authenticity, as the fecal matter that we all carry in our entrails is putrefaction, a bit of death that we are constantly in contact with,[46] like Ferdinand is with his shit-covered bottom.

We've seen how Céline's treatment and foregrounding of shit is motivated and has a variety of formal functions. But shit in Céline is more than just a formal element—it is material. To understand what this means, we must first understand Céline's relation to materiality, which is that he hates it. Matter, for Céline, is aligned with death against life, as matter is what the human body is reduced to upon death. No longer animated by life, able to resist the heaviness of gravity and break inertia, the body, deprived of force, becomes literal dead weight, inanimate matter.[47] Céline's hatred of materiality is so intense that his oeuvre could be described simply as "a struggle against matter"[48] in Godard's terms. Alice Kaplan describes Céline's sense of abject, morbid materiality as "a decaying positivism, that obsessive interest in disintegration that keeps the writing close to the body."[49] The same interest that leads Céline to describe bodies in their basest state—an assertion of the abominable matter we all end as—also animates his fascination for what in French is called the *féerique*,[50] manifested in his lifelong fascination for dancers as those human bodies who are able to, through their graceful movements, resist the inertia, weight, and rigidity that are wedded to death in Céline's imagination.[51]

Where Céline's poetics can be described as an attempt at escaping the body and as a repudiation of materiality insofar as materiality is a sign of accursed mortality, it is not so much materiality in itself that is a problem for Céline, but the incapacity of materiality in its human forms—the body, the objects and goods that we create—to resist time. The problem, in other words, is that materiality, like the human, bows the knee to time, and cannot help but be changed and deformed in its existence in time. Is it any surprise, then, given our predilection to framing literature (and art in general) as a way to thwart mortality by according to the text (and by extension, its creator) an afterlife or legacy that long outlives the one who makes it, that Céline, in his disgust at mortality, would turn to writing to not so much redeem materiality but force it to stand up against time? Céline uses the excremental, via literature, to reject the kind of materiality of which our mortal, weak bodies are disgraceful and defective exemplars, and experience a materiality that does not degrade—the materiality, the stuff, of literature.

For Céline, fecal matter is a particularly strong signifier of death, its matter pointing more directly at the death that all matter is than do other, less abject or odious forms of matter. But shit in Céline functions both as a figuration of death and as a way to resist it. Pierre-Marie Miroux, in a work consecrated to examining death in Céline's oeuvre, argues that "if this imprisoned [in our intestines] shit signifies death and all that it implies, doesn't the relaxing of the sphincters signify, inversely, life?"[52] I would argue that it is not simply the act of loosening the sphincters to allow defecation to occur that signifies life, but, more precisely, where the shit ends up.

Excrement, as we know, is an important part of the ecosystem, playing a crucial role in the cycle of life by acting as a vector of germination by spreading seeds, as food for certain species, and as fertilizer. Shit, in other words, holds the potential for life. But with modern waste management methods, which flush away our excrement and remove it from the ecosystem, shit is not in the service of life.[53] Shit must be allowed to be in contact with the systems and lifeforms it sustains if it is to produce life. Shit can and does signify life, within a literary ecosystem that puts it in contact with language.

In Céline's struggle against matter and death, writing, like medicine, is a way of resisting death and the effects of time. After the body gives up and is reduced to matter, our texts, if we are lucky, remain.[54] Shit's vital potential is unleashed when it is introduced by a writer like Céline into a literary context. Shit, in his writing, is effectively a transhistorical *fuck you* to time, where time *is* death, as it is the passage of time that produces mortality. Shit, unlike virtually everything else about the human body and the ways in which we inhabit it, and the ways in which it inhabits its environment, is stable. Even as everything about what our bodies signify and what kind of technologies we have for mediating the body evolves, shit remains a constant—remarkably impervious to the conventional teleological narratives of progress humankind is invested in. Just as was the case with the earliest humans, we are still confronted with the materiality of our shit, which, once it is produced, presents us with the imperative to manage it. Despite the development of forms of plumbing that minimize the contact we have with our fecal matter, the material experience of defecation—of eating, digesting, and then having waste that must be evacuated, and of feeling physically our feces transition from inside to outside our bodies—remains remarkably stable, timeless, and unaffected by progress.

This resistance to time, this hiccup in our narratives of progress that is shit, makes shit particularly well suited to making texts resistant to time as well, able to weather the effects of time and remain read and readable. In the context of writing, shit's materiality, which is all too undeniable in our lived lives, accords to the text as well an undeniable materiality, as intimated by the vocabulary of "coarseness" that is used to describe language like Céline's scatological, vulgar, profane vocabulary, his capacity for inventing an entirely new (crass) lexical field constituting a kind of genius.[55] A word like "coarse" points to language's having a texture, and hence, being material, as texture is a material phenomenon. And here, I would argue, following Monique Wittig, for the texture of language having real material status,[56] as opposed to standing merely figuratively for the physical textures we encounter in the world.

Céline, through the abrasiveness of his language, reveals the surface of language just as impressionist painters revealed the canvas as the site of representation and paint as the material by which images were created—an act that, as with Céline's language, seemed obscene to the impressionists' contemporaries even as it revolutionized art and brought painting into modernity. Given the relative immateriality of language vis-à-vis a medium like paint—if you touch a canvas painted in impasto, you can feel the paint itself, whereas running your fingers on the pages of even the most iconoclastic or revolutionary literary works doesn't deliver up the materiality of language or feel different than the pages of the most conventional works—it can be difficult to conceptualize language as a material.[57] But it is a material, as the narratives that literature produces are not made of immaterial concepts but through the language that gives them form.

Céline, in making recourse to so much coarse language, much of which is scatological, does so to disturb what, until him, had been the very smooth surface of the French language and the texts it was used to construct. His shit language calls attention to language as language—as a set of possibilities from which writers must choose, within which writers must work. He makes language viscous and gives to the language at our disposal a kind of heft. Through his carefully and deliberately coarse language, Céline gestures toward texture, thereby drawing attention to the way narrative is not simply a vertical, immersive experience, in which we as readers get to plunge into a simulation of the world, but a surface—a material. And for Céline's readers back in 1936, this surface with which he confronted them was obscene, as nauseating as the Passage Ferdinand calls home.

In the case of *Mort à crédit,* it was Céline's sex scenes, not his shit scenes, that got him censored, but in the terrible reception his novel had, it was the excremental that commanded attention, so that his critics couldn't see the novel's literariness for all the shit. Much attention has been paid to Céline's revolutionary use of slang and popular language, through which the language of the gutter, of the streets and sewers, became the literary language of a high-brow modernism whose self-conscious fragmentation and linguistic delirium lend themselves perfectly to the attentions of a perhaps higher-brow postmodernism embodied by the heady textual productions of poststructuralist theory.[58] But at the time of publication, Céline's readers had a much more straightforward relation to his shit language. For them, writing about shit using shit language made Céline "the biggest producer of waste *in the world,* a kind of Ford of sludge," and "behind this pruritis of bestial images and triviality, this erethism of waste, this opulent eruption of the vocabulary of the sewers, this compendium of urinals . . . and this commitment to the stercoraceous, what is there to justify or attenuate our nausea? Nothing."[59]

Céline's critics were united in excluding *Mort à crédit* from literature, as determined by these guardians of taste and culture, and it was this exclusion from the literary—from the thing that could give Céline an afterlife—that Céline could not abide. Céline was, to Céline, a writer, belonging firmly in the territory of literature and art. He responded to one review that faulted him for his unprecedented use of argot, or slang—and let us recall that Céline's argot is decidedly in an excremental mode—claiming that it was a dated language that would make *Mort à crédit* age quickly, by turning the charge against his accuser: "You say this language dies quickly. So it has lived, it LIVES as long as I use it."[60] Céline's shit language, which he carefully and copiously spreads around his text, rather than aligned with death, is aligned with life—it transforms from useless waste to vital fertilizer.

In *Bagatelles pour un massacre,* written after Céline's disappointment and anger at seeing *Mort à crédit* humiliated in the literary sphere, Céline diagnoses literature as being an odorless corpse.[61] Writing into what, for him, was the sanitized void of French literature, his own writing, full of shit whose stench Céline insists upon, is an antidote. To be alive is to produce shit; to be dead is to be shit. In Céline's hands, literature will produce shit—lots of it—and accordingly announce its vitality. Céline thus turns to a shit language, which, as language, proclaims its materiality more than the elevated and polished language of his confrères. As mentioned earlier, the coarseness of scatological language evokes the idea of texture and surface, but beyond that, it is permeated with greater materiality than other forms of language because it draws from the sort of staying power shit has as a material, seen in its capacity to contaminate other materials. Take, for example, the aversion most of us feel at the mere idea of eating or drinking from a previously used bedpan or chamber pot, no matter how thoroughly it has been cleaned and disinfected. The idea that shit was once there allows it to linger in the present, endowed with a materiality that outlasts its real presence. Or, put another way, shit seems to be able to cross boundaries more than other materials. It is this traversal quality that had Céline's critics in such a tizzy: simply the evocation of shit through the use of scatological language seems to conjure up actual fecal matter, as if the boundary between referent and sign were more porous than in other instances of language. Certainly, the fecal matter that is shit's referent is a particularly charged material—our aversion to contact with feces is biologically programmed, our disgust toward fecal matter an evolutionary instinct for self-preservation.[62] Shit's staying power is thus directly proportional to our disgust.

Céline harnesses this same staying power, and disgust, for his writing. A work like *Mort à crédit,* full of a shit language that lives because it has the power to overcome the inertia and static quality of the sort of polished language that had been the only authorized language at literature's disposal, is able to last, to outlast the more acceptable works of literature that were published at the same moment as *Mort à crédit,* which no one reads any more. Those other works, which have fallen into oblivion, have ended up in the dung heap of literary history, while it is Céline, with his seemingly boundless capacity to disgust his reader, who remains an integral part of the French literary canon—the body of works transmitted from one generation of readers to another as an important constitutive part of French identity—despite his politics. His shit, far from consigning his work to datedness, has enabled his work to become that most timeless of literary works—a classic.

Céline's legacy, through a work like *Mort à crédit,* is to fight against the deodorization of the French literary imaginary and to integrate the modern and contemporary canon of twentieth-century writing with the early modern canon that precedes it, whose scatological nature is a given and is even celebrated as an instance of Rabelaisian carnality—a corporeality that is denied in twentieth-century literature, or relegated to the terrain of sexuality instead (which, unlike the corporeality of fecality, shores up, rather than levels, difference).[63] If we take seriously the narrative that Céline is a revolutionary French writer whose transgressive use of a colorful, coarse, popular language modernizes French literature, the logical consequence is that the twentieth-century canon that Céline is a central part of and helps inaugurate is itself excremental—we know shit to be a viscous material that sticks to whatever surfaces it comes into contact with, like Ferdinand's bottom, the pages of *Mort à crédit,* the minds of his contemporaries, or the canon. Céline uses shit to resuscitate literature and issues to his successors a challenge: will you let literature die or will you use this material that produces life and is able to make matter resist the death of which it is part?

Exit through the Bathroom

I want to end by turning to the novel's own ending, which isn't really an end so much as an unresolved non-closing—one which crystallizes the challenge that Céline makes to French literature. Ferdinand, having returned to Paris after Courtial des Pereire's gory suicide, stays with his uncle Édouard and has a bout of vomiting and diarrhea, as he did after having nearly killed Auguste at the end of the first part of the novel. Ferdinand has an odd, manic conversation with his uncle, where he keeps stating the need to leave, citing the army as an option, while his uncle keeps trying to convince him to stay. The novel ends with Uncle Édouard putting Ferdinand to bed as if he were still a small child and telling him he knows where the bathroom is. Céline has already demonstrated for us how to bring a narrative passage to an end—by hurling Ferdinand into the toilets and covering him with the shit that is both a connection with mortality and a possibility for transcending it. *Mort à crédit,* which up to this point has seemed like one unending misadventure after another, also gestures to the toilet as a way out, but, unlike in the maritime crossing, leaves it to the reader to get us out of the text via the toilet, which is on the textual horizon just beyond the novel's end, rather than drawing upon a deus ex machina that hurls Ferdinand into it.

What will we as readers do? Will we use our imagination to fill the toilet with Ferdinand's shit? Will we allow Ferdinand to produce yet again the material to which we owe the narrative that we've been immersed in? The challenge, or invitation, is in some ways a disingenuous one: after hundreds of pages of Ferdinand's excremental adventures, the novel has developed in us a certain excremental instinct, and I would submit that we cannot but fill in the excremental ellipsis that is the novel's ending. Our readerly collaboration with Céline on this front is one more reinforcement of his recasting the modern canon as an excremental one, and while it may seem minor, if multiplied by all the readers this work has had and will have, it accumulates, just as the shit on Ferdinand's ass does.

By making us exit his text through the toilet, Céline seems to want the last odor of his text to be a fecal one. Going from *Mort à crédit* into the other works we read, won't this odor follow us like it does Ferdinand? As we read the works that follow his, that become integrated into the canon, won't there be that slight odor that presents itself to us and reminds us to look down beneath the surface of whatever text we read and recognize the excrementality that is there? The hermeneutics of suspicion that are a trademark of twentieth-century ways of reading are, in a post-Célinian moment, necessarily tainted with excrement. In whatever text we read, we can ask, "Where is the shit?" And if it isn't there, I would suggest that we should ask, "What happened to it?"

) 2 (

BECKETT
Shit for Brains

***

Samuel Beckett's response to the question of where shit is, is that it's everywhere—we are in it, we are of it, and we are headed to it. We don't have to look very far to get to the scatological in Beckett, when his writing, both literary and personal, is filled with scatological interludes, references, and jokes: we find in the Beckettian landscape scatological place-names like the villages Shit and Hole; characters named Krapp and Comtesse Caca are hardly subtle; and Beckett suggests throughout his letters that his books be used as toilet paper.[1] This author, hailed by some as *the* major modernist writer of the twentieth century, by others as the first postmodernist writer, functions as a literary Rorschach test: tell me what you have to say about Beckett and I will tell you who you are. Indeed, Beckett has given rise to a breathtakingly broad range of criticism, and the decades devoted to interpreting Beckett have given rise to as many critical angles as there are critics: a lot.

We have psychoanalytic interpretations of Beckett that read him through Jungian, Freudian, and Lacanian perspectives; we have Deleuzian readings of Beckett that use him to work against a Kantian bent in literary criticism more interested in what texts mean than what and how they do; we have the Beckett of animal studies, which gives accounts of, for example, the birds and the bees that can be found in his work; we have the Beckett of waste studies, which reads Beckett for the discarded objects that figure in and anchor his sparse landscapes or for the way his humans are themselves wasted; we have the Beckett of shit studies, where accounts are given of the evidently scatological dimension of his writing, showing how shit renders subjectivity porous, for instance, or how it is used to critique religion; we have the Beckett who's mobilized to illustrate the desolation of a post-Holocaust world and the emptiness of a broken human subject; we have the philosophical Beckett brought into conversation with René Descartes and Arthur Schopenhauer.[2] That Beckett criticism is this rich carnival is to be expected, perhaps: in addition to writing across genres, producing works of art criticism, literary criticism, poetry, fiction, as well as theater, Beckett was a bilingual writer. His transcultural trajectory—he was born and raised in Dublin, only to move to Paris, where he would spend the rest of his life—has thrown him into multiple canons, claimed as he is by both the Anglophones and the Francophones, with arguments made also for his Irish specificity.

You already know where my critical investments in Beckett take me—to his shit—and in what follows I seek not simply to supplement the scatologically oriented criticism that already exists, which does a fine job of giving different accounts of the many significations and functions that shit takes on in Beckett, of what shit can mean. Instead, I want to explore *why* it needs to be there—why Beckett's literary enterprise would fall apart without all the shit in it. In order to get there, we need to go back to Céline, as Céline is the scatological germ that, as we'll see, accounts for Beckett's turn to French as his first writing language and acts as a sounding board for the themes that emerge as obsessions for Beckett. To put it as Beckett or Céline themselves might: Beckett is the fart that follows Céline's turd.

Under a Célinian Sky

We know that Beckett was an admirer of Céline's writing, and a much-annotated copy of *Voyage au bout de la nuit* can be found in

Beckett's personal library, but the impact of Céline's work on Beckett's is infrequently discussed, unlike, for instance, James Joyce's and Marcel Proust's influence. Perhaps the infamy of Céline's political views makes him too toxic a figure to bring into the orbit of a politically good Beckett, who can be lauded not simply for his literary accomplishments but for his leftist political credentials, seen in his work for the French Resistance during World War II.[3] And yet, for Jean-Michel Rabaté, one of the central figures in Beckett scholarship, Céline is an even more important influence on Beckett than the aforementioned Joyce and Proust.[4]

In fact, for Rabaté, Céline is the reason that Beckett switches to writing in French, a move that would be instrumental in putting Beckett down the path of literary stardom, as it is the famous so-called trilogy—*Molloy, Malone meurt* (*Malone Dies*), and *L'Innommable* (*The Unnamable*)—written in French in the aftermath of World War II, which gets narrated as a turning point for Beckett's career. It is during this time of intense Francophonization that Beckett would produce the novels credited with dramatically reshaping the modern novel, and that he would write *En attendant Godot* (*Waiting for Godot*), undoubtedly Beckett's most famous play and one that would establish him as the modernist playwright of the twentieth century. As Rabaté puts it, "It's as if Beckett needed to go into French to be able to write not 'like Céline' but 'with' or 'after Céline.' Beckett would have thus 'translated' Céline—not into English, but into his own French."[5] This is a considerably different account of Beckett's French turn than the usual narrative that turns to Beckett himself for an explanation: that French, more so than English, enabled Beckett to write without style, to achieve a "flat" writing.[6] And yet, to read Beckett is to be confronted with one of the strongest styles of the twentieth century, one whose strength rivals and resonates with Céline's, with which it seems to vibrate on the same wavelength.[7]

Indeed, if you put the two writers side by side, the resonances and affinities become clear: both are transforming French, writing in French in such a way as to defamiliarize it and make it strange. Céline busts through literature's doors with a rocket launcher loaded with argot and the crassest language the century had seen, and Beckett's status as a non-native speaker of French affords him a consciousness and self-awareness about the process of language acquisition; both are obsessed with death, with the ontological dump that is human existence, and with figuring out a way to write death; and both are wickedly funny, endowed with a comic sensibility and a humor that is all too rare in twentieth-century French literature, which is weighed down by a certain ponderous seriousness.

Céline's exploding French literature open makes it possible for Beckett to come and write in Céline's wake, his own scatological language and brand of argot no longer shocking or novel, the way it was for Céline's readers. Leland de La Durantaye has described Beckett as a *logoclast*—literature's response to the iconoclasm associated with visual modernism's rejection of tradition (e.g., Marcel Duchamp's infamous urinal)—where logoclasm entails taking "stumbling, staggering, stunning aim at words and their concerted use" in an attempt to attack "the reason (or *logos*) for language's being."[8] Where Céline attacks words in order to make language live, seeing a linguistic and literary violence as the way to preserve and resuscitate a dying language and the literary bodies it produces, Beckett attacks words in order to destroy language, reduce words to dust, prevent them from making meaning, and quash out the seemingly inextinguishable pilot light of signification.

If we were to depict the two writers in the kind of caricature that was often used in the nineteenth century to critique its writers (e.g., Achille Lemot's famous caricature of Flaubert as a surgeon dissecting Madame Bovary on his table), we might come up with something like the following: Céline throttling language, represented as a wimpy man of uninspiring physique, while yelling all sorts of expletives and crying out "Live, damn it, live!" Beckett, on the other hand, could be depicted as holding a hammer playing a game of whack-a-mole with language and crying out "Stop meaning!" While each writer has a different end for language in mind, they are joined together in an antagonistic and conflictual relation with language, the medium and material to which they owe their posterity.

In what follows, I want to turn to Beckett's *Molloy* to see what it means for Beckett to write "not 'like Céline' but 'with' or 'after'" him. Beckett has a different vision for language and literature than does Céline, but he shares with his inassimilable, inadmissible, and yet indispensable predecessor an excremental sensibility that, as it was for Céline, serves not simply as an offensive or crass ornamentation for his writing, but is structurally necessary. I focus on *Molloy* in particular for a few reasons: first, it is Beckett's first novel written in French and in that respect, following Rabaté, his first Célinian novel, which makes it a logical point of comparison for the writers' excremental literary projects; second, *Molloy,* more so than Beckett's other works, elaborates a kind of excremental ontology and is the site of a sustained conceptualization of shit, which makes it a suitable text from which to extrapolate a model of excrementality as a system.[9]

"I Hardly Fart at All"

As we saw in the previous chapter, Céline's Ferdinand is a narrator whose ass is always covered in shit, such that the entirety of *Mort à crédit* is placed under a malodorous excremental sign and is structured narratively through and by shit. Like *Mort à crédit, Molloy* is picaresque, its hapless narrators carried along in the narrative by random forces that take them from one misadventure to another within the framework of each narrator's failed quest: Molloy, in the first part, recounts his failed quest to find his mother; Moran, in the second part, recounts his failed quest as some sort of agent to find Molloy.[10] Beckett's Molloy, as the first part's narrator and the second part's object, gives to the novel its narrative coherence or gravity, and functions as a kind of echo or distortion of Ferdinand, *Mort à crédit*'s narrative center. Even before *Molloy,* Beckett was already thinking with Céline, modeling his narratives on Céline's, fashioning his own version of Ferdinand. Beckett's short story, "L'Expulsé" (1946),[11] written and published before *Molloy* (which was written between 1947 and 1950 and published in 1951), can be seen as a kind of preparatory text for *Molloy,* with both texts featuring a peripatetic narrator who has been cut off from his family. Early on, the narrator of "L'Expulsé" reveals himself to also have had a shit-covered bottom, like Ferdinand, in a description that makes no attempt at hiding the Célinian intertext:

> I had then the deplorable habit, having pissed in my trousers, or shat there, which I did fairly regularly in the morning, about ten or half past ten, of persisting in going on and finishing my days as if nothing had happened. The very idea of changing my trousers, or of confiding in mother, who goodness knows asked nothing better than to help me, was unbearable, I don't know why, and till bedtime I dragged on with burning and stinking [*brûlant, croustillant et puant*] between my little thighs, or sticking to my bottom, the result of my incontinence.[12]

Where this intertextual resonance is particularly fecal and strong in this earlier text, in *Molloy,* we see Beckett putting more distance between himself and Céline, assuming a subtler intertextual position, and making Céline's influence less obvious. However, as both texts demonstrate, Céline is there as an abundantly fecal source for Beckett's own writing.

In Céline, the persistence and constancy of Ferdinand's fecal accretions undergird and shape the narrative. In Beckett, while Molloy is associated with feces, certainly, as intimated by his own admission of a Ferdinand-esque malodorousness[13] and the way he always has newspaper on hand with which to wipe himself (26; 26), the strongest parallel to Ferdinand is not found in Molloy's shit (of which we don't encounter much, except by implication) but rather, in his flatulence:

> Mimetic in spite of himself, there you have Molloy, viewed from a certain angle. And in winter, under my greatcoat, I wrapped myself in swathes of newspaper, and did not shed them until the earth awoke, for good, in April. The Times Literary Supplement was admirably adapted to this purpose, of a neverfailing toughness and impermeability. Even farts made no impression on it. I can't help it, gas escapes from my fundament on the least pretext, it's hard not to mention it now and then, however great my distaste. One day I counted them. Three hundred and fifteen farts in nineteen hours, or an average of over sixteen farts an hour. After all it's not exces-

sive. Four farts every fifteen minutes. It's unbelievable. Damn it, I hardly fart at all, I should never have mentioned it. Extraordinary how mathematics help you to know yourself. (39; 39–40)[14]

The fart scene is often cited as one of the most memorable from *Molloy*, often to illustrate Beckett's humor, where it is framed as a comic interlude or a joke.[15] I propose to take this scene, however, not simply as a joke, but as a confession of as much narrative import as Ferdinand's confession about his fecality.

Molloy's farts, which are as constant and as malodorous a presence as is Ferdinand's shit, have a similar function as the latter in structuring the narrative and placing it under an excremental sign without having to utter the excremental at every moment. With Beckett, as for Céline, the smell lingers, so that you know that in the one, a fart was recently passed at any given moment, and in the other, shit is still on that ass. Both texts' readers are forced to pay this corporeal toll: the narrative will not be delivered to us in a sanitized or deodorized format. Certainly, we can opt to ignore the odor, and the excrementality it signals, but at what price to the narrative's integrity? Pretending that we don't hear or smell a fart, out of politeness, doesn't mean that it's not there, that it hasn't changed the composition of our immediate atmosphere, that we haven't taken it in.

What does it look like to read Molloy's farts as a meta-narrative disclosure about the structure and operation of the text? Let's begin with the first sentence in this passage, where Molloy, describing himself in the third person, declares that he is "mimetic in spite of himself . . . viewed from a certain angle." The declaration seemingly comes out of nowhere, as the text that precedes the declaration has to do with what kind of weather Molloy likes, which is to say cloudy, rainy days more so than sunny ones, a predilection Molloy chalks up to the way the "pale gloom" (*pâles ombres*) (39) cast on rainy days are able to hide him better. And the text that follows the declaration of mimetic capacity takes Molloy's flatulence as its subject. What is the angle from which we can ascertain Molloy's mimesis? What is being imitated and how is Molloy enacting said imitation?

Beckett is not a careless writer: if he places this mysterious

declaration of mimesis between a reflection on weather and his relation to it and a mathematically precise accounting of his self via his
flatulence, it is surely for a reason. Indeed, after the flatulence interlude, the text returns to the question of weather: "In any case this
whole question of climate left me cold, I could stomach any mess"
(39; 40). Molloy's relation to the climate, to the weather, is the first
instance of a mimesis via the body that furthermore contains another
instance of mimesis in the same way that a fart is contained by a body.

In sum, in the text before the farting passage, Molloy speaks
of how certain weather conditions hide his body better than other
weather conditions do. Then we have the declaration of mimesis. Following that, we have Molloy's description of how he hides his body
under text—the layers of the *Times Literary Supplement,* a venerable
publication that stands in for a certain kind of elite literary culture[16]—
during the winter, which mirrors the way life itself hides underneath
the surface of the earth during this season. Molloy's rhythms mimic
the rhythms of the earth and he reveals his body only when the earth
wakes up again and reveals the life that had been lying dormant,
such that we can establish an analogy between Molloy's body and the
living bodies (animal and plant) that the earth contains.[17]

Molloy's body is cast as a mimetic object, where it responds to
the world by mirroring it—something we can also see in all of Beckett's characters, who mimic the decomposing environments they find
themselves in by themselves decomposing. Molloy's wrapped body
is thus a representation of winter and the passage of time, and if the
earth's awakening and the irruption of new life that spring constitutes
is tied to Molloy's shedding his filthy layers of newspaper—filthy they
must be, from having stayed in contact with his living, excreting body
for months[18]—it has the consequence of casting Molloy's body as life
itself, where the unveiling of his body corresponds to the earth's unveiling of life. What is considered abject—Molloy's failing body, with
its odors, its bum leg, its agedness—is recast as vernal, or more precisely, as a representation of the vernal. Through this close association of Molloy's body with the earth's, of the abject with the vital,
Beckett thereby ties excrement to life, even as it can also function as

an expression of death: its function as waste, loss, or excess is key to its ecological role as fertilizer. To put it simply, shit is the transformation of food, and food is the transformation of shit,[19] and the body is the site for this shit–food interface, or alchemy.

This reading accounts for the focus on climate and nature that precedes the fart passage by making Molloy's body an expression of those things. How, then, do we get from here to flatulence and mimesis? The body, which is not a unitary or unified object, but itself composite—an ecosystem and world unto itself—contains another mimetic object, which is of it without necessarily being it: the fart. Beckett, in the latter part of the passage, moves from placing the body in relation to the world, to its environment, to placing the fart in relation to the body that is its environment by framing the fart as the central object, one that is expressed involuntarily. Via its expressivity, its status as an expression, the fart *is* mimetic, insofar as mimesis, in both its imitative and representational dimensions, is a product of expression such that unexpressed mimesis is a contradiction in terms. The question raised here, then, is that of what Molloy's prolific gas represents and what it imitates in order to do so. This is where the resonance between Molloy's constantly farting bottom and Ferdinand's constantly shit-covered one comes into relief.

Just as Ferdinand took the anus of his dog, Tom, as a guide and point of orientation, following it, Molloy takes Ferdinand's fecal behind as his, following it. To have cast Molloy as as fecal a narrator as Ferdinand would have been too close of an imitation. Beckett thus introduces an interval between his narrator and Céline's, transforming constant fecality into constant flatulence. By doing so, Beckett is able, like Céline, to place the entire text under an excremental sign, while still asserting his distinction from his predecessor. The distinction between feces and flatulence is consequential as an expression, on Beckett's part, of the will for a different poetics from Céline's, despite their shared investment in writing death and the degradation of the body wrought by mortality.

Some might argue that flatulence is not actually excremental, being gas as opposed to the solid matter we associate with the feces that are the referent for excrement, properly speaking, while others could point to the shared anal provenance and malodorousness as being enough to place flatulence with shit in the category of excrement. In the case of flatulence versus feces, within a mimetic framework, one can posit flatulence as an imitation of feces, able to imitate and reproduce the odor but unable to reproduce the materiality of shit. Where Céline's narrator, Ferdinand, produces solid matter—shit—Molloy produces nothing but air. But there is an inherent ambiguity to flatulence: while it is still in the intestinal tract, not yet expressed, it feels similar to feces in the way both occupy space in the tract. While we are often able to distinguish whether that feeling of fullness in our gut is due to feces or to flatulence, there are times where it is unclear what matter we are dealing with—hence the coining of the term *shart,* a portmanteau combining *shit* and *fart,* which refers to the accidental expulsion of fecal matter when one is simply trying to pass gas. When still inside the body, not yet expressed, both farts and feces can be taken one for the other, and the process of expression is the same for both, passing through the release of the sphincter. This tension between feces and flatulence is an interesting one and Beckett, I would argue, mobilizes it to enact the tension that inheres between the object of mimesis (the referent) and the mimesis itself (the representation or imitation): the representation depends on the referent for its existence and yet by existing it calls attention to the way it fails to fully reproduce the referent that is the ground of its existence. The very thing that causes the representation to exist is what causes it to fail.

Beckett, by insisting on Molloy's flatulence over and against his fecality, asserts a fundamental difference between his writing and Céline's, so that he is not simply translating Céline, to return to Rabaté, but writing after and with him. Where Céline's narrative stinks because of the solid matter that adheres to its narrator's ass, Beckett's narrative's stinkiness is produced through Molloy's immaterial farts that dissipate into the air. Beckett would appear to be insisting on a less material and more cerebral text than what we get with Céline. Where, in Céline, we have characters actually dealing with shit, rolling up their sleeves and handling the abject material, in Beckett, the encounters with that kind of base materiality are a degree removed and remain on the olfactory level instead, captured by the repugnant fart, which is effectively shit without the physical matter of shit. Beckett's narrative might smell like shit, the way Céline's does, but when it comes to confronting it, we are always placed at a certain remove, as the first-person subjectivities occupied by both Molloy and Moran never actually have to touch the stuff themselves. *Mort à crédit*, as a form of mimesis, is a fuller or truer imitation of its abject object than Beckett's text, which is diluted in comparison. The confrontation with the foul odor of Molloy's flatulence occurs for the reader, as it does for Molloy himself, purely inside one's head: the foul odor of the text reveals, when you follow your nose, that there isn't anything solid there.

Just as Beckett's topographies become abstract and flattened, as opposed to the traceable Parisian cartography of *Mort à crédit* with its real place-names, so too does the odor lose its depth by being untethered from the materiality of shit. Where Ferdinand's shittiness ascribes to the text a kind of physical depth and materiality, Molloy's flatulence saps the text of those qualities, which accounts, perhaps, for the sudden move by which Molloy turns his counting of his farts into an existential statement by which his self is conjured up as an epistemological object that can be captured by placing farts within a mathematical, as opposed to material and embodied, frame. In other words, Céline sends us back into our bodies with the sorts of nauseating passages he writes, while Beckett sends us out of our bodies and into the ideal realm of mathematics, and by extension, a Cartesian kind of philosophy dedicated to the mind and to cogito over the body.[20] While Beckett himself protested against a philosophizing reading of his work, claiming that if he'd wanted to philosophize, he would have written philosophy,[21] that has not stopped his critics from ascribing to his work a philosophical weight and impetus.

I want to override Beckett's own anti- or nonphilosophical declaration and say that he philosophizes despite himself, and that we can track this "in spite of himself" to the involuntary nature of Molloy's farts, which come out of him "on the least pretext" (*à propos de tout et de rien*), implying that there's nothing he could do to stop their expulsion every four minutes on average. The mimesis evoked at the beginning of the fart passage is also cast as involuntary: Molloy is mimetic *in spite of himself*. If we take mimesis to mean representation, broadly speaking, this implicates expression, as a representation is necessarily expressed. So, we can rephrase the mimetic declaration to read that Molloy expresses despite himself, which maps neatly onto Molloy's flatulence as a form of expression in its etymological sense, wherein his body expresses, or pushes out, gas, but also in its figurative sense, as a kind of representation. Molloy expresses and farts despite himself, and so too does Beckett philosophize despite himself, as the involuntary farts assume philosophical weight here, mobilized as they are toward an ontological and epistemological end. Perhaps the most precise reading of *mimetic in spite of himself* (*mimétique malgré lui*) is to read *lui* (*him*) as referring not to Molloy but to Beckett as Molloy's creator, in which case the sentence becomes one where Molloy is mimetic, or expressive, despite Beckett. Beckett does not want to express, he does not want to philosophize, he wants to shatter words in a logoclasmic project, and yet *Molloy*, despite his best attempts at flattening and destroying language, continues to mean: something philosophical is to be found in the constant cloud of flatulent gas that surrounds his constantly farting narrator, both there *in spite of himself*.

Philosophy is not so much in the fart itself, but in what is done with the fart, which is to say, its being counted, measured, and transformed into a law or principle rendered in mathematical terms: to be Molloy is to be flatulent, and to be flatulent is to have a concrete if gaseous means of knowing oneself. In the silent, smelly intervals between farts is where this knowledge of self can be attained. But how does fart-counting lead to knowledge of the self, to this philosophical end? The answer lies in the way the fart for Molloy is a measure of time, an experience of duration, such that to count farts is to express the passage of time, and the passage of time is the truth of mortality, and death is ultimately the beginning and the end of Beckett's knowledge and philosophy.[22] In Beckett, we see combined Beckett's narration of the anus as the birth canal by which Molloy sees the first light of his first day (20; 20) and Leo Bersani's assertion that the rectum is a grave.[23] The anus is where everything begins and ends, and the flatus and the feces that come out of this ontological passage, described by Molloy as "the true portal of our being" (107; 109), are thus both philosophically inflected.

However, importantly, the fart is not the philosophical object to be strived toward, but rather, a prelude to the shit that is the real philosophical substance. Molloy's constant flatulence translates to a constant calling attention to his anus[24] without having to explicitly narrate each fart, which has been expressed as a mathematical principle. This flatulent anality automatically conjures up the presence of shit—both gas and solid share the same orifice—but as an absent or looming one, offstage or, rather, off the page. The real material of the narrative is not found in the words, the marks on the page, or in the fart, but in the silence, the blank, the absent excrement that flatus is in constant contact with, both sharing the gut as their home—the gut, this organ, this second mind, which turns life into death, but a death that itself gives rise to life.

It is the solid shit, formal and silent, like the creases in Beckett's face, that is the philosophical material of a writing that philosophizes in spite of himself, through which self-awareness might be obtained. The flatulent cloud that surrounds Molloy—a profane analogue of the mandorlas that surround Christ and the Virgin Mary—is thus a sign pointing toward the silence as the space for the real stuff. And recall that in the winter, Molloy's farts are captured by the solid paper of the *Times Literary Supplement*—captured by text. The fart is thus doubly framed—first by mathematics, but more importantly, by language. And it is the latter—the text, with the language it uses to bring the self's shit to the very edge of the text—which proves to be the most important.

Molloy, by farting his way through his narrative, is in essence directing his reader to follow the odor to its origin—the anus—and to find there the silence and the shit that is the true knowledge of the death that is our existential foundation. It is in the fundament that the fundamental truth of death can be found, and it is to be found not in the immaterial fart, but rather the solid shit that is the fullest expression of the passage of time, of the transformation of life into death, of the only future and possibility that awaits us. In other words, Molloy's countable farts, which appear to take us out of the body into the realm of the mind, end up taking us right back to the anus, which, for Beckett, is the philosophical space par excellence. The human is a philosophical creature, and the philosophy it produces is shit.

Shit Philosophy

What sort of philosophy is happening in *Molloy* despite Beckett? Or rather, what sort of philosophy is happening through and by the novel despite Beckett? The subject of Beckett and philosophy is "old hat"[25] and has been taken up repeatedly, most often to identify the traces or influence of specific philosophies as they work their ways into Beckett: in the rich body of scholarship that works through some iteration of the configuration "Beckett + X philosopher," we can find readings of Beckett and Schopenhauer, Beckett and Aristotle, Beckett and Descartes, Beckett and Democritus and Plato, Beckett and Spinoza, Beckett and Geulincx, and so on.[26] This work enables us to piece together how Beckett became Beckett, and illuminates his writing insofar as it reveals which kinds of overarching philosophical questions were principal concerns, what sort of a conceptual orientation he had toward the world. What I am interested in, however, is not this work of reconstructing, excavating, and identifying which philosophers had what kind of influence where in Beckett's writing, but rather, how the expressivity of the text, in the representation that Beckett writes despite himself, constitutes a meta-philosophical discourse in the same way that flatulence, as we've seen, constitutes a meta-narrative one.

For the project of figuring out what sort of a status philosophy has in *Molloy,* and its necessary relation to the excremental, it is useful to turn to what was excluded from the novel. In the manuscript version of the novel can be found a thirteen-page passage in Moran's narrative dedicated to an exposition of the excremental economy of

Ballyba.[27] As Edouard O'Reilly describes it, this passage is "possibly the only major variant with regards to content that can be found in what is generally assumed to be the first draft of *Molloy*. . . . Though the manuscript contains many variants, they are arguably all of a (predominantly) stylistic nature. Only this one adds any significant semantic value."[28] This lost semantic value is situated in part 2 of the novel, just after Moran expounds to the reader in his report what he knows of Molloy's hometown, Bally, and the region it's located in, Ballyba (adding that Moran himself hails from the town of Shit in the region of Shitba) (183–85; 183–85). In Moran's account of Ballyba, as was published in the final version:

> The population of Ballyba was small. I confess this thought gave me great satisfaction. The land did not lend itself to cultivation. No sooner did a tilth, or a meadow, begin to be sizeable than it fell foul of a sacred grove or a stretch of marsh from which nothing could be obtained beyond a little inferior turf or scraps of bogoak used for making amulets, paper-knives, napkin-rings, rosaries and other knick-knacks. Martha's Madonna, for example, came from Ballyba. The pastures, in spite of the torrential rains, were exceedingly meagre and strewn with boulders. Here only quitchweed grew in abundance, and a curious bitter blue grass fatal to cows and horses, though tolerated apparently by the ass, the goat and the black sheep. What then was the source of Ballyba's prosperity? I'll tell you. No, I'll tell you nothing. Nothing. (184; 185)

The excised passage is found after the last lines, as a response to the question of Ballyba's wealth. Before Beckett decided that Moran would not say anything, he had decided to say a lot.

O'Reilly describes the passage at great length, explaining how Beckett lays out Ballyba's opulence as deriving from its excremental economy, where its citizens' feces are turned into fertilizer that enables the region to grow an abundant quantity and assortment of vegetables. The region's stability is built on shit: Ballyba's citizens are given a fecal quota that they must meet, and few Ballybaians ever leave as travel away requires them to compensate the local government for the shit they'll be depriving Ballyba of during their time away. Moran's report further elaborates on the impact that profession has on the quality of one's excrement as fertilizer (clergymen's shit makes the best fertilizer), on the way excrement has given rise to an advanced septic tank technology that ensures the most efficient distribution of shit, on excrement's informing the region's idiomatic expressions, and on the medicinal benefits of shit baths (a proposed use of shit that was turned down because of fears that bathers would contaminate the shit, rendering it unusable). O'Reilly succinctly describes Ballyba's relation to shit: "In creating Ballyba's economy, Beckett has touched upon matters of civic duty and civic pride, of bureaucracy, folklore and tradition, science and technology, poetry, celebrity, social status and sainthood. In Ballyba, it would appear, all these are built on shit."[29]

O'Reilly is intrigued, like I am, by the dramatic excision of such a substantial and colorful passage and attempts to give an account of why Beckett would develop this fecality at such great length only to delete it. For O'Reilly, Beckett develops Ballyba's fecality as an expression of Buddhist philosophy, where "shit is the symbol of the transience of all things, as they break down into feces."[30] O'Reilly draws parallels between Beckett's passage and Buddhism, where shit's fertilizing ethos frames feces in relation to food (both the production of and the breaking down of) as does Buddhism, and between the way both Beckett and Buddhism cast the material world as lacking intrinsic value. As evidence of Beckett's familiarity with Buddhism, O'Reilly points to two allusions to Buddhism in Beckett's corpus—in the essay "Henri Hayden, homme-peintre" ("Henri Hayden") and *Comment c'est* (*How It Is*)—as proof that Beckett was aware of Buddhism to at least some degree. In O'Reilly's estimation, if Beckett deleted this expression of a kind of Buddhist philosophy regarding the transience of life and the material world, it is due to a combination of readerly prudishness and the desire not to have this Buddhist treatment of shit interpreted in a psychoanalytic context, where "[Beckett] may have decided that faeces took on, in the Freudian framework, an inappropriate valence."[31]

Even if one accepts the interpretation of *Molloy* as a psychoanalytically informed work, consenting to J. D. O'Hara's reading of the
work, which claims Beckett is consciously working through Jungian
themes in Molloy's narrative and Freudian ones in Moran's,[32] the argument that Beckett deleted this Ballyba shit passage to avoid having
shit be read psychoanalytically doesn't account for the instances of
shit that still occur in the rest of the novel. If Beckett didn't want shit
to be misread by being placed in a psychoanalytic framework, why
leave any shit behind at all? Why have Molloy remark on his mother's defecatory habits and call attention to defecation as a process by
having the only papers he carries be not identification papers but
newspaper for wiping his bottom with? Why have Moran adminis-
tering an enema to his son and observing the contents of the latter's
chamber pot? O'Reilly's reading, while having the merit of opening
up the question of Beckett and philosophy to non-Western philosophy, resisting thus the Eurocentrism of virtually all philosophical
readings of Beckett, nonetheless remains limited in its inability to
account for Beckett's inclusion of shit in other parts of the novel.

I want to step back from O'Reilly's reading and offer up an alternative account for why Beckett would go to the trouble of writing
thirteen pages on shit only to cut them. I would argue that Beckett
wrote those pages for himself, as a way of figuring out what kind of a
setting the novel takes place in and what kind of a character Molloy,
as the novel's logic and central object, is. In this reading, it's important
for Beckett and the narrator to be speaking and writing in a universe
that's built on the excremental, as Molloy's Ballyba and Moran's
Shitba are.[33] It's important for Beckett to work out a world where
every single dimension of life is undergirded by the excremental. But,
having figured that out, he decides he doesn't need to leave it in there:
what the excision tells us, quite simply, is that Beckett didn't feel that
the reader needed to have the textual world's excremental foundation
made explicitly visible to them, and that it was more important for
the writing side of things than for the reading side. He had needed
to write his way into his text, just as academic writers often have to
write their way into their argument, not knowing what it is they are

going to say or where they are going until they've written their way there. And just as some of those words that enable us to figure out our argument are to be discarded as preparatory material once we've figured out where we want to go, so too does Beckett cut out those thirteen pages once they've allowed him to map out the contours and nature of the world he is creating in *Molloy*.

As a result of the excision, we as readers are put in the position of pursuing *Molloy* with limited information, mirroring Moran pursuing Molloy, and Molloy pursuing his mother. We thereby engage in the kind of quests that our narrators do, which are both excremental: Moran tracks Molloy down to the most excremental Ballyba, and Molloy's mother is cast as Comtesse Caca, an incontinent woman who shits herself and stinks of her waste, who birthed him through her anus, such that the quest for the mother, taken in its metaphorical sense of a return to origins, is, in Molloy's mind, a return to the shit whence he came.

By being inadequately equipped or informed questers, as are Molloy and Moran, by being deprived of the knowledge of the excremental foundation that Beckett has written for himself, we are forced to do the work of building that foundation on our own. Beckett, rather than deliver up the excremental to the reader, making the reader a passive recipient or receptacle for shit, compels us instead to assume an active role in working through and making sense of the shit that we do find in the novel, turning us in that sense into handlers and workers of shit. Just as Moran examines his son's chamber pot to arrive at a conclusion about his son's health, so too do we read the bits of shit that have been made visible in the text in order to draw conclusions about what sort of a state the text is in and what sort of a text it is. Beckett gives us just enough shit to place his work in an excremental key, and then leaves it to us to uncover and sustain its excrementality. In this sense, Beckett, like Céline, primes the reader to read for and think in the excremental.[34]

I agree with O'Reilly that the Ballyba report is a philosophical matter. But rather than simply translate Buddhist philosophy into fiction, I see the report as Beckett working out the philosophical ground of *Molloy* and establishing it as an excremental one, which, once cut, is dispersed into the entire text rather than being confined to the imaginary territories that Ballyba and Shitba map onto. The entire text, rather than these thirteen pages alone, becomes the means to express a philosophy that exceeds the seemingly legible philosophical content of an attitude toward the transience of life that evokes Buddhism for O'Reilly. The excision of the Ballyba report effectively alters the text's expressivity by liberating the excrement from the localized site of the Ballyba passage so that the entire text can express excrementality, similarly to the way that Molloy expresses farts and their excremental odor throughout. While this total excrementality might be invisible to the reader initially, the Ballybaian excremental economy becomes apprehensible or consequential through the action of Molloy's constant flatulence, whose atmospheric excrementality is the less material expression of Ballyba's shit-foundation and environment. Just as a fart punctuates and colors whatever non-flatulent situation or context Molloy might be caught up in, so too does Ballyba's prodigious excrementality seep out into seemingly non-excremental contexts in *Molloy*'s writing.

The escape of shit into the non-shit: this is where we can find a distinctively Beckettian philosophy wherein no concept, no activity, no philosophy can be free from shit, can be untainted by the excrementality that is the origin of life and its end. Expressivity and the expression that issues from it are always already compromised, and whatever philosophy one can try to mine from Beckett's text is grounded in shit. Unlike Céline, where the shit doesn't appear to have a philosophical valence and exists as pure materiality, and the death that that materiality encodes, Beckett's shit is philosophical. Beckett moves from Céline's shit-language and the shit-literature it instantiates toward a shit-philosophy contained within a shit-literature, toward a tainted literature-concept. Where Céline says all of literature smells of shit, Beckett is saying that all of *thought* smells. All of philosophy smells.

Any fruitful concept that is produced, is produced at the cost of shit, cultivated through the collection and distribution of excrement that is offered up as a material to be turned into philosophical substance. Beckett thus articulates a kind of alchemy, which takes seriously both the invocation of philosophy in the philosopher's stone and the excrement that was commonly understood to be a necessary component of the stone.[35] Where the alchemical tradition would posit a necessary relation between gold and shit, Beckett modifies it for his own purposes to posit a necessary relation between philosophy and shit, with the flatulent narrative serving as a reminder to follow our noses to the smell's anal origins and the shit that is the material of philosophy, the matter from which a knowledge of self and an ontological foundation can be constructed. If philosophy is shit, then fiction is the fart that reminds us of where shit comes from—the excremental ground of being, the excrement as the ground to which we return.

Toward an Ontological *Sabbat*: The Joy of Shit

Beckett ties philosophy to literature and places both in an excremental register. While it is possible to read this excrementality as an anti-hierarchical, transgressive position that aligns Beckett with Bakhtin and Bataille, Beckett's willful leveling of philosophy and literature through turning them into shit and farts is more than a negative gesture of upheaval. The overturn serves as a prelude to a perhaps unexpected posture of un-Beckettian joy, to be found in and through shit as transformation.

Beckett, by positing philosophy as shit, overthrows, in a Rabelaisian way, the traditional hierarchy wherein mind reigns over body, philosophy over shit. Rabelais, in Mikhail Bakhtin's view, counteracts the sanitization of the grotesque body and its various functions (the euphemistic language of "bodily functions" already a product of the sanitization process wherein the grotesque body is transformed into a smooth, clean, classical one) in order to tap into the philosophical functions of the grotesque body. The grotesque body, defined as such by the body's transgression of the boundary between it and the world, serves as the figure through which cosmic hierarchy (understood as the way in which the elements of the cosmos, in premodern

views, are structured and ordered), the process of (re)generation, and
the intimate relation between life and death can be grasped.[36] What
the grotesque body does conceptually for Rabelais is at the heart
of Beckett's philosophical concerns: the conundrum of being born
into a miserable existence, the anguish of the death sentence that is
life, and the cruel joke of having our consciousness contained in and
dependent on the grotesque bodies that are our point of contact with
the world.

Beckett joins Rabelais in dethroning philosophy as the highest or
"purest" form of thought or concept-production by finding philosophy in the excremental, claiming it to be a product of a humble orifice
like the anus. Like Rabelais, Beckett dismisses the sort of rarefied
culture associated with high culture (literary modernism, in Beckett's case, and classical Renaissance culture in Rabelais's) in order to
elevate the base and material—shit taken as the material par excellence of baseness—in its stead. In a carnivalesque gesture—carnival
epitomizing for Bakhtin the overturning of usual hierarchy[37]—abject
bodies are centered, hierarchy no longer makes sense, and the world
of *Molloy* is characterized by chaos and disorientation over order and
self-possession.

Another way of framing Beckett's move, besides as a Rabelaisian
return to a grotesque body, is to see Beckett as privileging what is discarded under the usual order of things as waste and discarding what
is privileged by said order. Jonathan Boulter, in discussing Beckett's
Texts for Nothing, a collection of short stories first published in French
in 1955, offers up the provocative suggestion "that we reconfigure
these texts as waste and observe the degree to which there is a reciprocal, perhaps constitutive (though ultimately paradoxical) relation
between the narrating subject and its waste." He does so to "explore
the possible implications of the notion that language—that which defines and configures the subjectivity of the subject, contains it in the
narrative it tells of itself—is also that which by definition, as waste,
must be cast out, rejected (disjected). Narrative thus becomes what
Georges Bataille calls the 'accursed share,' the excess which defines
the subject even as it is cast out."[38] Boulter reads both bodies and

texts as waste, which amounts to, from a Bataillean perspective, reading literature as the waste through which culture defines itself, the expelled material on which culture depends for its identity. Following Bataille's intuition about the ambiguity and ambivalence of waste, wherein waste becomes constitutive of a culture by virtue of being expelled by it,[39] Boulter sees waste having a similarly ambiguous and ambivalent role in Beckett's writing, where waste instigates a "blurring of boundaries between waste and its producer, a blurring that reflects ultimately the blurring of metaphysics that occurs in Beckett's entire oeuvre."[40] The consequences of this blurred metaphysics are seen in the uncertain and troubled status of the subject in Beckett's work, where the human subject cannot be completely destroyed because the act of destroying it and turning it to waste has the unwelcome consequence of reconstituting said subject, where any negative action winds up dragging in the positive. This is Beckett's ontological conundrum, one that Boulter sees Beckett as unable to overcome, leaving himself and his texts in a state of productive paradox.

Both the Bakhtinian and Bataillean points of view draw attention to the way Beckett uses the excremental to resist hierarchy and an idolatrous elevation of the human subject as the center of cultural and philosophical systems. Beckett's overthrowing of hierarchy might only function within the space of his texts, and he might not be able to overcome or eliminate "the agonizing fact of being,"[41] but *Molloy* gives us a glimpse of how a space of ontological celebration can be carved out through the excremental, where excrement is not simply an economic element, or a manifestation of the materiality of death, or a reminder of the abjection that entering into life is—all configurations that appear at various points throughout the text. Instead, excrement becomes an experience of what we might call joy.

At the beginning of the novel, before Molloy narrates his quest to find his mother, he engages in narrating two characters named, simply, A and B—a kind of warmup for the larger narrative task that will be the rest of *Molloy*—hesitantly talking his reader through the process of describing A and B, of communicating their actions, and of situating them in a setting. In the middle of this narration, Molloy turns from a description of the landscape, which up till this point has been fairly objective and quite detailed, in ways that resonate with the sorts of description a New Novelist like Alain Robbe-Grillet would engage in during the following decade, and inserts a phrase that Ruby Cohn has described as a moment of "lyrical mastery."[42] And indeed, the sentence leaps out from the page, propelled by its embrace of a lyricism that Beckett, for the greatest part of the novel, otherwise eschews in order to stage a language that is as faltering and inadequate as are the bodies of Molloy and Moran (and the human body tout court in the face of mortality): "But now he knows these hills, that is to say he knows them better, and if ever again he sees them from afar it will be I think with other eyes, and not only that but the within, all that inner space one never sees, the brain and heart and other caverns where thought and feeling dance their sabbath [où sentiment et pensée tiennent leur sabbat], all that too quite differently disposed" (10; 11).

Cohn describes this sentence as a sudden move "from the landscape to the human core,"[43] but I see it not so much as a move from the one thing to the other, but rather, the transformation of the two into each other: here, our insides are in effect a landscape that can be seen, and the distinction between interiority and exteriority, between the visible and invisible, no longer holds, as all are brought to exist on the same plane, the whole constituting a human topography wherein the inside of the human is sounded out in the same way that the human maps out the hills in which it wanders, the one a negative of the other (what is a cavern if not the negative of a hill, a hill that's been hollowed out?). The positive and its negative converge and are caught up together in the singular act of seeing, of perceiving the world, of taking it in with the body, and of turning the body into a world.

Beckett overturns the usual processes of apperception not simply by shifting what is seen—turning the insides into a landscape—but also by transforming the means through which we see. In the passage, there is an extraordinary moment of ambiguity, where not only does seeing differently, "with other eyes," evoke the possibility of seeing a different kind of landscape than usual, but the possibility of having that internal landscape be the means by which one sees, so that one sees not simply with one's eyes, but with "all that inner space one never sees." The inner space, described as "the brain and heart and other caverns," is thus transformed into organs of perception, of sight. The notion of seeing with one's brain or one's heart isn't particularly striking or novel—the idea of perceiving things either cerebrally or emotionally seems basic. But Beckett, through insisting on the other caverns, extends the faculty of sight to other parts of the body—in particular, the gut.

Beckett shifts mid-sentence from the question of sight, from framing the body's inner space as itself seeing, to being the space where *sentiment et pensée tiennent leur sabbat*. Again, here, the brain and the heart, as those organs associated with thought and sentiment, make perfect sense as sites where these meet to hold their sabbath (meant here in the occult sense). But the question of which other caverns inside our bodies can hold such a sabbath has only one answer, and an obvious one at that: the gut. The gut, long spoken of popularly as a site of feeling—as when we speak of a pit in one's stomach, or butterflies, of one's gut feeling, of the gut as something to be followed—has been recognized by scientists as constituting a second brain in the human body.[44] The gut-brain, known as the enteric nervous system, comprises neurons that line the long tube of the gut, in higher numbers than are found in either the spinal cord or the peripheral nervous system, and is responsible for overseeing digestion and ensuring that waste is moved through the gastrointestinal tract and eliminated from the body. But beyond driving digestion, the enteric nervous system sends information from the gut to the brain, which has been credited for the gut's impact on our emotional state.[45] The gut is thus where brain and emotion come together.

To see otherwise, to see the inside that we normally do not see—and to see with parts of our bodies that we do not normally see with—is to transform the insides of our bodies into thought and feeling made visible, to see the heart and the brain and the gut, and to see with them. To see—and see through—the gut as this other cavern is in effect to see the shit that fills it, that it is always in contact with, that it is always moving out into the world whence it came, the world that it used to be. We cannot normally see our guts, contained as they are by our bodies, but the shit we expel from them, as the positive to our guts' negative, is in effect a way of seeing our gut. And in casting the gut as a set of different eyes, Beckett in effect turns the hills that our usual eyes see into shit, which is what our gut sees—this figuration of shit as hills a different disposition of the hills indeed. It is in this fecal matter—this way of seeing (with) our insides, this transformation of food into waste, into the remainder that our body produces, into that which no longer has any use for our bodies—that *sentiment et pensée tiennent leur sabbat.*

It is in the gut that feeling, as a way of seizing and being in contact with the world and existence, and thought, as a way of understanding said world and existence, come together in an ontological celebration that takes on occult connotations—their convergence a mysterious and unsettling phenomenon that cannot be understood and that appears unseemly.[46] Excrement, far from being simply the sign and material of death, is in fact a site of a celebration, of existence cast as joy. In this regard, Beckett makes good on the paradoxical nature of shit, which makes it both a sign of death and a source of life, both vile shit and the food that it used to be. This one compact lyrical passage thus expresses the essence of the thirteen pages of Moran's report on Ballyba, which cast excrement as a positive and necessary material, as opposed to the abject and dirty matter it is figured as in the rest of the novel.

I want to return to Beckett's scatological jokes and the seemingly ironic and deprecatory humor with which he described his writing as shit. While these references have been interpreted, understandably, as Beckett's dismissal of his writing, when read in the light of *Molloy* as an excremental and flatulent response to Céline, the equivalence between Beckett's writing and shit begins to look different. Rather than a value judgment about Beckett's writing, in which it comes out wanting, to take his texts as shit is to strip them of their surface connotations of abjection, disgust, waste, and see beneath all that the ontological *sabbat* that they are writing toward—a necessary interruption of the existential agony and absurdity epitomized in such famous declarations as "I can't go on. I'll go on," and the Schopenhauerian view that life is a pensum, or chore.[47] Digestion and defecation, like life, is also a chore: you can't not defecate and you must keep on defecating[48] over and over and over, for as long as you live. Yet shit can be more than a dirty chore, an inconvenience that keeps you from being maximally productive, or a waste of time. It can be a reminder to see otherwise, and to see in our bodies' digestive work of transformation an ontological *sabbat*—a raucous, excessive coming together of thought and emotion that takes the convergence of these two things in the caverns of the body as the key to changing a shitty world into creative shit.

Just as shit is waste that the body no longer has any use for, but that is vital to the growth of the food that the body requires, so too is Beckett's writing a life-giving material that can only function in an ontologically positive sense insofar as it is useless, waste, shit. In a sense, despite the technological and scientific creatures that we have become as a species, we have never stopped being alchemists. The difference between the medieval era and the twentieth and twenty-first centuries is that instead of trying to turn shit into gold, we moderns get to the gold by adding an intermediary step, where we first turn shit into culture, into art, which, as we know all too well, can easily be monetized. In the case of a cultural producer like Beckett, whose excrementality remains within the linguistic realm, unlike those cheeky shit-artists who confront the art world with the truth of how valuable shit becomes in the right circumstances, his faltering, limping logoclasm—as hard as he tries to keep his words from meaning, they continue to keep meaning—leans on the excremental. If Beckett can't ever succeed in breaking words down into dust, at least he can break them down into shit—a shit that, unlike the shit of our sanitized Western plumbing systems, which we whisk away with potable water that we do not drink, is allowed to circulate freely in his writing and his readers' minds as a transformative force that will unceasingly turn into what is transformed into what transforms into what is transformed into what transforms into what is transformed into what transforms . . . ad nauseum.

Part II
SHITTY IDEAS

) 3 (

FECAL FREEDOM
Sartre and Genet's))< >((

***

. . . the turd Genet and his excrementalist buddy, Sartre.
—George H. Bauer, "Pretexts for Texts"

Chapters 1 and 2 treated Céline and Beckett as points of entry into French literature that demand excrementality of literature. In this part of the book, I move beyond the first part's argument—that literature requires shit—in order to demonstrate what kinds of concepts can be produced by fecality. In this chapter, I turn to the Sartre–Genet pair—an odd couple, perhaps, with Sartre's eminence as a public intellectual vibrating on a different plane than the mystique Genet cultivated with his bad-boy artist persona—to show how their literary sensibilities converge in fecality as a means of figuring and giving form to the idea of freedom.[1]

If ever there was a bromance gone bad, it would be the story of the love built and lost between Jean-Paul Sartre and Jean Genet.[2] But before they went their separate ways—or rather, before Genet took his distance from Sartre following the latter's publication of his monumental, obsessive *Saint Genet, comédien et martyr* (*Saint Genet, Actor and Martyr*)—they were friends bound by excrementality. Sartre scholar George Bauer's formulation in the epigraph is telling. Genet is a turd: an identity is established between Genet and fecal matter, with Genet accorded a materiality that is withheld from Sartre, who is instead

105

described as an "excrementalist."[3] This adjectival construction defines Sartre in relation to the excremental—Sartre is excrementalist insofar as he is drawn to excrement—without his sharing the same material, fecal constitution as Genet-*cum*-turd. Bauer's pithy and irreverent turn of phrase captures the essence of *Saint Genet,* a text that turns Genet into shit in order to feast on his fecal body of work.[4] Genet is the shit and Sartre is the excremental philosopher-fly that circles around Genet, deriving nourishment from the latter. (However, as we'll see in this chapter, it is when Sartre is producing fiction, not philosophy—when he is writing with Genet rather than about him—that he passes from a *mouche à merde* to a producer of excrement.)

When it comes to discussions of Genet, *Saint Genet* looms as an unavoidable reference. It is nearly impossible to take up Genet without recognizing, at least in passing, Sartre's reading/hagiography of Genet,[5] which seems hellbent on fixing and giving a full account of an oeuvre that had just begun, thereby closing a book that had barely been written (literally, if we are to believe Genet's claim that he had writer's block for six years after reading *Saint Genet*).[6] *Saint Genet,* which explains Genet's transformation/rehabilitation from criminal to artist, maps Genet's picaresque trajectory onto the existentialist happy ending of shedding bad faith—where bad faith is flight from one's inescapable, compulsory freedom—in order to assume fully one's freedom in the face of the vertiginous, nauseating contingency of existence. In this story, it is when Genet assumes his freedom that he is able to transform himself from the pariah that society has made him out to be into the writer who will go on (albeit with the help of luminaries such as Cocteau and Sartre himself) to burst into the French canon and reshape it.[7]

There have been pointed and substantive critiques of Sartre's perhaps overdetermined insistence on reading Genet through his existentialism-tinged optics of freedom. Leo Bersani, for instance, writes that "it would also blunt the originality of [Genet's] work to claim, as Sartre does, that his embrace of criminality is designed to transform a stigmatizing essence imposed on him by others into a freely chosen destiny."[8] Whether or not one agrees with Sartre's read-

ing of Genet, if the brick that is *Saint Genet* proves anything, it is that
it is not difficult to read freedom onto Genet's life and work, as seen,
for instance, in his seemingly insouciant disregard for the rule of law
and for poetic convention. My point in this chapter is not to perform
an existentialist reading of Genet—we already have that in the ma-
gistral *Saint Genet*—but rather to tease out the way Sartre's unceasing
investment in freedom (a foundational concept for his entire life and
work)[9] resonates excrementally with Genet's own literary project in
a way that makes visible the way fecality serves as a singular expression of freedom, such that existentialism, when understood as
a project of radical and absolute freedom, cannot be anything other
than an excrementialism.

The focus on freedom reveals something crucial about fecality:
namely, that it is both an antisocial, anti-relational, anti-hegemonic
force (as manifested spectacularly by Genet, whose topsy-turvy
poetic and moral cosmogonies channel both Bakhtinian carnival
dynamics—the inversion of power, the elevation of the grotesque
body—and the anti-communitarian force of queerness as elaborated
in the anti-relational thread of queer theory)[10] *and* a way to combat
Sartrean bad faith. In other words, shit is both antisocial and ethical,
capturing the complexity of sharing a world with others from whom
we are always apart, and of whom we are always a part. Reading Sartre and Genet together through shit provides us with a richer vision
of freedom where each writer's work can be seen as constituting two
sides of the same fecal coin, where fecality is an immanently ethical
conceptual site, as will be developed in the next chapter via the concept of care.

In order to read Sartre and Genet together, I must first read them
apart. I'll do this by examining Sartre's *La Nausée* (1938) and *L'Enfance d'un chef* (1939) and Genet's *Notre-Dame-des-Fleurs* (1943)—works
that were written before Sartre and Genet came to know each other
or each other's work.[11] This decoupling or turning to writing produced before their first encounter in 1944[12] allows for putting Sartre
and Genet back together in ways that are concerned not with the biographical drama and fallout instigated by *Saint Genet,* but rather with

fecality's philosophical and ethical function. Each writer's work, both of which have proven to be enormously influential on the course of French thought and culture, builds on excrementality—an excrementality they come to independently even as they would eventually converge in their shared articles of fecal faith.

Sartre, Excrementialist

Sartre is an odd figure to grapple with. The most famous public intellectual of the twentieth century, Sartre refused to stay in any one generic lane, producing philosophical treatises, plays, fiction, biographies, literary and art criticism, in addition to public-facing essays. Despite this spectacularly multivalent output, Sartre's work, regardless of form, was always in service of philosophy—a philosophy that, under the name of existentialism, stands for an unwavering commitment to human freedom as a capacity that must not be refused, but rather, assumed in order to create a more just world.[13] If Sartre turned to literature, it was because of what he saw as literature's capacity to express philosophical concepts.[14] And the idea that drove his literary turn was contingency, the bedrock of the existentialist doctrine of freedom:[15] contingency, as the lack of a reason for one's existence, is a refusal of determinism, and the lack of determinism means that we have freedom to choose what we will do and be. Sartre would work on contingency continually until its expression was transformed from a "factum sur la contingence" (pamphlet/polemic on contingency)[16] into the novel *La Nausée* (*Nausea*) (1938), which Sartre himself named as one of the few works he would wish to be remembered by[17]—a literary precursor to Sartre's philosophical magnum opus, *L'Être et le néant* (*Being and Nothingness*) (1943), which would be published a few years later.

While *La Nausée* is lauded as one of Sartre's major works and a definitive treatment of his conception of contingency as a philosophical concept,[18] it was followed the next year by the publication of *Le Mur* (*The Wall*) (1939), a collection of short stories closed out by the novella *L'Enfance d'un chef* (*The Childhood of a Leader*), a parody of a bildungsroman that has been largely passed over in scholarly discussions of Sartre's work and thought, which have found it more fruitful to focus on *La Nausée* as an exemplary convergence of Sartre's philosophical and aesthetic orientations.[19] I see *L'Enfance d'un chef* (hereafter referred to as *L'Enfance*) as a significant sequel to *La Nausée* that mobilizes fecality to produce a fuller experience and understanding of freedom in its embeddedness in contingency.

Both texts were written before World War II, the historical event that would shake Sartre out of his apolitical bad faith[20] into the political engagement that would mark the rest of his career. This was a period during which Sartre was focused on abstraction, much like the protagonist of *La Nausée,* on giving a phenomenological (i.e., internal) account of the contingency of existence, rather than on the external, concrete, social, and political questions he would devote himself to after the war. In other words, Sartre's primary concern was philosophical and he was exploring how to render his philosophical thought in literary terms.[21] *La Nausée* and *L'Enfance* both track the development of their solitary young male protagonists: *La Nausée* is a kind of bildungsroman following its protagonist Antoine Roquentin's journey from existentialist angst at his incomprehension of contingency to his plunge into art (by taking up literature's *plume*) following an epiphanic revelation of existence's contingent nature; *L'Enfance* is a parody of the bildungsroman that tracks its protagonist, Lucien Fleurier, the son of a bourgeois industrialist, who transforms from a boy floating in his unmoored, unmotivated, contingent life when he discovers a way to combat this contingency by embracing anti-Semitic, fascist politics.

The two texts are two sides of a looking glass, with Roquentin a kind of existentialist hero (although not a particularly likeable one) who finds a way out of the problem of contingency by embracing it, and Fleurier an existentialist antihero who epitomizes bad faith by allowing far-right ideology to determine him. The tain that separates and joins these two mirrored experiences of contingency takes the shape of *La Nausée*'s chestnut tree, which reappears on the other side in *L'Enfance* as an *étron,* or turd. The famous *marronier* root scene—the chestnut tree's root an object that, in its iconicity, could be likened to Proust's madeleine insofar as it stands in for an entire oeuvre—is transformed in *L'Enfance* into fecal matter. If *L'Enfance* has as much shit as it does, this is no accident: *L'Enfance* is scatological because *La Nausée* wasn't. *L'Enfance* supplies the shit that *La Nausée* needed.

From Nausea to Diarrhea

La Nausée derives its title from the nausea Roquentin identifies as his response to experiencing what Marie-Ève Morin describes as "the undifferentiated and nauseating contact with worldly things in their sheer existence."[22] This contact with things in their thingliness is so stomach-turning because their existence, their contingency, is excessive. Indeed, one can tie Roquentin's existential nausea to everyday nausea: the physical desire to vomit, to expel the contents of one's stomach following alimentary excess, can be mapped onto existential nausea as a reaction to the excess of existence itself, the incapacity to digest what one has eaten metaphorizing the incapacity to digest contingency. As Chris Falzon puts it, "The feeling of nausea is the rationalist's sickness in the face of the conceptual indigestibility of the world."[23] This existential nausea is brought to its climax in the chestnut tree scene.

Roquentin, who begins his journey as a rationalist—a biographer of the Marquis de Rollebon who undertakes the immensely rational project of ordering and making sense out of the life of this fictional eighteenth-century man—has his rationalist worldview completely shattered when, while sitting on a park bench, he notices the chestnut tree root sticking up out of the ground beneath his feet. He can no longer make sense of the chestnut tree root as being a chestnut tree root because *root* is an idea tacked onto the thing after the fact:

> I couldn't remember it was a root anymore. The words had vanished and with them the significance of things, their methods of use, and the feeble points of reference which men have traced on their surface. I was sitting, stooping forward, head bowed, alone in front of this black, knotty mass, entirely beastly, which frightened me. Then I had this vision.[24]

This vision, or revelation, is of the contingency of existence, where its arbitrariness places it outside the grasp of rational apprehension or cognition, rendering it absurd. As Roquentin writes, trying to make sense of the physical fact of the tree root, "This root, on the other hand, existed in such a way that I could not explain it" (129; 184). As an example of its inexplicable nature, Roquentin grapples with the fact that the root appears to him to be black: "Black? The root *was not* black, there was no black on this piece of wood—there was . . . something else: black, like the circle, did not exist" (130; 185). The circle is an idea, the color black is an idea as well, and no idea, or concept, can possibly participate in the same order of reality and existence as this "black," knotted, raw, frightening mass in its inertness, its resistance to being made to signify.

Existence cannot be explained—it just is. This contingency, succinctly captured in the phrase "*They did not want* to exist, only they could not help themselves" (133; 190), sends Roquentin into a rage at participating in the same meaningless, unwilled, arbitrary existence as the trees, as their roots:

> And I was inside, I with the garden. I was frightened, furious, I
> thought it was so stupid, so out of place, I hated this ignoble
> mess. . . . It didn't make sense, the World was everywhere, in
> front, behind. There had been nothing *before* it. Nothing. There
> had never been a moment in which it could not have existed. That
> was what worried me: of course there was no *reason* for this flowing
> larva to exist. *But it was impossible* for it not to exist. (134; 191)

What interests me here is not Roquentin's understandable reaction to the unpleasant, shattering experience of learning that the meaning and depth that we are so attached to as an essential and singular part of human experience is an illusion. What interests me is the description of the chestnut tree root as the object that triggers this spiral into contingency (and hence, to freedom, as the only ethical response to contingency). In the passages cited above, we have an image of the root as black, inert, knobbly, obscene in its excess, its excessively raw quality. Elsewhere in the chestnut tree scene, we have a more detailed description of the root: "this hard and compact skin of a sea lion . . . this oily, callous, headstrong look" (129; 185).

This description of the tree root does not correspond in any way with my own phenomenological repertoire of tree roots. First, the color is wrong: a chestnut tree, like most trees, is brown and has brown roots, not black ones. Second, the description of the root as having skin akin to sea lion skin is odd. Why a sea lion skin of all epidermal possibilities? Sartre's evocation of a sea lion's sleek wetness would better map onto a turd, in its sleek wetness,[25] than to a tree root. Fecal matter also has that animal oiliness Sartre evokes and a turd that has been expelled from the body has an obscene and completely tranquil autonomy that conveys the same kind of stubbornness and entirely raw presence Sartre ascribes to the root. And if Sartre insists on the blackness of the root, I would argue that he is using blackness not as an objective chromatic descriptor—again, chestnut trees and their roots are not black—but as a figurative descriptor of impurity, where fecal matter, which is normally dark-colored, signifies, as we've seen earlier, death and putrefaction—ideas that are antipodes to the whiteness and lightness associated with cleanliness and purity. Where whiteness would stand for the fantasy of being able to be pure consciousness—*being-for-itself (pour-soi)*, in Sartre's terms—the blackness attributed to the root is its denial, the assertion that we as humans cannot help but also participate in *being-in-itself (en-soi)*, as equally contingent in our existence as the root that triggers this cascade of emotion and existential turmoil.

The association of tree root with turd with contingence becomes manifestly clear in *L'Enfance,* which brings together both fecality and the tree root as an exemplary manifestation of contingency. What Sartre suggests in *Nausea*—the evocation of the excess of overconsumption—is turned, in *L'Enfance,* into another existential digestive crisis, one that finds egress not through the mouth but rather, through the anus. (In this regard, Sartre and Beckett could be seen as sharing the view that the anus is indeed the *portail de l'être* [portal of our being], the existential passage par excellence.)

L'Enfance is an imminently scatological text: in it we find plenty of fecal scenes, from Lucien's toilet training (in stark contrast to his cousin Riri who isn't as quick a study as Lucien and continues to

soil himself long past toddlerhood) to pretentious adolescent conversations about Freudian theory, from a solid figurine of a turd to
the violent diarrhea Lucien experiences at his homosexual initiation.
This is a text that would give plenty of ammunition to Sartre's critics
who, as alluded to in this chapter's epigraph, charged him with being
a gratuitous coprophile, the creator of "L'Excrémentialisme," a writer
guiding his readers on miasmic "excremental paths."[26] Indeed, even a
reader as sympathetic to Sartre's philosophy as Albert Camus would
write, in a review of *Le Mur,* the collection of stories that *L'Enfance*
was originally published in, that "the only criticism one could make
would have to do with the author's use of obscenity."[27] *L'Enfance* is
a sufficiently scatological text that the literary scholar C. J. Harvey
would be compelled to publish a defense of it that explains Sartre's
use of "disquieting . . . scatological details" by claiming that he uses
shit the way he uses parody—"both scandalize the reader, jolting him
out of his aesthetic and philosophical complacency"—and concludes
that "like some verbal alchemist, Sartre transmutes baser metals into
gold," the text's "sordid, obscene or grotesque images . . . provocative in their complexity but never gratuitous."[28] I agree with Harvey
that the shit in the text is not gratuitous, but its function goes beyond
jolting readers out of complacency into aesthetic and philosophical
attention—it serves instead as the aesthetic and philosophical mes-
sage, where the concept of contingency finds its fullest realization in
fecal form.

Let's turn now to the text to see how Sartre does this, beginning
with the toilet-training scene that occurs just five pages in:

> But the next day when she was sitting near him holding his hands
> while he was on the pot and said to him, "Push, Lucien, push, little
> darling . . . please." He suddenly stopped pushing and asked her,
> a little breathlessly, "But you're my real mother, aren't you?" She
> said, "Silly," and asked him if it wasn't going to come soon.[29]

This scene has been read as staging Freud's theory of infantile sexuality, evoking not so subtly the Oedipal scene of a son's sexual desire for
his mother and framing the toilet training as a coital scene, where we

see superposed "in scandalous fashion defecation and fornication."[30] While the fecal is associated with the sexual throughout, as we will see later with Lucien's homosexual initiation, I want to bracket the sexual and leave it on the surface to instead see how the notion of freedom, in its existentialist sense, is already being sketched out here, through the fecal. While Sartre leaves unwritten the actual transmission of the fecal gift from son to mother—the scene concludes without telling us if Lucien actually produces a bowel movement—what is written is feces as centered around will: Lucien is the fecal agent and if he only assumes his agency, he can produce the feces his mother implores him to produce.

The first instance in the text of Lucien as a subjectivity endowed with freedom is thus grounded in fecality. The character of his cousin Riri serves as a foil to Lucien's freedom-endowed person: "Lucien could not keep himself from thinking that Riri, seven years ago, still did number two in his pants and after that walked with his legs wide apart like a duck and looked at his mother with candid eyes saying, 'No, mamma, I didn't do it, I promise'" (98; 36). Nothing in this scene indicates that Riri voluntarily defecated in his pants—rather, this memory, spurred by the sight of a Riri who "had become a very handsome young man, a little too elegant" (98; 36), is meant to remove from Riri the dignity and maturity he now has by revealing what an incontinent mess he used to be, unable to control his sphincter. Unlike Riri, who cannot control his bowel movements, who does not have freedom but whose body instead acts as an *en-soi* rather than a *pour-soi*, Lucien fancies himself someone who has always had that control, that freedom. That is, until Lucien himself loses control of his sphincter in his sexual encounter with Bergère, the older, erudite, artsy-fartsy boy who takes Lucien under his wing and tries to pass himself off as being a modern-day Rimbaud, smoking hashish, engaging in automatic writing, owning bizarre objects such as a "diabolical turd" (109; 59),[31] saying, in all seriousness, that that turd and other joke objects like it have "a revolutionary value. They disturb. There is more destructive power in them than in all the works of Lenin" (205; 60).

Part of Lucien's revolutionary education in a Rimbaudian "dérèglement de sens" (disorganization of the senses) involves having sex with Bergère on a trip they take together. Lucien, in effect, asks Bergère to initiate him even as he is filled with dread. Humiliated by his inability to become aroused, Lucien takes refuge in the bathroom: "'It isn't my fault,' he hissed, 'you made me drink too much, I want to puke'" (217; 72–73). What follows is the transformation of Roquentin's existential nausea into Lucien's existential diarrhea:

> In vain he pushed his fingers down his throat, he could not vomit. Then he dropped his trousers mechanically and sat on the toilet, shivering. "The bastard," he thought, "the bastard." He was atrociously humiliated but he did not know whether he was ashamed for having submitted to Bergère's caresses or for not getting excited . . . he fell back on the seat in despair. After a while he was seized with violent diarrhea which soothed him a little: "It's going out by the back," he thought, "I like that better." In fact, he had no further desire to vomit. (116; 73)

Where Roquentin felt nauseated at his helplessness in the face of the excess of a contingent existence, the excessive existence of all that exists around him, Lucien feels nauseated at his helplessness in the face of someone else's will that would reduce him to an object, but not the placid *en-soi* existence of an unselfconscious object such as a tree root, but rather, the agonizing passive existence of a consciousness that knows it has been reduced to an object. In this situation of excess, Lucien, overwhelmed, seeks relief in being able to force himself to vomit, in being able to will that expulsion of his insides. Instead, what he experiences is the relief of involuntary defecation.

Unlike the solid turd of the text's opening,[32] which, like the diabolical turd, symbolizes freedom—but in the distorted sense of power over something (power over his mother, in this case, who is left begging him to please push out his feces) rather than the existentialist sense of responsibility for and toward one's own life and freedom, where one's freedom is its own object—the liquid feces here, shapeless and formless, symbolize lack of freedom. It is after renouncing the voluntary projection of one's will (Lucien stops trying to make himself vomit) and being subjected to corporeal forces beyond his control, that Lucien is able to emerge from the bathroom and successfully go through with his homosexual initiation. It is in embracing not freedom but passivity—a textbook case of Sartrean bad faith—that Lucien, rather than leaving a situation that distresses him, submits instead to the body and will of Bergère, allowing the older boy to shepherd him into a sexual encounter. We see this embrace of passivity in Lucien's finally having an erection when he imagines himself to be a doll, completely at the mercy of whoever handles him: "'I'm his little doll!' Then Bergère shouted in triumph. 'At last!' he said, 'you've decided. All right,' he added, breathing heavily, 'we'll make something out of you.' Lucien slipped out of his pajamas" (117; 74). The illusion that Lucien succumbs to is the idea that he has been able to choose the abdication of his freedom, that this giving up is actually an expression of will.[33]

How, you may be wondering, does this fecality connect back to the chestnut tree root that I argue is the hinge between *La Nausée* and *L'Enfance*? For the answer, we must return to the beginning of *L'Enfance*, to a few pages after the toilet-training scene that dramatically pits Lucien's will against his mother's, in an arch rendering of Freud's theory on anal retentivity—an expression of will that informs the rest of Lucien's development in the text.[34] Shortly after this scene, a chestnut tree makes its appearance in a heavy-handed reprise of Roquentin's epiphanic scene, which merits citing at length:

> The air trembled about the red crest of the wall and the sunlight
> made burning spots on the earth and on Lucien's hands. "Chestnut
> tree!" It was shocking: when Lucien told mamma, "My pretty little
> mamma" she smiled and when he called Germaine "stinkweed"
> she cried and went complaining to mamma. But when he said
> "chestnut tree" nothing at all happened. He muttered between
> his teeth "Nasty old tree" and was not reassured, but since the
> tree did not move he repeated, louder, "Nasty old tree, nasty old
> chestnut tree, you wait, you just wait and see!" and he kicked it.
> But the tree stayed still—just as though it were made of wood. That

evening at dinner Lucien told mamma, "You know, mamma, the trees, well . . . they're made of wood," making a surprised little face which mamma liked. But Mme. Fleurier had received no mail at noon. She said dryly, "Don't act like a fool." Lucien became a little roughneck. He broke his toys to see how they were made, he whittled the arm of a chair with one of papa's old razors, he knocked down a Tanagra figure in the living room to see if it were hollow and if there were anything inside; when he walked he struck the heads from plants and flowers with his cane: each time he was deeply disappointed, things were stupid, nothing really and truly existed. Often mamma showed him flowers and asked him "What's the name of this." But Lucien shook his head and answered, "That isn't anything, that doesn't have any name."
(89; 18–19)

In this scene, Sartre, in a parodic tone, rearticulates all the main aspects of Roquentin's epiphany: the *marronnier* as trigger; rage at the contingency of things existing *en-soi* as experienced by a being endowed with consciousness; the inadequacy of language to capture anything about the reality of the object it would claim to name. What Lucien's encounter with the *marronnier* brings out that is muted in Roquentin's is the self-deception humans subject themselves to in bad faith when they refuse the contingency of existence, of being *en-soi*, and only admit being *pour-soi* as truly existing. The incapacity to accept contingency—as Roquentin does, in recognizing that his own existence participates in the same order of existence as the chestnut tree—leads Lucien to lash out in destructive violence against objects, presaging the violence against humans with which the novella will close when Lucien throws himself into the feeling of having a real existence when he assaults a presumably Jewish reader of the communist paper *L'Humanité*, egged on by his fellow right-wing *camelots*, all of them happy to delude themselves into thinking that this external identity is what they *are*.

The chestnut tree serves, in both *La Nausée* and *L'Enfance*, as the site of a first encounter with contingency, but with radically different results. One protagonist assumes his freedom to take on a creative project, the other refuses his freedom to instead allow himself to be determined by an ideology and an action that are external to him, his seeming agency and initiative themselves the product of an existential passivity. If Sartre followed up *La Nausée* with this rewriting of its story of contingency in *L'Enfance,* I would argue that it is because it wasn't enough to demonstrate what a proper response to contingency looks like; for the reader to be fully informed of their existential choices, it was necessary to portray an improper, unethical response to contingency as a cautionary tale.

By beginning *L'Enfance* with the potty-training and chestnut tree scenes, Sartre places the whole text under the sign of both fecality and contingency, tying them together, and it is in taking back up the chestnut tree scene so unambiguously that Sartre is effectively exhorting the reader to read *L'Enfance* together with *La Nausée.* It is no coincidence that the object that stages contingency in both texts is a chestnut tree root (although Lucien engages with the whole tree and not just the root, the fact that it so clearly references *La Nausée* means that Lucien's *marronnier* sends the reader back to Roquentin's root—Sartre does not need to explicitly name the root a second time for the root to be present): a tree root resembles feces through its shape and color. There is something, then, about fecality that enables it to get at the contingency–freedom pairing in a way that the tree root as a source of nausea cannot. We move from *La Nausée* to *L'Enfance,* from nausea to defecation as a response to the excess of existence, as we saw in *L'Enfance*'s diarrhea scene. What does this shift along the axis of conceptual indigestibility from nausea to defecation signal?

The shift from the desire to purge via vomiting and the desire to purge via defecation marks a shift in the relation between human freedom and the world in which that freedom can be exercised. Harkening back to Céline's use of vomit as opposed to feces, the primary distinction between these two forms of expulsion maps onto the question of processing. Vomit is the production of undigested, unprocessed food. Feces are the sign that the body has processed and taken in food. Read existentially, vomit would be the result of the incapacity to process contingency, the reality of one's situation in the world; feces would then be the result of having properly digested contingency. In *L'Enfance,* however, we do not have a single instance of healthy and proper defecation—we do not ever see an *étron sain,* a healthy turd, as opposed to an *étron diabolique,* a diabolic one. The toilet-training scene does not actually give us any access to fecal matter; Riri, while his feces might be healthy, has a pathological incapacity to control his sphincter; Lucien's diarrhea is certainly not healthy; and immediately following the chestnut tree scene, Lucien becomes heavily constipated (90; 19). The only solid feces described in the text are Bergère's *étron diabolique,* which is not real.

All this bad shit is a sign of Lucien's bad faith, and the text, through the omission of good shit, suggests that good faith, and the assumption of one's freedom in the face of contingency, could be represented through a healthy, normal bowel movement. To be the producer of healthy, solid shit is to accept contingency—as embodied, very concretely, in the unceasing and repetitive need to defecate, day in and day out, a need over which we have no influence—and respond to it by the exercise of our freedom via the voluntary control of our sphincter muscles. Fecality thus permits Sartre to both articulate what bad faith looks like (Lucien) and to suggest what good faith looks like (an offstage good defecator), and to frame fecality in terms of freedom, of how we respond to the unpleasant fact of contingency (contingency, like feces, isn't particularly pretty, and provokes more repulsion than attraction).

One of the things we can take away from Sartre's revisiting, in *L'Enfance,* Roquentin's adventure in contingency is that he, on some level, grasps that bad faith, even as it has largely been cast in purely intellectual terms as a question of consciousness, is in fact a visceral and embodied condition and cannot be understood except as such.[35] Sartre's introduction of so much excrement in *L'Enfance* allows us to reframe the flight from freedom as a flight from a certain kind of embodiment: Sartrean freedom is responsibility, a freedom that constrains you to use it. Fecality is a freedom that constrains you to use it—we are free to control when and where we defecate (if we have a normal use of our sphincters) but we are not free to refuse to defecate if we are invested in remaining alive.[36] To be in good faith is not simply a conscious orientation toward the world, it is also an orientation toward one's body: Sartre is not nearly as Cartesian as he has been made out to be. Reading *L'Enfance* and *La Nausée* together and attending to the fecality *L'Enfance* prohibits us from ignoring is instructive: unlike Roquentin and Lucien, we do not need to go outside and encounter a tree to learn this crucial lesson about contingency; we need only to sit on the toilet and encounter the embodied subjectivity that expressed fecality interpellates.

Genet, Shitter of Poems

I want to shift gears from Sartrean contingency and the freedom that fecality dramatizes to the fecal text Genet produced in solitude in the prison of Fresnes: his first novel, *Notre-Dame-des-Fleurs,* the text that put him on the literary map and made Sartre learn of his existence. This shifting of gears will turn out to not be much of a shift at all but rather an extension into the same territory of fecal freedom that Sartre began to explore in *L'Enfance*. *Notre-Dame-des-Fleurs* was written without Genet knowing of Sartre's work[37] but it can be seen as a response to Sartre's fecal call, a text that would bring Sartre out of his excremental solitude into a fecal solidarity with Genet.

Sartre and Genet would appear not to have much in common with each other literarily. Edmund White articulates this contrast succinctly:

> Although Genet may have had recurring ideas, and may have
> imposed a design on his novels, his themes and schemes never mit-
> igate the reader's sense that the author is improvising notions and
> discovering linguistic possibilities line by line, word by word. The
> action in Genet's books occurs primarily on the local, not the glob-
> al, level, in the language, not in the plot, whereas the interest in
> Sartre's imaginative work is best served by a *précis* of the contents.
> Sartre is more fun to discuss, Genet more absorbing to read.[38]

Despite this difference, they are both intuitively drawn toward fecality as a way of elaborating freedom as a fundamental principle.

Sartre, as Annie Cohen-Solal puts it, was fiercely anti-hierarchical, anti-establishment[39]—anti-power, in other words. This refusal would align Sartre with Genet's spectacular refusal of the social order and we can describe both persons' oeuvres, then, as a quest for freedom from power. Fecality, in both writers' hands, expresses this freedom: in Sartre's case, fecality serves as the germ of what would come later in his life to be his overtly political anti-power stance while in Genet's case, that desire for freedom from power was always roiling on the surface of his writing.

Where Sartre's fecality operates in the service of a project of philosophical persuasion, Genet's fecality strikes at our bodies, offering an experience of freedom that passes through an experience of excrementality, just as the manuscript of *Notre-Dame-des-Fleurs* had to do to see the light of day: as Genet recounts in *Miracle de la rose,* he began to write in prison by hiding his manuscripts in the *tinette,* the waste receptacle of a toilet.[40] *Notre-Dame-des-Fleurs* blooms from a literal wasteland and it is to this first fecal flowering that I now turn.

Genet is a rare canonical author whose work has not been purged of its shit in its general and critical reception. Perhaps because of his homosexuality and his raw and lyrical descriptions of anal sexuality, which are impossible to ignore, the excremental, by being tied to the same anality, has avoided the sanitized fate that the other authors in *Cacaphonies* have been met with. By and large, however, this excrementality has been so tightly tethered to either abjection or homosexuality (or the two together, where Genet's writing of homosexuality is taken as an embrace of an abject sexuality that flouts proper society's norms) so that these two themes have dominated most readings of Genet. In my reading of Genet, I want to tie Genet's excrementality instead to a literary project that embodies a particular conceptualization of freedom. It is in Genet's writing that we can see an expression of the freedom he experienced in, through, and with regard to literature.

Deeply cultured (Genet, while a vagabond and a criminal, was a voracious reader and often ended up in jail for having stolen books), Genet draws freely from "high" literature, having his way with such established literary figures as André Gide and Marcel Proust. While Genet's embrace of an anti-normative freedom has been linked to an embrace of abjection as a way of freeing oneself from an oppressive society,[41] where Genet renders abject all the parts of the social order—what Sartre would refer to as *gens de bien*—that he brushes up against, I see Genet doing the opposite.

Instead of an embrace of the abject that preserves and proliferates abjection, I see Genet's excrementality as a refusal of abjection through the exercise of a freedom borne out in literary form. It is the recuperative logic of queerness, where the inhabiting of queerness has deprived it of its pejorative power. By embracing what has been considered abject—criminality, homosexuality, excrementality—and treating as abject what has been deemed good—law-abidingness, heterosexuality, cleanliness—Genet hollows out the abject so that it can no longer signify as it used to. Abjection becomes a desiccated, empty shell.

A scene from *Notre-Dame-des-Fleurs* illustrates Genet's abjection-annihilating action well: a flashback to the child the protagonist Divine was (a boy named Lou Culafroy) testing the limits of the divine power he has been asked to learn about and accept. With terror in his heart, Culafroy decides to cast the body of Jesus Christ, contained in eucharistic wafers, onto the floor and experience God's punishment of his sacrilegious action:

> The silence rushed at the child, bowled him over like a team of
> boxers, pinned his shoulders to the floor. He let go of the ciborium, which made a hollow sound as it fell on the wool.
>   And the miracle occurred. There was no miracle. God had
> been debunked. God was hollow. Just a hole with any old thing
> around it. A pretty shape, like the plaster head of Marie-Antoinette
> and the little soldiers, which were holes with a bit of thin lead
> around them.[42]

This scene echoes Lucien's wanton destruction of his toys and objects around him, with both boys finding out that the objects that make up the world are devoid of real existence. Nothing happens to Culafroy—the stories of God he has been regaled with are false. This is Genet's rewriting of Sartrean contingency: what we thought was the motor of existence is a decoy—there is no determining force to drive our lives. Abjection cannot but be defined in relation to the good—the imposition of normativity—and in this scene both ideas (the abject and the pure, the impure and the good) are deflated and hollowed out at the same time, revealed to be nothing more than contingent narratives, empty figures.

Genet's treatment of all that is considered abject is a calling out of the emperor's nudity: it places pressure on our internalized embrace of the "good" as an illusion that we have collectively consented to. If we follow Genet's treatment of excrementality, we must move away from the abject, because there is nothing in the way he uses and is used by shit in his text that casts it as abject. While Genet has used the term *abject* to refer to his work ("My imagination is plunged in the abject, but on that point, it is noble, it is pure. I reject deception; and if I've been known to exaggerate from time to time in pushing heroes and adventures toward the horrible or obscene, it's in the direction of truth"),[43] I see this as a concession to the poverty of his readers' and interlocutors' imaginations. As Geoffrey Hartman writes, "Genet's scatology is human physicality curiously ennobled, as if nothing, in art, remained impure because of the force of art."[44]

It is because we cannot stretch our minds enough to be able to make the terms *noble, pure* encompass those things we have rather arbitrarily expelled and shut out from their semantic purview that Genet must use the word *abject,* when, as he clearly states, to him they are pure and noble. Genet offers up a rotten, shitty potato to society's pristine potahto. While abjection, I would argue, is a projection onto the text, Genet's shit is a positive material by which he is able to project himself out into the world (to use Sartre's terms for the exercise of one's freedom). Shit is a positive expression of a mode of being in the world. We should take Genet at his word when he calls poetry—this thing to which he devoted his life, this thing that he risked his freedom for—shit: "This poem has relieved me. I have shat it out" (202; 210).

Notre-Dame-des-Fleurs opens with the narrator (usually referred to as Genet himself) fantasizing about a photograph of German serial murderer Eugen Weidmann (France's last publicly guillotined criminal), the convergence in Weidmann's image of criminality and masculinity spiraling out into an imagined universe of criminal masculinity—criminals, pimps, prisoners—centered in the figure of Divine, the drag queen / prostitute protagonist whose perspective the narrator inhabits. Both the prison—the narrator's space from which he writes—and the Paris in which Divine and the cast of the men she loves live, are sustained by the excremental in an intricate intermingling of farts and shit, solid matter and the odor that announces that that matter is nearby.

In the novel, shit is cast as both an origin and an end, the alpha and omega of this imagined universe. Genet describes the origins of Darling (Mignon), the virile, masculine pimp counterweight to Divine's transcendent femininity, in excremental terms: "He was probably born in one of those neighborhoods that smell of the excrement which people wrap in newspapers and drop from their windows, at each of which hangs a heart of lilacs" (96; 59). Genet is always operating in a hybrid mode—where there is masculinity there is femininity, where there is shit there are flowers, where there is repulsion there is beauty. Here is no exception, and the excrementality that is cast as the origin of this exemplar of masculinity is also cast as the end of an exemplar of femininity (that of Divine, who knew how to rework the masculinity that she had been born into): "A vast physical peace relaxed Divine. Filth, an almost liquid shit, spread out beneath her like a warm little lake, into which she gently, very gently—as the vessel of a hopeless emperor sinks, still warm, into the waters of Lake Nemi—was engulfed, and with this relief she heaved another sigh, which rose to her mouth with blood, then another sigh, the last" (315; 373).

In between an excremental beginning and ending, we find an excremental milieu: the intimate space of Divine's Montmartre garret, in which she lives with her men, is described as a "darkness the more massive for having been mildewed for years (as by a scent of chilled incense) by the subtle essence of the farts that had blossomed there" (159; 148), each subtle trace of a fart a reminder of what an anus can release into the world. The public space of the Paris outside the garret is also cast in excremental terms, mapped out by Darling as follows:

> He knows all the cafés in Paris where the toilets have seats.
> "To do a good job," he says, "I've got to be sitting down."
> He walks for miles, preciously carrying in his bowels the desire to shit, which he will gravely deposit in the mauve tiled toilets of the Café Terminus at the Saint-Lazare Station. (96; 58–59)

Darling knows Paris through how it welcomes his shit, through where he can place his bottom and carry out the solemn ritual of relieving himself. The other spaces we find in the novel are also permeated by the excremental. Genet's childhood is remembered along Proustian lines, the fecal odors of prison triggering a fond recollection of the toilet that was his refuge: "The atmosphere of the night, the smell rising from the blocked latrines, overflowing with shit and yellow water, stir childhood memories which rise up like a black soil mined by moles. . . . The reminiscence that really tugs at my heart is that of the toilet of the slate house. It was my refuge" (107–8; 75).

If the novel's settings are all excremental, it serves as a way of emphasizing that the story Genet is telling through his cast of criminal, deviant characters is a human—that is, a universal—one: "Alone in the cell, in almost breastlike rhythm (it beats like a mouth), the white tile latrine gives its comforting breath. It alone is human" (261; 295).[45] The excremental is a sign for the human—Genet's embrace of and identification with the excremental is thus an identification with the human, an identification that society has refused him. Genet's writing is antisocial, not anti-human, and this refusal of the one and appropriation of the other is exemplarily figured in excrement, which is likewise antisocial but deeply human.

Just as there is a complex interrelation between Genet's prison environment and the poetic environment that he imagines and writes for himself—between the real and the fictional—so too is there a complex interrelation between odor and matter. In one of the most memorable passages of the novel, Genet writes:

> I have already spoken of my fondness for odors, the strong odors of the earth, of latrines, of the loins of Arabs and, above all, the odor of my farts, which is not the odor of my shit, a loathsome odor, so much so that here again I bury myself beneath the covers and gather in my cupped hands my crushed farts, which I carry to my nose. They open to me the hidden treasures of happiness. I inhale, I suck in. I feel them, almost solid, going down through my nostrils. But only the odor of my own farts delights me, and those of the most handsome boy repel me. Even the faintest doubt as to whether an odor comes from me or someone else is enough for me to stop relishing it. (176–77; 174–75)

Why would Genet love his farts but not his shit? Why would Genet be horrified by someone else's farts but not his own? We can make sense of this somewhat mystifying passage by aligning farts with fantasy and shit with reality, a fart's gaseous, dissipating odor similar to the way fantasy punctuates but cannot override the real in its solidity and intractability.

If Genet loves his own farts but not that of others, it is because Genet is invested in his own fantasies, not someone else's imagined desire;[46] and we can see in this investment in fantasy an investment in a certain kind of freedom, the freedom to be oneself and someone else at the same time: "Like me and like the dead child for whom I am writing, his [Darling's] name is Jean. . . . It is another Jean, here, who is telling me his story. I am no longer alone, but I am thereby more alone than ever. I mean that the solitude of prison gave me the freedom to be with the hundred Jean Genets glimpsed in a hundred passers-by, for I am quite like Darling, who also stole" (267; 304–5). This freedom is the freedom to be oneself by becoming someone else, which is exactly the freedom that Divine exercises and imparts to the men in her life, as when Notre-Dame (Our Lady) is permitted to still be masculine, hard, even while being penetrated by another male, Gorgui Seck (243–44; 272). To adopt someone else's fantasy would be to allow them to refashion you, while what one's own fantasy is able to tap into is the power to refashion oneself. Genet expresses this potential when he calls himself "the Genet material" (*la matière Genet*) (139; 120)—a formulation that, even as it evokes malleability and the capacity to be shaped and reshaped, evokes fecality, as with *matière fécale,* a fecality that is lost in translation, fecal *matter* unable to connote *material* as *matière* does.[47]

The flatulent freedom of fantasy played out above, as we've seen, has incarceration and the loss of freedom as its condition of possibility. That flatulent freedom is then a consolation, an approximate rendering of a freedom that has been lost. There is freedom and there is freedom, and despite Genet's celebration of penality in his descriptions of life in the penal colony of Mettray and his elevation of prison sociality throughout his oeuvre, it was his post-carceral situation that allowed him to become the writer he had always wanted to be. Between the freedom of fantasy and the freedom that the literary enterprise offered him—both promising to allow Genet to become someone else—Genet chose the latter freedom, a freedom that maps onto feces, to the shat-out poem, rather than to flatulence.[48]

We can see this relation between the flatulent and the fecal worked out within the text itself, when Genet maps farts and feces onto different kinds of language. Genet writes, "Here, I cannot refrain from coming back to those words of argot which stream from pimps' lips as his farts (pearls) stream from Darling's downy behind" (252; 283). If farts are a kind of secret language, the shit it juxtaposes and commingles with is, by contrast, a public language, as dramatized by the following scene, which depicts the anal inspection Darling undergoes when imprisoned:

> He bent. The guard looked at his anus and saw a black spot.
> "... eeze" [*oussez*], he cried. Darling sneezed. But he had misunderstood. It was "squeeze" [*poussez*] that the guard had cried. The black spot was a rather big lump of dung, which got bigger every day and which Darling had already several times tried to pull away, but he would have had to pull the hairs out with it, or take a hot bath. (258; 290-91)

Shit is no longer one's own property, but is called out into public, such that it is as much the prison guard's as it is Darling's. In the description of Darling's origins, there too excrement takes on a public valence, as it is thrown out of windows, out of private homes, into the public streets below. Where fantasy, as a flatulent freedom, is private, transient, ephemeral, the fecal is public, solid, endowed with staying power through its form unlike the gas that dissipates into the atmosphere.

Here, you may counter that the public fecality depicted in the previous passage is one of coercion and has lack of freedom as its context. While this is certainly true if we take it as a simple fecal scene, if we take the scene as a comment on the kind of freedom literature affords as a public act of self-transformation, it becomes instead a Sartrean elevation of will. As Genet writes elsewhere, "Poetry is a vision of the world obtained by an effort, sometimes exhausting, of the taut, buttressed will. Poetry is willful. It is not an abandonment, a free and gratuitous entry by the senses" (236; 260). This description completes Genet's earlier claim that he has shit out a poem. The poem is a turd and it is produced through labor, through the effortful exercising of one's sphincter. The drive to create it may be contained in one's own body, but it is one's readers who drive the writer on, saying "Poussez! Push!"—"Give us a text!" And it is in the production of that text that Genet, inscribing his ephemeral farted fantasies into something as durable as a text, is able to enjoy a lasting freedom from and for himself. To use the religious language that permeates the text, what Genet gives his readers is a perpetual adoration of the blessed sacrament of transformation: of flowers into shit, shit into flowers; Culafroy into Divine, Divine into Culafroy; *la matière Genet* into *la matière littéraire*.[49] The birth of the author is the end of the person—what will allow Genet to be, forever, a proliferation of Genets, Darlings, Divines, Our Ladies of Flowers.

Certainly, there is ambivalence on Genet's part—a tenderness and affection expressed for farts that are not extended to shit. This ambivalence between flatulence and fecality as two different modalities of freedom is the ambivalence between involuntary fantasy and voluntary fiction. When we read Genet describing his flatulence-induced fantasies, describing the treasures that his farts reveal, those revelations are Proustian—involuntary, like the memories triggered by Proust's madeleine. The transformation of that fantasy into literature, however, is an exercise of will, of effort—unlike the pleasure of being transported by one's farts, it is *not* a "free and gratuitous entry by the senses." Flatulence is freedom from, but fecality is freedom to, and it is this latter freedom that Genet chooses.[50]

This freedom to is the freedom obtained through literature, and if fecality is elected as its sign, it may have to do with the convergence, in shit, of fecal matter with phallic form. The penis—revered object of Divine's, and Genet's, worship—is an objective correlative to shit. Much ink has been devoted to discussing Genet's reverence for the penis, which is beauty incarnate—Divine, extending her transformative magic to Darling in an act of feminization, says to him, "You're pretty . . . like a prick" (94; 56). But despite how much of Genet's writing is driven by the phallic (by the penis as object and as signifier, as the raison d'être of a whole host of Genetian characters), I would argue that Genet's poetics are excremental—that this phallic textual universe must be anchored in the excremental because the turd, as a phallic object, can still be worked in its materiality, can undergo the transformations in form that Genet effects through his writing. The penis, on the other hand, in its rigidity, in its capacity to work others, cannot be worked on in the same manner.

In this regard, I turn away from the "phallic flower"[51] that Derrida erects as a figure for Genet's poetics, where the proliferation of floral meanings and uses in Genet—"flowers of rhetoric, the broomflower ('genêt'), specific examples of flowers in Genet's fiction, the hermaphroditic quality of flowers which contain male and female reproductive organs (just as the name 'Genet' carries the mother and the son), *Our Lady of the Flowers* as character and as text and finally . . . the lost flower of Camille Gabrielle [Genet], Genet's unmarried mother"[52]—registers the constitutive undecidability of Genet's writing. The floral framework is thus an important one for understanding Genet's undecidable poetics, demonstrating Genet's erection of a phallus that deconstructs itself[53] and inscribing him in the maternal—the maternal that generated Genet in throwing him away, such that Sartre would come to identify Genet's origins as his becoming-excrement—thereby complicating Genet's relation to sexuality and the categories of sex that would claim to account for it.[54] What the excremental poetics I point to and insist on here does, however, is enable us to understand where that productive figure of the flower comes from. I turn, in other words, to the excrement in which *Genet* grows.

The phallus might be what drives Genet's writing, but it is in shit that that writing is wrought, permeated by the kind of *féerie* that flatulence is able to bring to the excremental medium at hand. The penis gives rise to stars, to constellations made of sperm: "their warm sperm, spurting high, maps out on the sky a milky way where other constellations which I can read take shape. . . . Thus a new map of the heavens is outlined on the wall of Divine's garret" (99; 63). The penis inscribes an unattainable limit, a sky that can only be gazed at longingly from below. The below in which Genet writes, the literary space that can be inhabited, is the excremental, the latrines that exhale humanity in their acceptance of shit and piss, the toilets in which Darling deposits his desire. Sartre described *Notre-Dame-des-Fleurs* as an "epic of masturbation"[55] but the novel is just as easily an epic of excrementality, an essay on how literature is shit, on how Genet must strain and labor to shit out his poem.

This tension between penis as object of desire (and desiring object) and shit as material of literary desire reaches its climax at the novel's ending. A few pages before, Divine dies in a pool of her nearly liquid shit, in shit that lacks the phallic form that had been her raison d'être—her life's object has been liquidated. Divine, as an agent of transformation, as someone who arranged for her wall to become a Milky Way, must die—just as farts are fleeting, so too is Divine, who lived in an atmosphere of farts. Divine, as a creative agent, is no match for Genet, who, unlike her, continues on. At novel's end, Genet performs a kind of transfiguration of Darling, installing him in the position of writer and giving him the last word in the form of a letter Darling writes to Divine from prison:

"Dearest,

I'm writing a few lines to give you the news, which isn't good. I've
been arrested for stealing. . . . Dearest, I'm awfully sorry about
what's happened to me. Let's face it, I'm plain unlucky [*Je n'ai pas
de pot, reconnais-le*]. So I'm counting on you to help me out. I only
wish I could have you in my arms so I could hold you and squeeze
you tight. Remember the things we used to do together. Try to
recognize the dotted lines. And kiss it. A thousand big kisses
sweetheart, from

Your Darling."

The dotted line that Darling refers to is the outline of his prick. I
once saw a pimp who had a hard-on while writing to his girl place
his heavy cock on the paper and trace its contours. I would like
that line to portray Darling. (317–18; 376–77)

Je n'ai pas de pot, while indeed meaning being unlucky, has excremental origins: in an argotic sense, *pot* means "both the extremely
important orifice serving to evacuate waste produced by our intestinal factory, that is to say, the anus, but also, what surrounds it—the
'ass' or posterior."[56] The English translation of "I'm plain unlucky"
is unable to convey the excrementality of the expression. Darling is
shit out of luck, or rather, his luck is out of shit: he doesn't have an
anus or an ass to fall back on, and in this plaintive, tender missive
to Divine where he asks for help, he offers her an empty signifier:
an empty outline of his penis, which, in its form, can double as an
outline of the turd he cannot produce, no longer having a *pot* (recall
that in the prison inspection scene, the turd is never evacuated, that
exercise of will is never realized).

Genet, writing from prison, like Darling, has managed to transform his own carceral situation into literature. Darling sends Divine
the outline of his penis and asks her to fill it in with the memory of
his penis in action, as a maker of stars. Genet writes to his readers
from prison and gives to us the same outline, tracing its contours,
and asks us to fill it in. While Divine, as Darling's reader, will fill

that outline in with his penis, we, as Genet's readers, are invited to fill in that negative space with *la matière Genet,* with the shit that Genet identifies himself as so that he might be able to seize for himself the freedom that literature affords, the relief obtained from shitting out a poem—from becoming someone else, lastingly.

)) < > ((

Sartre and Genet converge literarily in their use of excrement to figure their respective investments in freedom: in Sartre's case, the existentialist freedom that is the only good faith response to the contingency of existence; in Genet's case, the literary freedom that enables him to transform himself into something else, to project himself into an elsewhere and a someone else. Their shared preoccupation with freedom is what ties them together as turd and excrementalist (although, given the way Sartre writes, his identification with the chestnut tree root, we might as well call him a turd as well). In the friendship they shared, until they didn't, Sartre and Genet's working and reworking of freedom as a consistent through-line in each one's literary projects can be captured by an emoji that comes to us via Miranda July's film *Me and You and Everyone We Know* (2005). In an iconic scene, a six-year-old boy, Robby, pretending to be an adult, chats online with a lonely forty-year-old, and in an attempt at talking dirty, proposes to "poop back and forth": "I'll poop in your butthole and then you will poop it back into my butt and we will keep doing it back and forth with the same poop. Forever." Robby translates this visually, creating the emoji)) < > ((to represent what this eternal pooping back and forth would look like.

Despite the distance Sartre and Genet would eventually take from each other, this fecal freedom can be seen as a turd-idea that gets passed back and forth from each other once they landed on each other's radars: each person considering the freedom that the other produced and then returning or revisiting it with the next work. Beauvoir, in *The Prime of Life,* describes their convergence around freedom during their friendship:

The paradoxical quality about [Genet] during this period was that though he ran to certain set attitudes, which camouflaged his true nature, he remained nonetheless wholly attached to freedom. The whole basis of his fellow feeling for Sartre was this idea of liberty they shared, which nothing could suppress, and their common abhorrence of all that stood in its way: nobility of soul, spiritual values, universal justice, and other such lofty words and principles, together with established institutions or ideals.[57]

The freedom that would bind them together is the freedom that would permit their tie to be severed. While Sartre would be replaced by Derrida as the philosopher-reader of Genet, Derrida's *Glas* competing with *Saint Genet* for hermeneutical primacy,[58] nothing can clear out that excremental, human odor that wafts out of Genet and Sartre's works. Readers come and go, but shit stays—freedom cannot and must not be contravened. Shit cannot and must not be ignored.

The promise of forever contained in))< >((as a model of literary and intellectual exchange came to an end after the publication of *Saint Genet,* each set of parentheses moving away from each other, but what remained was the < >, the turd that signifies freedom.[59] For both Sartre and Genet, shit crystallizes the relation of the self with its other. Sartre's shit addresses the relation between self and world, tracing the contours of contingency (captured in the turd-like form of the chestnut tree root) and the obligation to freedom it inspires. Genet's shit addresses the relation between a free self and a constrained self, between the self one has been made out to be and the self one can be, capturing both the freedom to be and not to be. To have the fullest understanding of ourselves, it is best not to look to a mirror—to this narcissistic reflective surface—but rather to the dark, resistant, impassive, malleable material that is our shit.

) 4 (

TO WIPE THE OTHER
Duras's and Gary's Fecal Care Ethics

***

Shit, as Sartre and Genet demonstrate, is both a poetic and an ontological material, allowing us to understand ourselves and the freedom that defines us. But it is also an ethical material, one that interrogates relationality as it forms it. Shit is always a question of interrelation, be it the relation between ourselves and our bodies, where defecation gives us a glimpse of our insides; the relation between our waste and our environment, where our methods of waste management have profound and most often pernicious consequences for the ecological systems we are part of; or, as this chapter examines, the relation between ourselves and others. In this last relation, shit is an excremental situation that, just as it reminds us of the boundary between inside and outside, forces a calibration or configuration of what acts as a border between ourselves and the others that we enter into contact with. It's at this border that we find the space in which to create and take up an ethics of care that transcends identity.

Marguerite Duras's *La Douleur* (*War*) and Romain Gary's *La Vie devant soi* (*The Life before Us*) are about as dissimilar as two texts can be, yet they both stage the fecal as precisely the site for working through this ethics of care, arriving at the same conclusion despite their diametrically opposed textual strategies. If the twain do meet, making for strange bedfellows, it is because of the shit each writer draws upon—a shit that exercises an ethical gravity that transcends whatever political, aesthetic, or biographical differences might exist between Gary and Duras. Indeed, Duras and Gary have had very different literary destinies: the former became the iconic and much fêted face of a certain postwar French avant-garde, known for her leftist politics, quickly canonized as one of the most important voices in modern French literature; the latter was a career diplomat who remained a staunch Gaullist his entire life, whose prolificity and ability to sell books deprived him of the highbrow sheen so prized by the French intelligentsia, such that he has become canonized despite his books' success, not because of it.[1] Nonetheless, Duras's highbrow seriousness and Gary's middlebrow humanism and lowbrow scatological humor converge in the shit that ties their works to each other and that ties us all to each other, imposing the question of care as one that cannot go unanswered.

Duras: Shit's Nonhumanity

In 1985, nearly forty years after the publication of Robert Antelme's work of Holocaust testimony, *L'Espèce humaine* (*The Human Race*) (1947), Duras, Antelme's ex-wife, published "La Douleur"—the narrative that constitutes the first part of *La Douleur* and gives this collection of war fictions its name.[2] Ostensibly taken from wartime journals that had been tucked away in her country home in Neauphle-le-Château and forgotten about for decades, "La Douleur" was conveniently unearthed when the journal *Sorcières* asked Duras if they could publish her juvenilia.

In the terse preface to "La Douleur," which recounts her time waiting to see if her then husband, Robert L. (the alias Duras uses for Robert Antelme), would be returning home from Dachau, and the struggle to keep Antelme from dying following his return, Duras disavows this text even as she attests to its veracity, its documentary status as a found object: she claims that she has no memory of having written it, doesn't know when she could have written it, and finds it absolutely impossible that she could have written such a text during the period in which it was ostensibly written.[3] The page-long preface engages in a peculiar sort of back-and-forth between denial (*"I have no recollection of having written it. . . . How could I have written this thing I still can't name"*; 3–4; 12) and ownership (*"I know I did, I know it was I who wrote it. I recognize my own handwriting and the details of the story"*; 3; 12).[4]

This oscillation anticipates the relation she will have to Antelme himself and his shit, the inhumanness of which she will describe over the course of four pages in a scene that is central to the operation of "La Douleur," which exists to communicate just how much war costs—specifically, what it took from Antelme as a survivor of a Nazi concentration camp, and what it took from Duras as a survivor of his survival. The shit scene takes place after Antelme's return home, at a moment when his survival seems nearly impossible, and describes the unrecognizable fecal matter that is expulsed from Antelme's skeletal body, as his body, deprived of nourishment for so long, is subjected to bouts of diarrhea in a long passage that merits being cited at length to give a sense of the duration that Duras wanted this fecal passage to impose on the reader:

> Gruel, said the doctor, a teaspoonful at a time. Six or seven times a day we gave him gruel. Just a teaspoonful nearly choked him, he clung to our hands, gasped for air, and fell back on the bed. But he swallowed some. Six or seven times a day, too, he asked to go to the toilet. We lifted him up, supported him under the arms and knees. . . . Once he was sitting on his pail he **excreted** in one go, in one enormous, astonishing gurgle [*Une fois assis sur son seau, il faisait sur son seau, il faisait d'un seul coup, dans un glou-glou énorme, inattendu, démesuré*]. What the heart held back the anus couldn't: it let out all that was in it. . . . So, he **excreted** [*faisait*] this dark green, slimy, gushing thing, a **turd** [*merde*] such as no one had ever seen before. When he'd finished we put him back to bed. He lay for a long time with his eyes half shut, prostrated.
>
> For seventeen days the **turd** [*merde*] looked the same. It was inhuman. It separated him from us more than the fever, the thinness, the nailless fingers, the marks of SS blows. We gave him gruel that was golden yellow, gruel for infants, and it came out of him dark green like slime from a swamp. After the sanitary pail

was closed you could hear the bubbles bursting as they rose to the surface inside. Viscous and slimy, it was almost like a great gob of spit. When it emerged the room filled with a smell, not of putrefaction or corpses—did his body still have the wherewithal to make a corpse?—but rather of humus, of dead leaves, of dense undergrowth. It was a somber smell, dark reflection of the dark night from which he was emerging and which we would never know. . . .

Of course he'd rummaged in trashcans for food, he'd eaten wild plants, drunk water from engines. But that didn't explain it. Faced with this strange phenomenon we tried to find explanations. We thought that perhaps there, under our very eyes, he was consuming his own liver or spleen. How were we to know? How were we to know what strangeness that belly still contained, what pain?

For seventeen whole days that **turd** still looks the same. For seventeen days it's unlike anything ever known. Every one of the seven times he **excretes** each day, we smell it, look at it, but can't recognize it. For seventeen days we hide from him that which comes out of him, just as we hide from him his own legs and feet and whole unbelievable body. . . .

After seventeen days, death grows weary. In the pail [it][5] doesn't bubble any more, it becomes liquid. It's still green, but it smells more human, it smells human. [*Au bout de dix-sept*[6] *jours la mort se fatigue. Dans le seau elle ne bouillonne plus, elle devient liquide, elle reste verte, mais elle a une odeur plus humaine, une odeur humaine.*] (56–59; 72–75)[7]

Before commenting on this passage, I want first to discuss the ways the translation fails the text, and have bolded words in the passage and its translation to point out the ways that the translation distorts its excremental register.[8] In the first instance, we see Duras using the verb *faire,* which can be translated as *to go,* which Bray renders as *excreted,* replacing the informal *faire* with the formal *excrete.* Duras's insistence on the *faire* emphasizes the materiality of shit—this inhuman, incomprehensible bubbling fecal matter is something that Antelme makes, that his body manufactures. In this way, we see that on the level of language, in French, *faire* has a material, concrete conception of defecation that is lacking in English's *to go,* which, instead of insisting on shit as matter, places it in a spatialized framework, where shit is defined not through its material nature but through where one goes—the bathroom, ideally, and not one's pants—to do the work of defecating, which remains offstage.

While this replacement of *faire* by *excrete* is regrettable, the translation of *merde* as *turd* is incomprehensible. This passage describes Antelme's shit as something that is formless, or *informe*, but, through translation, it is transformed into something well-formed—a turd is solid, with clear contours, which is clearly a misnomer for the bubbling, gushing substance coming out of Antelme's anus. In the translator's desire to avoid using a word as profane as *shit,* she winds up establishing a wholly different relation between shit and materiality, shit and form, than what Duras writes. Why Barbara Bray chose *turd* over *shit* is unclear: *turd* is not a particularly polite or elegant word, and while less profane than *shit,* perhaps, still carries something of the obscene. Perhaps she did so because of the way both *turd* and *merde* share that hard "d," opting for a similarity in sound at the cost of a loss of meaning. Or perhaps she did so because *shit* is messy: it does not have the limited referentiality of *turd,* which refers only to fecal matter, or, by extension, a person one sees as being as contemptible as said matter. *Shit,* on the other hand, exceeds the fecal to seize for itself all kinds of signification, functioning as expletive, as a general term for a situation or for objects, its referentiality extraordinarily capacious—what can't be mapped onto shit? But to sanitize *shit,* turning it into a more manageable *turd,* is to foreclose the messiness and ambiguity that the writers of *Cacaphonies* exploit.

In this passage, which constitutes one of the most extraordinary descriptions of shit to be found in literature, we have Antelme's fecal matter doing remarkable signifying work through, precisely, the messiness that inheres in *shit.* It is quite long, delivering up four pages of tight narration and description that enclose the reader in an excremental passage that mirrors the intestinal passage, over the course of which Antelme's shit stands in for the inhuman, for suffering, for the unspeakable horrors of the concentrationary universe, for death, while at the same time evoking life in its resemblance to humus—the rich soil that enables vegetal life to grow.

Cast firmly under the sign of the nonhuman, Antelme's shit bridges life and death, the unthinkable past and a possible future. As long as Antelme continues to produce this nonhuman shit, more vegetal than animal, his life is suspended, the nature of his waste matter determinant of what his existential fate will be. As material, his shit is nonsensical: Duras and her fellow carers have no idea of what could be producing such unknown material, and Antelme's body's output is completely disproportionate to what is being taken in. He eats a few teaspoons of mush a day and expels bucketfuls of what we might describe as formless matter, or the *informe*,[9] which signifies violence, forest, dark, night, the mysteries of the unknowable. This matter exceeds—it exceeds Antelme, it exceeds Duras's powers of comprehension and apprehension, and it exceeds us as readers.

As matter, Antelme's shit is thus protean in its capacity to signify multiply, but it is a signifying matter that is beyond our mastery. It is beyond anyone's control, and the seventeen-day vigil at his bedside is a measure of how at its mercy they are, as helpless before it as one is before death, which is what Duras calls this fascinating material from which she cannot turn away (the English translation unfortunately erases this identification of shit with death). It is no coincidence, then, that Duras would choose to communicate this experience of shit as death by holding the reader captive within an experience of duration. Our helplessness vis-à-vis time, where time will always have the upper hand, outliving, outlasting, and outwaiting us, finds reiterations in the narrated impotence before this shit and before the death it would figure.

The shit passage acts as the narrative threshold between life and death, without which Duras's account of Antelme's survival cannot cohere. Duras needs this liminal scene in order to be able to conclude the text as she does with the words, "He didn't die in the concentration camp" (68; 85), and impart to them their full weight and polysemic potential. This simple sentence acts not only as an affirmation of Antelme's livingness, but also as the tacit articulation of its dark underside, coming as it does after a description of the manifold ways in which both Duras and Antelme are haunted by his concentrationary experience even after the end of the war, after his return to health from having been reduced to a mere echo of himself, an unrecognizable "wreck" (*déchet*) (54; 69), a mere "form" (55; 70).[10]

If Antelme did not die in the camp, he died outside it, a seemingly simple declaration that extends death's reach beyond the concentrationary universe it is equated with to non-concentrationary spaces as well. The death that Antelme's body expelled over the course of those seventeen days lived between life and death changes form. Before, it had been contained within the *informe* matter of his bubbling inhuman shit, taken as an exemplary, necessary, and singular representation of the horrors of the Holocaust—what Bruno Chaouat sees as the only sign capable of beginning to communicate to readers the deeply human inhumanity of the Holocaust.[11] Now, death is to be found outside the suffering body, in the indifferent world that carries on regardless of what happens in it. "He didn't die in the concentration camp," despite its declarative construction, functions as a question, interrogating what death is, and what the relation between life and non-death is. It is in the shit scene that life and death become crystallized as well as immediately rendered senseless, producing, on an ontological level, the kind of vacillation and ambivalence that Duras expresses in the preface with regard to the text and the fact of having written it. The shit is inhuman, but it's human; she cannot recognize it but she must recognize it as belonging to Antelme, as being produced by him. The thing it is is both so clearly itself and an abolition of all comprehensibility.

Duras's writing of shit resembles Céline's treatment of shit. Like Céline's deployment of a shit that establishes difference only to destroy it, Duras's writing of Antelme's shit also raises difference—the difference between the human and nonhuman, between being and nonbeing—only to destroy it. Duras insists, as does Céline, on shit's capacity both to break and to bond, when she cites Antelme's shit as being what separates him from his carers more than the more intelligible signs of the atrocities he's lived through—"fever, the thinness, the nailless fingers, the marks of SS blows." Shit is both what repulses Duras, rupturing her relation to Antelme, and what ties her to him, when, six or seven times per day, she aids Antelme in his defecation and takes care of his shit and his shitting body for him. And like Céline, Duras ties death and shit together as caught up in one signifying project—the writing of a human truth that exceeds writing, that, as Duras puts it, shames literature (4; 12).

This shit passage, upon which "La Douleur" hinges, has, remarkably, been passed over in Duras scholarship, with critics either omitting the passage or describing it laconically,[12] referring to Antelme's diarrhea as if it were an ordinary bout of involuntary defecation, rather than the drawn-out, dramatic, and narratively vital passage it is for Duras, who relies on it to communicate just how gaping the schism was between her, in the land of the living, and Antelme, more dead than alive, and to convey the incomprehensible depth of the inhumanity Antelme lived through. One of the rare discussions of this shit passage that ties it to Duras's literary project writ large is found in Jane Bradley Winston's *Postcolonial Duras: Cultural Memory in Postwar France*. In this work, Winston recuperates for Duras's oeuvre the political substance that she sees criticism and scholarship as having effaced and removed over the course of Duras's long career, where the earlier, communist Duras is treated as political while the later Duras, the psychoanalytical Duras, is depoliticized for her trademark writing of the sexual and the personal.

Winston's strategy, which restores to Duras's full corpus the political continuity denied it, is to read *La Douleur* with Duras's first novel, *Un barrage contre le Pacifique* (*The Sea Wall*) (1950), seeing the former, 1985 text as being animated by the same political, anti-colonial impetus as Duras's early novel, which was written at the same time that Duras's lover, Dionys Mascolo, was writing his treatise *Le Communisme*. Winston sees Mascolo's politics informing Duras's literary response to a shared question of human need. Duras's politics can thus be explicated or grasped via Mascolo's, whose conceptualization of revolutionary politics is not grounded in traditional class-driven materialist thought, but insists instead on a category-dissolving, universalizing quest for self-creation or self-actualization, which, in Mascolo's mind, results in the subject's recognizing itself as being subject to material need, where it is the human subjection to material conditions and needs that provides the common ground for a communism, for a collectivity that comes together by communicating its universally shared vulnerability and needs. Winston sees Robert Antelme's shit as the figuration of what she takes to be one of the central points of *La Douleur*: the fact that we, as one human race, are both human and nonhuman, as made manifest by the Holocaust. The nonhuman shit that Antelme produces is taken as the "material sign of the Nazi crimes and his victimization."[13]

Winston, drawing on Kristeva's *Powers of Horror,* reads his shit, in its fluidity, as abjection incarnate, able to move between categories such as inside and outside, rendering their boundaries less solid. The consequence of this abjection is to present all those who behold Antelme's shit, either as direct witnesses or as recipients of Duras's testimony, with the epiphany "that all of us, as human beings, have human and nonhuman potential; that we are thus one human race."[14] Winston ties Duras's writing of Antelme's shit to *Un barrage contre le Pacifique* to argue that Antelme's shit in fact represents and reprises the political substance associated with the early, communist Duras so that the boundary-dissolving abjection of Antelme's shit, which leads to the intermingling of categories such as the human and nonhuman, is brought to bear in a critique of French empire and its shoring up of boundaries, imputing thus to Duras's signature style—associated with blurring and fluidity—a political project that aligns Duras with the oppressed.

Winston's reading of *La Douleur,* which aligns with Chaouat's, takes up Antelme's shit for what it has to say about the state of our humanity, for the way Duras, through Antelme's shit, is able to represent the inhumanity of our humanity, the commingling of the human and nonhuman, the human and the monstrous. I want to use Antelme's shit, however, to lean into the nonhumanness that is at work in the passage, which makes evident the way Duras makes space for a nonhuman humanism,[15] by which I mean an ethics that cares little for the human (or not) status of the one who cares, but renders the human—nonhuman boundary porous and open by turning care into a question of instinct.[16] Care becomes an instinct, an imperative response to a situation of need. Just as the animal licks its own or some other creature's wounds out of instinct, so too should the human response to someone else's shit—the assumption of the obligation to wipe someone else's bottom, to deal with their shit as if it were our own—become a question of instinct as well.

Granted, the question of instinct becomes complicated here by gender: it's difficult to imagine a man writing or narrating this scene of tending to Antelme's excremental vulnerability. Duras is a woman who seems to be assuming a different kind of instinctive position vis-à-vis Antelme than the sort of animal instinct I refer to here—that of the so-called maternal instinct. Antelme is reduced to eating mush, the stuff that babies eat, and she could be seen here as mothering Antelme. Reading this scene as a maternal one rather than an animal one doesn't change the framing of care as instinct—maternity, after all, is a kind of animalization of the human, where the woman becomes a body driven to care for her young in a kind of unthinking, animal way—but it is to miss the larger point of fecality as the force by which care might become an unparticularized, universal human position rather than the feminized practice it is currently.

I want to pause here to develop further the gendered nature of care because it is at the intersection of gender and care that feces' radical potential for recasting how we think care becomes evident—that shit's capacity to act on another concept in a literary environment is particularly visible. Care ethics, in the realm of ethics or moral philosophy, has always been feminized, with Carol Gilligan's classic work *In a Different Voice: Psychological Theory and Women's Development* (1982) considered the originary text for formulating a feminist care ethics, and Nel Noddings's *Caring: A Feminine Approach to Ethics and Moral Education* (1984) the main reference for its maternalist strand.[17] Just as care work—teaching, nursing, childcare, et cetera—is profoundly feminized, so too is thinking care. While Gilligan does not subscribe to the kind of essentialism Noddings does, considering the fact that women are society's caregivers to be a social rather than a natural state, both point to mothering as an exemplary site of care: the mother as the first and ultimate caregiver is the example by which all other instances of care will be measured, where the mother–child relationship is, in Noddings's words, "a very special relation—possibly the prototypical caring relation."[18] Noddings casts the maternal—our earliest experiences and memories of being cared for as an infant—as "universally accessible" (5) and sees this universal experience of being mothered as the "universal heart of the ethic" (6). And Gilligan presents the mother–child relationship as playing a crucial role in shaping a child's relational mode—their attachments and how they will navigate and experience care.[19]

I respect Gilligan's valorization of care in the face of a narrative of moral development that both establishes care as the basis for thinking of women as good and for thinking of them as morally immature compared to men,[20] and I can understand Noddings's recentering of the feminine via an elevation of the maternal even as I disagree with its essentialist bent. And I share with them and all thinkers of care the emphasis on care as a fundamentally relational practice.[21] This means that care is contingent, as a relation exists first and foremost as a practice dependent on the persons involved and not as a concept. I would argue that fecality—in particular, the work of attending to and dealing with someone else's feces—is what allows us to capture most profoundly the relational and contingent nature of the care relation in ways that establish it as a truly universal ethical foundation. Noddings's maternal, while deemed a universal experience, is still anchored in the particularity of the mothering body, whereas my focus on wiping detaches the action from the identity of the actor to argue instead for how the universality of fecality as an intimate experience shared by literally every body displaces care ethics from the particularized frame to which it has been constrained.

Particularized, gynocentric formulations of care ethics are animated by a femininity that also brings them to a halt. These recuperations, while important, are palliative rather than transformative: they are akin to organizing for higher wages for care work, for equal wages for women, when the problem is capitalism itself. There has been important conceptual work done to degender or universalize care, notably by Joan Tronto, who seeks to change the value associated with care so that it is no longer relegated to a gendered (and racialized) ghetto but is instead a universal, democratic value. While I agree with Tronto that an ethic of care ought to be universal, rather than feminine, we diverge on the question of instinct. Tronto rejects an instinctive conceptualization of care as "not part of the realm of moral choice," which leads to its dismissal as a "serious ethical idea" when her project is to elevate care on moral philosophical terms.[22]

My call to transform care into instinct is not an uncritical celebration of instinct or so-called nature—instinct can be cruel. Instead, I am arguing that casting care as instinctive rather than a practice stemming from some sort of "higher order" human sympathy or moral reasoning would allow for a lot more care to be in the world. And if there needs to be more care in the world, that need is an indictment of the currently inegalitarian and inequitable structure of care. Thinking care as instinct is not to paper over the very real inequality that inheres in care: were the tables turned, would Antelme have tended to Duras's shit? Certainly, he might have, but it's just as plausible that he would have delegated that work to a woman or that he might have left Duras altogether, just like the many men who leave their wives when the latter are diagnosed with cancer or some other life-threatening disease, leaving their care to someone else.[23]

In short, I am not disputing that care is gendered—it obviously is, and the work of feminist theorists of care ethics amply demonstrates that reality. What I am pointing to, however, is the kind of conceptual, ethical work that fecality can do in a literary context, in a text like "La Douleur." Gilligan, Noddings, and Tronto *describe* the gendered inequality of care, but the descriptions Duras provides of Antelme's excremental body and her response operate on a different level.[24] Feminist work on care ethics, in its descriptive work, necessarily reproduces this inequality if only for the purpose of calling it out, of impressing on readers the need to change this reality. But "La Douleur," even though it is profoundly historically anchored, refuses both conventional description and prescription—two modes that theoretical articulations of feminist care ethics operate in.

Description in fiction is never description: it is always a call to imagine, to build with the writer a world. Duras's excremental passage, rather than a mere description of reality as lived and borne out by Antelme's suffering body and Duras's responsive one, uses fecality to work out an idea that is a compelling alternative to the gendered inequality of care as it functions in a society where the care instinct has been socialized out of men to be assigned nearly exclusively to women. In response to a horrifying world that could produce the Holocaust and the systematic dehumanization of millions of persons, Duras writes fecality in such a way as to point toward the universal instinctualization of care as a way of turning humans into animals of care, such an animalization a way of saving the human from itself.

Through Antelme's shit, we are encouraged to view care not as the gendered act that we know it to be, but as an animal act and positionality, as a species-wide imperative. If fecality is such an effective vector for this kind of conceptual work, it is because it is found here in fiction, which appeals not only to our minds but also to our bodies in the way it, as a fabulation, a fabrication, creates worlds for us to project into. Fiction's capacity to make us engage with a different form of thought, embodiment, and action than is ours in our day-to-day lives opens a space in which we have the opportunity, finally, to imagine and think differently. Let us return now to Duras's fecal fiction, to follow her instinctualization of care through shit to its conceptual conclusions.

Antelme, in Duras's description, is a suffering animal, a suffering body, and Duras is an animal body that responds to the former's weakness with its own strength. Here, there is never any question of whether Duras ought to care for Antelme or not—of course she must. There is no ink spent reflecting on Duras's reactions to the inhuman shit flowing out of Antelme's body, no description of repulsion or disgust that must be surmounted for Duras to be able to do the work of caring for Antelme. In the face of Antelme's need, manifested in his extreme excremental situation, there is no room for thought: one simply responds, and tends to the shit at hand. Such an instinctive response not only opens the human–nonhuman boundary so that

the human Duras can occupy the animal position of instinctive creature, it also makes porous an ontological boundary: Duras has been
contaminated by Antelme's shit—not by its physical matter, but by its
ontological substance, by the blurring of death and life that it entails.
To wipe—to enter into contact with shit—is to consent to take on that
living dead status, to consent to be a bit more dead so that someone
who is dead might be a bit more alive, to suspend the intra-human
distinction that would maintain subjectivities in a relation of I–you,
self–other.

It is in this last dissolution of subjective boundaries that we can
see the problematic nature of a Kristevan reading of Antelme's shit
that places it under the sign of abjection. Abjection is, ultimately, always about the self. The boundaries of subjectivity that are threatened are one's own—it's when one can no longer distinguish between
self and other, when one's own subjectivity is under assault, that the
abject exercises its power. In the kind of ethical imperative that we
find in this passage, however, to assume an ethical response or position is precisely to go beyond the sort of self-centered, self-concerned
posture abjection necessarily entails. Here we find an I–you relation,
but not a *you* in the usual sense of *you,* which serves to shore up the
I, where the ethics of care risks being reduced to the binarity of an *I*
that acts as an agent of care and a *you* that passively receives care as
its object. Care, in the kind of excremental context that Duras delivers up, is in fact an anti-identitarian act, one whose boundary dissolution does not trigger crisis but suspends the force of subjecthood
altogether so that what remains is the act of relation—a kind of pure
relationality, one that is marked by reciprocity, in which hierarchy is
nonsensical.

Relation here is a radical leveling. Shit lends itself to thinking such
a leveling, such an ethical indistinction, as crystallized in the simple
observation that there really isn't much of a difference between one's
own shit and someone else's. It's all a matter of projecting our own
constructed senses of self onto this material that, for what variations
one's diet and gut flora might produce, is the same thing, the byprod-
uct of our digestive process. When confronted with shit that comes

from someone else's body, we don't say, aha, this is clearly vegetarian-produced shit, or this is the shit of someone who eats meat, or this shit is produced by a person of such and such race—we are not able to draw conclusions about the identity of the body that produced it. What we see is shit, and this often abased matter that levels the aforementioned distinctions should also level another distinction to which we hold on dearly—the distinction between self and other, the recognition that we accord to the excrement that comes out of our own bodies that we deny to the excrement that comes out of others' to which we respond with disavowal, save in a context of care, which can afford no such distance.

The philosopher Bernard Stiegler, in his work on care, excavates the etymological history not of the word *soigner,* to care for, but of *penser,* to think, in order to posit thinking as a fundamental dimension of caring. As Stiegler explains, the verb *panser*—to bandage, to groom (a horse)—was first written as *penser.* In the convergence of these two homophonic verbs, which have, since the seventeenth century, come to have their current, divergent meanings, Stiegler sees a key philosophical insight, where the coming together of *panser* and *penser* directs us to think of thought as care, as also implicating the processes of nourishment and assimilation.[25] To care is thus to think, to think is to care, and both require assimilation. The assimilation of thinking with care, and the attribution of a unified assimilation to *panser/penser,* care/thought, is a complicated move, however, as the assimilation normally associated with *penser* is distinct from the assimilation associated with *panser.* Where *penser* is the site of a self-directed assimilation, where the thinker assimilates what is thought into their mind, the assimilation of *panser* is a transitive, not reflexive, act of assimilation, where another person assimilates the nourishment that the carer provides. Stiegler, by bringing together care and thought to propose care/thought, or care as thought and thought as care, is effectively attributing to *penser* an ethical imperative to turn outward, to take something other than oneself as the object of one's attentions.

Duras's shit scene dramatizes and enacts for the reader, decades before Stiegler, what care as thought and assimilation looks like. Her nourishing Antelme's body, and making it assimilate the lifegiving food she provides, produces what we could call a reciprocal action of care, which casts Duras as assimilating his inhuman shit—she effectively treats the shit she hides from him as her own, wiping him as she does herself, disposing of his shit as she might of her own. In so doing, she assimilates his survival: Duras does not coopt or ventriloquize his suffering but instead undergoes an authentic assimilation rendered possible by her assimilation of his shit. Duras's care brings Antelme to life, and her care for and assimilation of Antelme brings Duras to and through death, so that the two might coexist in this excremental situation and its wake as people who now know, viscerally, what life and death are, and take on a haunted, gut-wrenched postwar existence as the only position possible in the wake of the unthinkable war.

In this shared situation of extreme humanity, marked by its nonhumanity—Antelme reduced to a diarrheic skeleton and bag of organs that must be tended to, Duras reduced to a body that must care, that must tend—Duras and Antelme both move away from the human to make themselves open onto and traversed by the nonhuman as the only way in which to live.[26] The shit, once gone—wiped away, eventually transformed again into the recognizable human shit a human body is supposed to produce—persists, leaving indelible traces, its physical viscosity translating into existential viscosity, where two human subjectivities can blur into each other to become instead animals that *pansent* in order to *pensent*.

In the light of Duras's shitty writing, the Cartesian *cogito ergo sum* takes on a profoundly anti-Cartesian meaning, and makes more interesting the "writing the body" normally associated with Duras. No split of the body from the mind—instead, we have a kind of collective excremental existentiality where shit, which the body produces but is not, replaces thought with the kind of assimilation that our excremental bodies teach and impose on us, day after day. Instead of *je pense donc je suis* (I think therefore I am), we might say, *je chie donc j'essuie* (I shit therefore I wipe). What Duras shows us is that what is being wiped is not the self, distinct from the other, but a state of embodiment that assimilates me to you. And just as *panser* is heard as *penser, je chie donc j'essuie* is heard as *je chie donc je suis* (I shit therefore I am/follow), where *suis* is taken in its polysemy: to be is an act of following, as we cannot be without coming after someone else, after their shit. Just as how, in Céline, a dog's anus serves as Ferdinand's North Star, and Ferdinand's anus serves as Céline's narrative North Star, so too here: Antelme's anus is a star-shaped lodestone that guides us in the darkness that is the dis-aster[27] of the Holocaust, that most human of events.

Gary: Home Is Where the Shithole Is

Where Duras's *La Douleur* is traversed by a moral urgency that takes seriously the task of writing the Holocaust, of "restor[ing] the memory of the Nazi past unto the history of our present,"[28] enacting for the reader an experience of the *douleur* that gives the work its title, Gary's *La Vie devant soi* (1975) presents instead as an irreverent Holocaust comedy.[29] Like *La Douleur*, *La Vie devant soi* is written and narrated in the postwar by a narrator who has no direct experience of the camps. Unlike *La Douleur*, which presents us with the transition from the concentrationary universe back into the world outside it, *La Vie devant soi* is narrated by an Arab boy, Momo, who has no real understanding, historical or otherwise, of what his foster mother, Madame Rosa, a Polish Jew and former prostitute, experienced in Auschwitz. Where Duras crafts tragedy, Gary opts for farce—a revolving door of colorful characters and improbable scenarios set in Paris's working-class and ethnic Belleville neighborhood that quickly take us from Momo as a ten-year-old rascal and son of a murdered prostitute, who forges relationships with the marginal individuals he has as neighbors (e.g., the Victor Hugo–loving Arab shopkeeper, Monsieur Hamil; the transvestite ex-boxer prostitute, Lola), to a Momo who discovers he's actually a fourteen-year-old young man who's been lied to by Madame Rosa, who wanted to keep Momo closer to her by keeping him a child. We learn at the end of the novel that its narrative is being recounted by a deeply traumatized Momo, who has been discovered huddling in Madame Rosa's cellar (called her *trou juif,* or Jew hole) next to her corpse, which he's doused with perfume and put makeup on to hide the putrefaction that's set in, performing his own version of sitting Shiva, unable to accept the death of the woman who was both mother and child to him.

The novel has been the subject of much discussion and controversy because it is one of the most spectacular and mediatized literary hoaxes of the twentieth century.[30] Gary, in the 1970s, some twenty years after he had won the prestigious Goncourt prize for his autobiographical novel *Les Racines du ciel* (*The Roots of Heaven*), was washed up. By then he was an aging man unable to keep up with the literary movements of his time, left behind by the politically driven *littérature engagée* (committed literature) that Sartre advocated for and by the avant-garde New Novel, which set out to destroy those literary conventions of plot, character, and traditional narrative that Gary hewed to closely. Motivated by his sense of increasing irrelevance, he set out to shake up the French literary scene by starting the Émile Ajar con: under this pseudonym, Gary published *La Vie devant soi* while he continued to publish novels under his own name, and won a second Goncourt prize for the novel, when the prize rules forbid awarding the prize more than once to the same author.

Discussions of *La Vie devant soi,* generally speaking, have tended to focus on the work's Holocaust dimension, on the hoax and Gary's relation to and motivation for Ajar, Gary's deliberate grammatical disordering—his writing in an incorrect French—and on the work's humanism, part and parcel of Gary's lifelong humanism, which was responsible for both his commercial success and for the lack of critical consideration or prestige accorded to his work.[31] As with the other texts discussed in *Cacaphonies,* the excremental dimension of the work has been ignored, despite the fact that it is a source of narrative continuity, with the work beginning and ending in shit.[32]

In the novel's opening chapter, Momo explains that he came to be in Madame Rosa's care because it was she who looked after all the neighborhood prostitutes' children in exchange for money. Momo narrates how his becoming aware of being an orphan, unlike the other children, triggers an excremental situation that sets the tone of the novel. After hearing from another boy that his mother always appeared when he had a stomachache, Momo is seized by stomach cramps and convulsions in order to try to make his mother appear. When a mere stomachache doesn't result in his mother's coming, he escalates the situation:

> I even started to shit all over the apartment to get more atten-
> tion. . . . I yelled that I wanted to see my mother, and for weeks I
> went on shitting all over the place to get even. . . . I kept on shitting
> for the principle of the thing, but it was no life. There were seven
> more kids boarding with Madame Rosa at the time, and they all
> started shitting for all they were worth, because kids are terrible
> conformists, and there was so much shit all over the place that I
> went unnoticed.
>
> Madame Rosa was old and tired to begin with, and this kind
> of thing was very hard on her, because she'd already been per-
> secuted for being Jewish. She dragged her two hundred and ten
> pounds up the six flights several times a day on her two poor legs,
> and when she came in and smelled all the shit she collapsed in
> her chair with her bundles and burst into tears, which is easy to
> understand. She said there were fifty million Frenchmen in France
> and if they'd all done what we did even the Germans couldn't have
> resisted, they'd have skedaddled, every last one of them. Madame
> Rosa had been in Germany during the war, but now she was back.
> She came in, she smelled the shit, and she started yelling: "This is
> Auschwitz! Auschwitz!" because she'd been deported to Auschwitz
> for the Jews.[33]

In this farcical scene, which is the first real action we see in the novel, Gary foreshadows the novel's end, establishing shit as the source of a narrative symmetry and continuity that will become apparent only after one has finished the book.[34] This beginning anticipates the ending, which features Madame Rosa pissing and shitting on herself (263; 175), dying in her chair down in her Jew hole, which is trans-formed, through her bodily functions, into a literal shithole.

The novel's beginning, featuring Momo's contagious shitting, in which he is able to lose himself, blending into the shit décor that he and the other children create through their collective defecation, turning Madame Rosa's apartment into a shithole, thus acts as an excremental bookend to the novel's end, which features Momo once more losing himself in an excremental space at Madame Rosa's side. Madame Rosa's reacting to Momo's excremental protest by evoking Auschwitz might seem absurd initially because of the difference in scale—how can one compare a child's antics to Nazi atrocities?—but turns out to be a meaningful declaration, as opposed to the unmoored ramblings of an aging woman who is losing her wits to dementia. Madame Rosa's declaration neatly sums up Holocaust scholars' and writers' conceptualization of the concentrationary universe as a fundamentally excremental one. As literature and scholarship have made clear, the Holocaust entailed the reduction of huge swaths of humankind to shit, the familiar image of overflowing camp latrines and detainees walking on forced marches with diarrhea streaming down their legs—of the transformation of bodies into the waste they produce—serving as the most fitting representation of a Nazi ideology that treated the human as the sub- and nonhuman.[35]

Between the shithole where the novel begins and the shithole where it ends is the interval in which Momo is transformed from a ten-year-old boy characterized by the innocence associated with such youth, into the fourteen-year-old adolescent we discover him to be, his experience of Madame Rosa's death constituting the loss of innocence and his propulsion into the world of adulthood. To get from one point to the other, Gary has Momo and his reader pass through an interval marked by ever increasing excrementality. The education Momo receives in loss—the loss of one's mind (and hence of oneself as a stable entity able to be in relation to the world), the loss of a person through death, and the loss of childhood innocence that follows from these previous losses—operates in direct proportion to the body's loss of matter through defecation, or elimination. The more Momo masters the art of loss (to paraphrase Elizabeth Bishop), the more he is immersed in an excremental universe.

As part of Momo's education in loss, the novel's development, which maps onto Momo's development, has him assuming the responsibility of care. As Madame Rosa, the principal caregiver, is transformed into the principal object of care, Momo takes on the role of caregiver, motivated by nothing other than what he will eventually have to recognize is love. As Momo's narration makes clear, his understanding of care is anchored in the act of wiping shit. It is in his shifting attitude toward wiping—his evolving relation to shit that is not his—that he comes to assume an ethics of care. In so doing, he arrives at an understanding of himself as an entity that is not singular or isolated, but is instead defined as an immanently relational one, existing only insofar as he exists in relation to someone else, his self an exercise in and experience of porosity and permeability. What starts as a deep fear of being alone, of losing Madame Rosa—a fear that is self-centered, driven as it is by a concern primarily with what will happen to oneself—turns instead into the assumption of one's existence as being an existence for and with someone else. In other words, through his development of a wiping praxis, Momo moves from a centripetal inhabitation of his subjectivity toward a centrifugal one.

Even when Madame Rosa still has her wits about her, it falls on Momo to wipe the other foster children's bottoms, "because it was hard for Madame Rosa to bend down on account of her bulk. She had no waist and her ass went straight up to her shoulders nonstop. Every step she took was like moving a piano" (46; 74).[36] Momo is a reluctant wiper, and outsources the task of wiping to the children themselves: "I never wiped the kids' asses when they were past four, because I had my dignity and some of them used to shit on purpose. But I knew those creeps and I taught them a little game, wiping each other's asses, I got them to think it was more fun than each man for himself [*c'était plus marrant que rester chacun chez soi*]" (46; 74). While here we have what seems like a selfish act of getting the other children to wipe themselves by turning it into a game, this passage presages the centrifugal development of Momo's sense of self and his sense of responsibility toward Madame Rosa. Dignity, which calls for less wiping and a clear cutoff point for which bottoms are too old to be able to wipe, is intrinsically a centripetal, self-directed self-positioning. It is no coincidence that Gary transforms the selfish outsourcing into an instance of intersubjectivity, of bringing the children out of their "each man for himself," "chez soi" attitude in order to be together in a new form of collectivity. Momo too will move away from dignity, this static residing in himself, and move outward toward Madame Rosa as her failing body and mind compel him to make this movement outside himself.

Between Momo's holding on to some sense of dignity and Madame Rosa's complete reduction to an incontinent set of buttocks in need of wiping—the reversal of the directionality of their relationship of care—Gary gives us a glimpse of what it looks like for Momo to transform his wiping practice into a wiping praxis, when, at a moment where Madame Rosa has begun to decline, Momo sets aside his concern for his dignity and elevates wiping as the source of a certain kind of satisfaction. Describing Madame Rosa's decreased cashflow and the need to take on more children in order to be able to make ends meet, Momo states, "I'd never been happier to wipe asses, because they made the kettle boil, and when my fingers were full of shit, I didn't even feel the injustice of it" (55; 87). Wiping is cast now as a source of income and a way to care for Madame Rosa and himself: shit is no longer being mapped onto the self through the notion of dignity; rather, it is now the means by which to express care for someone other than oneself, to respond to the question of someone else's need and see it as tied up with his own. With Madame Rosa quickly deteriorating in mind and body, Momo moves from wiping the children in order to care for himself and Madame Rosa, to having to wipe Madame Rosa directly, acceding to an unmediated, direct form of care for her.

We've thus moved from the novel's opening gambit of spectacular shitting (and shittiness), where Momo responds to the loss of his mother with rageful defecation, thereby centering Momo's bowels, to focusing instead on Madame Rosa's. We've shifted from shit as a ploy to get one's biological mother back to shit as the means to recognize and care for the adoptive, nonbiological mother Madame Rosa is to

Momo. In the excremental relationality they forge through wiping and being wiped, they are joined together in a kind of coexistence that is rarely experienced in usual modalities of relation—one where you allow your body to become a kind of prosthetic body for the other. When Madame Rosa is no longer able to wipe herself, Momo allows his hands to be hers, accepts her shit as his, gets his fingers covered in the matter that had been inside her. Their relationship embodies what it means to exist outside of "chez soi," where the sense of propriety and property that normally governs our relation to our bodies—that establishes our bodies as indeed belonging to us—has become inoperative. The shit that had been chez Madame Rosa leaves her body to become Momo's shit instead. The distinction between Madame Rosa's ninety-five kilograms and Momo's diminutive stature (diminutive, since we know he was able to pass for a long time as a ten-year-old) becomes irrelevant: it matters little for Momo whether the shit was produced by Madame Rosa's body or by his own. The question of whose body it was does not figure. What matters is that this shit is out in the world and must be taken care of—existing thus as the site for the formulation and assumption of an unbounded ethics of care.

Many critics and readers have seen the novel as a humanistic tale of transcending identitarian differences, with the love between Madame Rosa and Momo demonstrating an inherently human capacity to love those with whom we share nothing in common, such a moral making up for the poor taste of joking about Auschwitz. We could also read Gary in a Rabelaisian light, seeing in his irreverence for matters as grave as genocide a carnivalesque inversion of values, where his bawdy, ass-centric narrative inverts the corporeal–cosmic hierarchy discussed by Bakhtin. I would submit, however, that Gary's insistence on the ass—Madame Rosa's, but also Momo's, given her repeated exhortations to him not to prostitute himself or sell his ass to make ends meet—and on the shit that comes out of it, is grounded in a particular vision of ethics anchored in the materiality of shit. Gary thus turns Emmanuel Levinas's model of a face-based ethical relation on its head, so that is not the confrontation with the face of the other

that spurs ethical response,[37] but rather confrontation with the ass—
that other face (as gestured to by the kind of symmetry we find between bottom and top, where the buttocks are cheeks and the anus,
another mouth)—that creates the ethical situation par excellence, the
one to which we must answer.

Momo's ethical stance leads him to spend the last part of the
novel doing all he can to keep Madame Rosa from being hospital-
ized, in keeping with her wishes expressed when she was still lucid.
The hospital and state healthcare system is triggering for Madame
Rosa, because of what she perceives as a shared concentrationary
dynamic—the gathering of people in a space where their deaths are
overseen and managed. When it becomes clear that he can no longer
keep her in her home, he brings her down, with great effort, to her
Jew hole, and stays with her in her shit as she effectively pisses and
shits out the remainder of her existence. It is no coincidence that
the weeks that Momo spends with Madame Rosa tending to her
body—the most intimate moments of their shared life—take place in
an analogue of the anus. It is in the Jew hole, which is by extension a
shit hole (indeed, Momo describes the area of the apartment building
basement as smelling of excrement; 21; 38), that Momo is able to experience and give full expression to the love that he feels for Madame
Rosa. In the dark anus of Madame Rosa's Jew hole, which is filled
with figurative shit like a rotting mattress and dilapidated furniture,
Momo is able to most completely be with Madame Rosa, the both of
them joined together by the shit that binds and by the shit that effaces
the I–you distinction that keeps subjectivities selfishly, non-ethically if
not unethically hunkered down in their respective *chez soi*—the bodies,
minds, and identities they call their own.

In It Together

It's here, in shit, that Gary and Duras converge. At first glance, Duras's anti-anthropocentric ethics, which has shit working to dissolve
the boundary between the human and nonhuman and casts care as
a question of the instinct triggered by shit, seems antipodal to the
bawdy humanism of a Gary who is still very much attached to the

human and marked by sentimentality—*La Vie devant soi* is nothing if not a tale meant to tug at the reader's heartstrings. This difference is a relatively superficial one, and to be expected: of course a resolutely humanist writer, as Gary was, will write shit in such a way that the humanity of the persons involved is preserved; of course an antihumanist writer, which I take Duras to be, given her critique of colonialism, capitalism, and a certain ecological sensibility, will write shit differently than a bourgeois humanist. What interests me here is the way Gary and Duras, despite being at odds politically and philosophically, both settle on the same material—shit—to convey to the reader what an affirmative response to an ethical imperative looks like. Shit is truly the leveler of difference, and just as it works within each writer's text to nullify key sites of distinction (human and nonhuman in Duras's case, my-versus-your body in Gary's), it operates across texts and authors to level the substantial differences we can cite to keep Gary and Duras at odds with each other.

Gary's and Duras's differences are ultimately overcome by the unicity of a shit that enjoys a certain kind of undefinability, or rather, that operates as an ipseity. What is shit? How can I convey to you what shit is? Shit is shit. Shit cannot be explained—it must be experienced to be understood. And in this way, it is also no coincidence that Gary and Duras would echo each other in setting their respective shit against the background of the Holocaust. If Duras's and Gary's ethics of care emerge in the excremental, it's because the excremental situation, linked intimately to the concentrationary context, is where boundaries of identity can be dissolved. Duras immerses herself in Antelme's concentrationary experience, Momo immerses himself in Madame Rosa's concentrationary experience. The concentration camp thus becomes a shared ground of experience, a kind of collective habitus, shared by writer, narrative, and reader.[38]

But where the ethical response to the Holocaust is one that takes the form of the oft-repeated mantra "Never again," the shit through which such an ethics might be thought is one that refuses the *never* and places ethics instead in a framework of *always,* of endless repetition. Shit is the thing that always happens over and over again, six, seven times a day even. And as often as it's repeated, it must be wiped, the ethical actor's hand restoring over and over again, in a Beckettian kind of repetition, the shit-covered ass to the state it used to be in: an expanse of clear skin that can be marked and written over and over again, in palimpsestic fashion, by shit. Each moment of wiping, of tending to another's shit, is a radical instance of an ethics of care that is driven by the dissolution of the distinctions that demarcate and divide. Through the act of wiping the other, which will occur over and over again, the other's alterity is wiped away, and the hand that wipes recognizes, in that gesture, that the difference between supposedly radically different states—clean and unclean, human and nonhuman, self and other—is created and undone by shit.

What brings us together then, the tie that binds, is not some rarefied and increasingly nostalgic humanity—the capacity for higher-order thinking and feeling, supposedly, than what animals and plants are capable of—but rather, shit. If ethics can be thought of as the ground for collectivity, then it's a ground full of shit. I'd like to give the last word to Woody Guthrie, whose "This Land Is Your Land," with its critique of territoriality and possession, is a rich source for framing Duras's and Gary's anti-proprietary, boundary-dissolving ethics: this shit is your shit, this shit is my shit, this shit was made for you and me.

Part III
POLITICAL SHIT

) 5 (

FIGHTING WORDS
Anne Garréta's Ultimate Weapon

***

Shit is the material of an ethics that would bind you to me, us to each other, but it is also the material with which we can construct the political: if ethics establish relationality as something unavoidable, then politics are the structures that determine how we relate to each other. Where Sartre, Genet, Duras, and Gary tap into fecality's conceptual power to demonstrate, in strikingly material terms, what freedom and ethics—the baseline parameters of relationality—look like, it's in turning to an author like Anne Garréta that we can see, in action, how we can use shit not simply to conceptualize but to contest, to act, to put up a political resistance to things as they are and as they've been.

In this chapter, I turn to Anne Garréta's latest novel, *Dans l'béton* (*In Concrete*) (2017), as a work that announces its political aims much more directly than is the case with the rest of Garréta's corpus, which, while consistently political, has often had its political valence overlooked.[1] Published sixteen years after her previous novel, *Pas un jour* (2001), for which Garréta won the Prix Médicis and became established in the contemporary French literary scene, *Dans l'béton* is unlike any of the works that precede it. Gone (or at least submerged) is the cynicism, the profound melancholia, the pervasive sense of loss. Present instead are humor and verve. Because the novel

163

presents as a *récit d'enfance* (narrative of childhood), one filled with unorthodox and humorous spelling (e.g., *week-end* as *ouikinde*), readers and reviewers immediately made comparisons with Raymond Queneau and his néo-français in *Zazie dans le métro* (*Zazie in the Metro*), with references to Céline, William Burroughs, Virginie Despentes, and Herman Melville thrown in as well.[2] The one comparison that wasn't made, despite Garréta's making the intertext patently clear by naming one of the key characters in *Dans l'béton* Catherine Legrand, was with Monique Wittig's *L'Opoponax* (*The Opoponax*), a *récit d'enfance* featuring a Catherine Legrand as its protagonist. Given Wittig's conviction that literature could and should function as a Trojan horse, a weapon for battling conventions that could reshape reality,[3] what we lose in completely dropping the novel's Wittigian point of reference is its political project, present in its will to break down the omnipresent structures of heterosexual kinship and race.[4] *Dans l'béton,* above and beyond being "une aventure familiale" (a familial adventure),[5] is a political adventure, one that passes, surprisingly, and necessarily, through *merde* and through *béton* (concrete) as an analogue of shit.

Beginning in It

Garréta's prolegomenon is a reflection on beginnings, but she doesn't begin, as does the apostle John, with the beginning—"In the beginning" (John 1:1)—but with a detour through concrete and family. The first sentence, "Le béton, c'est pas un métier de pédés" (Concrete's not a job for queers),[6] drops the reader into the middle of things, into the middle of the concrete that is the primordial and predominant material of the text. From the novel's very first words, we are, as the title announces, *dans l'béton*—in concrete. After this introduction to the matter and the material at hand—concrete—we are then introduced to the principal actors of the narrative: the narrator's father and her younger sister, who, along with the narrator, will form, not a love triangle but a concrete one, where, through the process of mixing and laying concrete, what will be rendered visible and material—if only to be broken—is a nuclear, heterosexual family structure that can no longer hold.

All of this will become clearer, but for now, let us proceed with the prolegomenon, where, after the introduction of concrete and a heterosexual family—recall that *le béton,* which is the activity that brings father and children together, isn't *un métier de pédés*—the narrator grapples with the question of beginning:

> Pour que ça soit clair, ce béton, faudrait que je vous explique une infinité de choses. Y faudrait que je mette tout bien en ordre. Et que je commence.
> Y faudrait.
> Mais par où commencer? Par la fin? Le début? Le milieu?
> Et où il est, le milieu?
> Dans la merde, ya pas de milieu. Ya juste la merde. C'est la merde, le milieu . . . Dans l'béton, c'est pareil.
> Alors, autant commencer par le commencement. (9)

For you to understand concrete, I'd have to explain an infinite number of things. I'd really have to get myself together. And I'd have to begin.
I'd have to.
But where to start? The end? The beginning? The middle?
And where is the middle, anyway?
In shit, there's no middle. There's just shit. Shit's the milieu . . .
In concrete, it's the same.
So, may swell begin at the beginning. (11–12)

From the very beginning, Garréta establishes a relation of analogy between concrete and shit, and it's to shit that the narrator's mind turns to try to think through what it means to tell the story of being *dans l'béton.* Garréta thus signals that this story of being *dans l'béton* is the story of being *dans la merde.* The narrative problem is how to tell a proper story—with a beginning, middle, and end—about concrete, when concrete, like shit, cannot be demarcated into those different stages. Concrete and shit are both only what they are, through and through, their uniform consistency trumping the kinds of division that time would seek to effect: one end of a turd is the same as the other end, one section of concrete is the same consistency and material as another section.

Certainly, one could place concrete into a temporalized structure so that one could say the preliminary steps of gathering the materials and mixing the concrete are a beginning, the laying of the concrete a kind of middle, and the fully hardened product an end, and do likewise with shit, where the digestive process of eating food and breaking it down in the gastrointestinal tract is the beginning of shit, where the process of defecating is a middle, and where the fully eliminated stool, a self-standing object now fully free from the body, is an end. But such an imposition of temporal markers is artificial, and the beginning, middle, and end are obtained through recourse to material outside and other than the material at hand: the materials from which concrete is mixed aren't yet in and of themselves concrete, just as the food we take in isn't shit.

The parallel drawn between concrete and shit is an important one, central to the proper functioning of the novel. We are meant to think shit through concrete, and, conversely, concrete through shit, and both function in the novel as weaponized materials that serve to crystallize or concretize human relational structures (the kinship structure of family, in the first case, and the challenges and imperatives posed by racial structures, in the second). Garréta deploys both concrete and shit as paired, twinned weapons against invidious and seemingly necessary social structures: How can you raise a child without a family—without a mother and father? How can you operate without a concept that accounts for the glaringly visible variations in skin pigmentation and the cultural and ideological trappings that follow from them? In this she takes her cue from Wittig, for whom the political potential of literary uses of language inheres in the way language is first and foremost matter—material that can be worked on, broken down, and remade in ways that have significant consequences for "reality" as "there is a plasticity of language on the real."[7]

As mentioned earlier, *Dans l'béton* is Garréta's foray into the *récit d'enfance,* a genre taken on already by such literary monuments as Marcel Proust, Georges Perec, and Raymond Queneau. The novel is a picaresque tale of the narrator's adventures, which fall into two categories. The first is the familial sphere, where the father's penchant for concrete leads to all sorts of mishaps and disasters: the destruction of the washing machines used to mix concrete; the family's roof falling in; the younger sister, Angélique, being covered in wet concrete, which leads to the father leaving the two children behind to find help to break Angélique safely out of her concrete shell. The second is the world of children, of school and play: it is here, in the sphere that schoolchildren occupy by themselves, that the narrator and her sister receive an education in hierarchy, in what it means to be singled out as different—they witness, for instance, a boy in the schoolyard get persecuted and teased as a *pédé* (queer, faggot), or an orphan girl (Catherine Legrand) get persecuted for being Black—and make the decision to fight back. Through the telescoping of family and school, of life in both its private and public spheres, hierarchy emerges as a through-line and foundational element of the narrator and her sister's lives. Garréta's *récit d'enfance* thus tells the story of a kind of political awakening or education.

The novel's political project follows in the explicitly anti-hierarchical, anti-difference path laid by Garréta's previous works, and is consonant with the political impetus that drove Garréta's entrance into literature, where her debut novel, *Sphinx* (1986), was written in order to "fuck difference."[8] The particular forms of difference and the ensuing hierarchy that *Dans l'béton* targets are those hypostatized in the nuclear heterosexual family and in race. With these political stakes thus articulated, the question of material arises: why does *Dans l'béton* require concrete and shit for its program of undermining the twinned structures of heterosexual kinship and racial difference?[9]

In what follows, I take us through the parallel operations of concrete and shit, looking first at the way Garréta deploys concrete to attack heterosexual kinship, then at shit to see how she mobilizes it to attack racial difference and racism. In doing so, it will become clear why concrete and shit are non-exchangeable vectors for Garréta's project: shit cannot do to the nuclear family what concrete can, and concrete cannot act against racism as shit can. But despite their non-interchangeability, concrete and shit possess shared material qualities that make them operate similarly on a formal level and in their relation to temporality, such that together, they point to language itself as being the ultimate political weapon—the material for breaking and refashioning the social contract.

A Concrete Family

The heterosexual kinship structure of the nuclear family—a mother, a father, and children—is from the very beginning of the novel tied to concrete. Concrete, as seen in the incipit, is the very first object introduced in the text, and following closely behind in the second sentence is "our father," whose role as the patriarch, the head of the household, is deeply implicated in concrete: "Le béton, c'est pas un métier de pédés. C'est peut-être pour ça que notre père a décidé, dès qu'on a été en âge, ma ptite sœur et moi, de nous entraîner au mortier, à la dalle, au coffrage" (Concrete's no job for queers. Maybe that's why our father decided, soon as we were old enough, my little sis and I, to educate us in cement, concrete, and casing) (9; 11). Under patriarchy, the father bears the responsibility for the well-being of his family, as well as its identity, as seen in the way the name of the father becomes the name of the children as well as of the mother. In heteronormative kinship structures, the father is thus akin to his home's foundation—the symbolic equivalent, then, of a house's foundation, which is poured out, not coincidentally, in concrete.

The project of ensuring the heterosexualization of his children, on which the reproduction of the heterosexual family depends, is tied to the father's penchant for concrete. Garréta's trademark irony is at play here, given that mixing and working with concrete is a decidedly masculine task, one hardly well suited to the project of rearing up girls in the ways of the femininity foundational to an operational heterosexuality. The only knowledge or education he transmits to his daughters revolves around concrete—how to mix it, how to diagnose a washing machine's weaknesses as a concrete mixer, how to fix a broken washing machine / concrete mixer, how to modernize through the manufacture and application of concrete (10–15;

12-17). The father, insofar as he is related to his wife and children, is described by the narrator as having these familial relations always mediated through concrete. He exists in the novel only through his compulsive and obsessive concrete mixing, and we never see him described or acting outside the context of concrete: making it, laying it, dealing with the consequences of it.

The father does not come out of the novel looking well: he is an authoritarian ("Il a toujours aimé pontifer. Poncifier aussi, parfois, et hardiment. Donner des ordres, surtout. C'est un chef et un pontife" [He's always loved to pontificate. To wax and buff philosophical, too, sometimes, and intrepidly. But mostly to give orders. He's a leader and a pontiff]; 13; 15) who insists on indulging his concrete mania with little or no regard for his children, whom he mobilizes as free labor, or for his wife, who is literally in tears and on the verge of nervous exhaustion from her incapacity to keep her children clean, as encrusted as they are—constantly—in bits of concrete that get everywhere, even in their food (10-11; 13-14). Against the father's mania for concrete, the mother's mania for cleanliness ("Notre mère, elle voulait nous garder propres, même le ouikinde. C'était une de ses manies" [Our mother wanted to keep us clean, even on the weekend. It was an obsession]; 10; 12) does not stand a chance—the father's will reigns supreme as the will around which the entire home is organized.

It isn't that the father doesn't care for his family or is uninvested in their well-being, but rather that he is so egocentric (with concrete always on his mind) that all his projects for improving the life of his family pass through the very concrete that makes that life terrible. For the father, concrete is a sign of modernization—a telos, the ultimate good and goal. So it is that when his wife inherits from "un vieux oncle" (an old uncle) a primitive shack in the middle of the French countryside, she returns to Paris to work ("Fallait qu'elle retourne travailler. Qui sans ça nous offrirait nos bétonneuses, nos machines à laver, nos générateurs?" [Necessary that she return to work. Who besides her would give us our concrete mixers, our washing machines, our generators?]; 30; 32), and he remains behind with his children to, as a surprise for his wife, modernize the shack, via concrete, of course:

> On allait lui moderniser sa bicoque isolée, vite fait bien fait. Une ou deux dalles de béton, mais du béton léger, hein! . . . un béton paillé par exemple. Un chouia d'électricité, à peine un peu de plomberie et ça srait une fermette de rêve pour Parisien ou même pour Anglais pas trop tordu. Calme, bucolique et moderne en même temps. (30)

> We would muddernize the hovel, we'd do it quick and dirty. One or two slabs of concrete, but lightweight concrete, you hear! A mix of chopped straw, gravel, and Portland[10] for example. A smidge of electricity, a pinch of plumbing, and it'd be a dream little farmhouse in the sticks for a Parisian or even a Brit who's not too queer. Calm, bucolic, and muddern at the same time. (32)

What we have here is a father who utterly fails at carrying out the patriarch's function as head and stabilizer of the family. In an inversion of gender roles, the father, who attempts to align himself with the straight masculinity of working with concrete, is in fact supported by his wife, who is the primary breadwinner and the source of funding for his stay-at-home DIY projects. The activity of working with concrete might itself be masculine, but the structure within which it occurs—financial dependence on his wife—is not.[11]

While the father's plan for the shack might seem noble, motivated by the desire to improve his wife's life and increase the value of her property, it quickly devolves. It is here that the father, totally caught up in his project of laying concrete on the dirt floor of the shack, fails to notice when the *lessiveuse* (washboiler) being used to carry fresh concrete tips over, entirely covering Angélique (or Poulette, translatable to Chicky, as she is affectionately called by her narrator-sister): "Si la lessiveuse, c'était le Vésuve, alors la bicoque, c'était Pompéi, et Poulette là-dessous ensevelie" (If the washboiler was Vesuvius then the hovel was Pompeii, with Poulette buried underneath) (69; 72). Once he does notice, his and the narrator's attempts at wiping off the concrete covering the little girl only succeed in further spreading the concrete over her body: "Plus on la taloche, plus on râcle cette morve de portland, plus notre Angélique en est tartinée et plus on s'tartine à son contact, plus on s'enlise dans la visqueux et s'embrenne dans le boulé" (The more we trowel, the more we scrape up that cement snot, the more our Angélique is slathered in it and the more we lather it when we come into contact with her, the more we sink into the slime and the more we're sucked into the muck ourselves) (75; 78).

To add to this catastrophe, the water pump completely breaks down so that there's no way to wash the concrete off Angélique. The father, failing to find his sledgehammer with which he had been intending on breaking the concrete shell open, despite the narrator's panicked protestations that he would kill Angélique ("Pourquoi papa, ô pourquoi tu veux l'assommer notre Angélique? Et à la masse encore! On ferait une omelette de la Poulette avant même d'avoir réussi à l'extraire de sa coquille" [Why, Papa, O why would you want to clobber our Angélique? And with a sledgehammer! We'd make an omelet of Poulette before we managed to crack her out of her shell]; 82; 85), abandons the two young girls to find help, leaving them behind, "dans le noir, dans la bicoque ouverte à tous vents, au plus profond trou du cul du monde" (in the dark, in the hovel exposed to the winds, in the deepest asshole in the world) (83; 86).

While Angélique sleeps, "bien à l'abri dans son sarcophagi" (sheltered in her sarcophagus) (152; 154), the narrator, exposed to the elements and completely in the dark, which terrifies her, tells stories, such as the story of battling the horde of racist boys to protect their friend Catherine Legrand "pour pas sentir la solitude et l'horreur de la nuit" (to stave off the solitude and horror of the night) (152; 154). The father, as in all his other enterprises, fails to secure help: in an absurd ludic turn, when his car breaks down, he tries to cut across the fields to return home, only to get lost, hopelessly scratched and torn up, finding and bringing back with him a gigantic bull that he had taken care of when it had been a calf. Salvation comes in the form of the narrator's grandmother, who, upon seeing that the children and father had not returned home the previous evening, leaves in the night to come to the shack to see what had happened.

At this point in the novel, which is nearly finished, the narrator, for the first time, reveals her gender, exclaiming, in joy, "Je chante que la rivière est profonde et si tu voulais on dormirait ensemble dans un grand lit carré et qu'on serait heureuses jusqu'à la fin du monde" (I sing that the river is deep and if you wanted, we could sleep together in a big square bed and we'd be happy until the end of the world) (153; 155). In a feat echoing that of *Sphinx,* Garréta's narrator had, up to this point, used gender-indeterminate language for the narrator so that the narrator's gender was suspended until the end, when who could have been Poulette's older brother is revealed to be in fact her older sister. This gendering and matriarchal alignment and identification with the grandmother—the narrator joins her sister and grandmother in the *on* described in the feminine as *heureuses* (happy)—is a repudiation of the model of heterosexual family embodied in the father as patriarch, who has failed to reproduce himself properly, lacking the son who would be able to transmit the family name.

The chain of endless catastrophes brought about by the father's misguided attempts at modernization and advancement serves to reveal patriarchy, and the familial structure of which the patriarch is the center and foundation, as being irreparably damaged and damaging, dysfunctional and counterproductive. The model of familial relation that passes through the father leads only to disaster. In the novel, the heterosexual nuclear family and its ultimately masculinist logic are rejected to instead privilege relationships and alliances forged between women, between sister and sister, between granddaughter and grandmother, and, as we'll see in the anti-racist part of the narrative, between girls.[12]

This outcome, in which the father is extraneous and useless, is to be expected in a work critiquing heterosexual kinship, and, at a much earlier point in the novel, Garréta foreshadows this breakdown of the traditional family via the breakdown of the paternal. In an episode demonstrating the father's general ineptitude, the father gets a shovelful of dirt and mouse droppings in his eyes, blinding him. With no water to flush out his eyes, he orders his daughters to spit into his face, which they do dutifully, imagining all sorts of delicious foods to stimulate their salivary glands. Looking back on this incident, the narrator describes it as "le jour où j'ai appris kya des fois où cracher à la gueule de ses ascendants, c'est un devoir filial. Et même, un devoir d'humanité" (the day I learned that there are times when spitting in the face of our elders is a matter of filial duty. A duty to all humankind, even) (39; 41). Spitting on one's father, in this case, which is extended to encompass spitting on one's entire lineage—where one's lineage is a representation of patriarchal success, measured by how many sons one's sons were able to beget—is a humanitarian duty. If humankind is to advance or to be preserved, the paternal must be spat upon and rejected.[13]

The War against Racism

The *devoir d'humanité* (duty toward humanity) in *Dans l'béton* is twofold, and in addition to tearing down the paternal—the foundation of the heterosexual family—Garréta targets another social structure, that of racism and the institution of racial difference that subtends it. While the narrator and Angélique are abandoned by their father, the stories the narrator tells to comfort herself are those of school and play, areas in which the authority and structure of the nuclear family are displaced in favor of the kinds of structures children create for themselves in the absence of adult supervision. The stories that the narrator draws on all have in common a structure where the narrator and Angélique are allied together in righteous opposition to the aspiring patriarchs-in-training with whom they share spaces of school and play: in addition to protecting a little boy bullied as a *pédé*, the most dramatic story, to which the narrator devotes the most time and attention, is that of their coming together to protect Catherine Legrand from the craven, cruel boys who would persecute her.

Catherine Legrand is notably the protagonist of Monique Wittig's 1964 Prix Médicis–winning novel *L'Opoponax*, whose coming of age operates through the awakening of a lesbian consciousness and desire, where it is through positioning and claiming herself as the minoritarian subject of *lesbian* that she is able to fully enter into and claim subjectivity, as represented in the appropriation of *je* (I) that occurs at the very end of the novel—a shock after hundreds of pages of third-person narration. Garréta's Catherine Legrand, however, is substantially transformed from Wittig's: Garréta's Legrand is an orphan and she is Black. We are first introduced to her when the narrator recounts having, in the countryside, engaged in reenactments of medieval jousts with other children, with bicycles serving as steeds, only to have a boy insult Legrand: "Un môme . . . s'avisa de faire le sang bleu et d'insulter une Dame, et des plus dignes et des plus belles. Parce qu'en effet, elle était noire, et même toute noire, sans famille avouable, car issue de l'Assistance et échouée chez la vieille pauvresse du bord de la rivière" (This one kid . . . got it in his head to act like a blue blood and insult a real Lady, a most dignified and beautiful Lady at that. And why? Because she was black, 100 percent black, with no pedigree since she came from the foster system and had washed up in the home of the poor old woman who lives by the river) (95; 97–98).

Legrand's Blackness reflects the ways in which the French political and demographic landscape has shifted, such that, in contrast to the implicit whiteness of France's women's and gay liberation movements, which Wittig was deeply involved in, the France of 2017 features in its political lexicon concepts such as *intersectionnalité* and *racisation,* which foreground racial politics.[14] And by being cast as an orphan, which effectively excludes her from the heterosexual structure of the nuclear family—she lives with an old, impoverished, presumably white woman—Garréta brings together in her person the failures of both the kinship structure and the racial structure that she would have *Dans l'béton* target.

But where Garréta uses concrete to break down the family, she turns to shit to attack racism. The narrator and Angélique, at the moment of the joust, immediately attacked the "jaune sire médisant" (slanderous callows[15] lord) (96; my translation) to defend Legrand's honor, who was "la première Dame à avoir honoré notre tribune, la première Dame noire sans doute à paraître en un tournoi à bicyclette tenue en ces lieux" (the first Lady to grace our bleachers, no doubt the first black Lady to ever show up at a bicycle joust held on these grounds) (95; 98). Immediately afterward, they begin planning another attack on the racist boy, reasoning that to avoid Legrand's being the object of a retaliatory attack, "une fois pour toutes, il nous faut défaire le jaune sire félon" (once and for all, we must defeat the perfidious callows lord) (102; 105). The key weapon in their campaign against a shitty ideology turns out to be shit, of the bovine variety.

The narrator, in a lengthy passage, outlines the qualities and virtues of cowshit, which make it eminently weaponizable. The passage is worth citing in its entirety because it is here that the parallel between shit and concrete as materials becomes evident, so that Garréta's deployment of concrete against the family must also be taken as an instance of weaponization:

> Et puis, on met au point et on teste notre arme secrète, notre arme suprême: la bouse-bombe.
>
> La bouse-bombe, perfectionnée par mes soins, c'est tout à la fois un projectile à large cône de dispersion, un gaz de combat suffoquant, et une arme bactériologique. En tout cas, c'est pas une arme conventionnelle, et les traités internationaux sont muets à son propos.
>
> Élaborée, comme son nom l'indique, à base de bouses de vache semi-sèches, c'est une arme redoutable, mais d'un maniement délicat.
>
> On va les cueillir vers midi sur la route où elles ont eu le temps de sécher après que les vaches les ont lâchées entre le pâturage et l'étable, aller et retour. Elles schlinguent d'autant plus que le bovin a tâté de l'ensilage. On sait les bonnes adresses, les bonnes étables. Un côté sec et rigide—celui qui a séché à l'air; un côté mou par en dessous.
>
> Toute la difficulté, c'est de la ramasser sans s'embouser; tout l'art, c'est de la stocker sur clayettes sans l'assécher trop et sans soucier grand-mère qui nous voit trafiquer ces galettes de merde du matin au soir et se demande ce qu'on peut bien faire de tout cet engrais.

La bouse-bombe, on la déploie à courte aussi bien qu'à longue portée et on la vectorise de préférence à la raquette de badminton. C'est un art de régler le tir d'un truc pareil, mais Poulette et moi on se rebute jamais à l'entraînement. (103–4)

And then we fine-tune and test our secret weapon, our ultimate weapon: the dung bomb.

The dung bomb, perfected by me, is a projectile with a wide cone of fire, a suffocating poison gas, and a biological weapon all in one. Clearly by no means a conventional weapon, and the international treaties are silent about it.

Developed, as its name indicates, from semidry cowdung, it's a formidable weapon, but quite delicate to handle.

We go around noon to collect them on the road where they've had time to dry after the cows have deposited them on the way between the pasture and the barn and back. They reek all the more when the bovines have been fed silage. We know the right places, the best barns. Dry and rigid on top—the air-dried side—and wet on the underside.

The tricky part is collecting them without soiling yourself; the key is to stockpile them up on crates without letting them dry out too much, and without alarming Grandma, who sees us mucking about with these shit-cakes morning and night and wonders what on earth we could be doing with so much manure.

The dung bomb can be deployed at short and long range, preferably with a badminton racket. Controlling the trajectory is an art unto itself, but Poulette and I never falter, never flag during training. (106–7)

And then, a few pages later, the narrator recounts how the *bouse-bombes* work to perfection:

C'est le moment crucial, le moment de dérouler notre carpette de bouse-bombes. . . .
    Tir cadencé!
    Feu roulant!

Nos bouse-bombes crépissent et immobilisent les rangs ennemis.
Arrivant en piqué, ça s'répand dans les bottes, ça s'insinue dans
les cols de chemises.

Quand, tir tendu, ça coeuille le fantassin en pleine poire, c'est
instantané. Y ferme les yeux, y ferme la bouche, il arrête de respir-
er. Ses mains lâchent la fourche, le manche de pioche, le caillou.
Y s'débarbouille frénétiquement, et plus y s'débarbouille, plus y
s'embouse. Et plus y s'embouse, moins il ose ouvrir les yeux et
plus y s'carambole avec le reste de son régiment.

Notre barrage de bouse-bombes a semé la plus totale confusion
sur le front Nord. (111)

This is the critical moment, the moment to unleash our stash of
dung bombs. . . .
    Rolling artillery barrage!
    Rapid rate of fire!
    Our dung bombs pebble-dash and pin the enemy ranks.
    Coming in at a nosedive, the dung splatters their boots, seeps
down their shirt collars.
    When a lobbed dung bomb hits a foot soldier right in the kisser,
the impact is instantaneous. He closes his eyes, closes his mouth,
stops breathing. His hands drop the pitchfork, the pickax, the peb-
ble. He starts frantically wiping himself, and the more he wipes,
the more he spreads the crap. And the more crap he spreads, the
less he dares open his eyes and the more he crashes into the rest of
his regiment.
    Our barrage of dung bombs has sown complete chaos on the
Northern front. (113–14)

Shit and concrete converge in their intractability as materials, and
each of the passages just cited deals with a particular dimension of
this intractability. The first, which relates the collection of the cowpies
and attends to their texture, points to the ways in which time plays an
essential role in rendering both shit and concrete intractable. The experience one has of both materials is temporally contingent: concrete
must be wet and fresh to be poured and shaped, shit must be dried

(but not too dried) to be deployed as a weapon. With both materials, if one waits too long or not long enough, one cannot manage or properly manipulate them. Concrete, when wet, cannot support weight but when dry, cannot be molded. Shit, when wet, is not a good projectile; but when too dry, cannot be spread around as is the case in the second passage, where the enemy winds up blinding and soiling themselves in their attempts at getting rid of it. As Garréta's narrator states, "Le temps, c'est de l'essence" (It's all a bladder of time) (28; 30), an observation that bears obvious consequence for the writer's task: the difficulty of writing is not so much one of inspiration, but of making and having the time to write, of managing to write within a particular interval, when life under capitalism multiplies demands on one's time even as it demands increased productivity.

The second passage, which relates the deployment of the *bouses* as *bombes,* has the particular viscosity of shit mirroring that of concrete: both Angélique and the boys who are the target of the *bouse-bombes* are covered in materials that they become more enmired in in direct proportion to the attempts made at getting rid of them. This mirroring encourages us to read the Angélique-in-concrete scene through the enemies-in-shit scene, such that the relation between father and daughter is framed not so much in familial terms, but adversarial ones. The father essentially treats his daughter as an enemy, which the narrator seems to understand when she cries out, "Papa, ô pourquoi tu veux l'assommer notre Angélique?" (Papa, O why would you want to clobber our Angélique?).

Shit and concrete are both intractable and essential. Shit is the girls' secret weapon, without which they would not have been able to defeat the racist boys, and concrete is the key to the father's projects of modernization, as well as a decisive material in concretizing the failures and limits of the father, and by extension, the heterosexual nuclear family he attempts to construct around himself. Through Garréta's insistence on the weaponizable quality of both concrete and shit, these materials are imbued with political force—the force to resist the weight of the parts of the social order to which they are in opposition: the family, in concrete's case, and racism, in shit's case.

We are still left, however, with the question of the specificity of these materials. Why concrete to attack the family and shit to attack racism? Couldn't Garréta have reversed them so that the father was a fertilizer maniac terrorizing his family by going out and collecting excrement, experimenting with creating different kinds of fertilizer so that his daughters and wife always stank, becoming social pariahs as a result? In which case, couldn't the girls have come up with ways of covering their racist enemies in fresh concrete instead by laying wet concrete traps for them to get stuck in?

I would submit that there is a particular logic governing why Garréta attributes these functions to the materials she is working with, which has to do with pointing to the ways in which the social structures of family and race (the concept that makes racism possible) are constructed, so that her readers might be better equipped to take them on themselves. Family is cast as an "essential" structure if a clearly social or cultural one[16]—see, for example, the pervasive narrative of children needing both a mother and father if they are to develop properly[17]—whereas race seems biological, or natural. One can construct alternative families, of which blended, queer, or single-parent families are a clear example, but constructing or inhabiting an alternative race seems ridiculous on its face, as demonstrated by the scandal of Rachel Dolezal and her claim to be a different race than the race she "is." And yet, race, like gender, is a social construct, and a fairly recent one at that.[18]

Garréta is aware of this divergence in the way the structures of family and race are perceived, and tailors the material of her resistance accordingly. Concrete—the material by which she targets the family, this cultural construct—is used primarily for the construction of industrial, commercial, and infrastructural structures meant for collective use. By using concrete, Garréta simultaneously insists on the constructed nature of the family and gives lie to the idea that it is somehow a private structure. While the space of the nuclear family might be mapped onto domesticity or the private sphere, it is an immanently public structure foundational to a certain kind of sociality—namely, patriarchy and the various ideologies that are reproduced in its name, including racism.[19] Kristin Ross, in *Fast Cars, Clean Bodies,* has shown how postwar France was deeply invested in a modernization tied to an Americanized culture of consumption and hygiene—to, in other words, technology. Garréta responds to this characterization of modernization by tying it to the family, arguing effectively that the family is also a technology, by which a nation can build itself—it is just as much an infrastructural project as are the concrete highways that connect the nation to itself.

And through shit, Garréta uses a "natural" material to target a "natural" phenomenon. It is important that the shit used for the *housebombes* is cowshit as the bovine nature of this material draws attention to the way cowshit, which seems natural, a biological product, is itself only available to us because of the process of domestication. The cow, in its common form, only exists as the consequence of significant human intervention, and the animality of the resulting species masks its human origins. It is also, in other words, the fruit of technology—animal husbandry. The decidedly nonnatural origins of the cow point also to the nonnatural origins of race. The weaponization of the shit that is a product of domestication places domestication itself under the sign of violence. The elevation of the family, the domestication of women, the domestication of race (e.g., the enslavement of Black people as chattel labor, the predominance of racial minorities in domestic service)—these are all structures obtained through physical and conceptual violence.

This, then, is the moral of *Dans l'béton*: everything that we have at our disposal comes to us through some sort of human or social intervention—if not the material itself, then the conceptual tools by which we make sense of it. This awareness of the processes by which we come to believe the things we do, by which we come to inhabit the structures that form us, is a necessary step in beginning to undo them if we are to ever replace them. *Dans l'béton* is thus a novel with a decidedly political bent, but that is not the only takeaway of the novel. Beyond a certain political awareness, Garréta is invested in a poetic awareness as evidenced in her will to have readers reading the novel through a Wittigian lens, seen in her appropriation of Catherine Legrand. Wittig's primary poetico–political intervention was to insist on the materiality of language as the principal matter through which political reality might be shaped. For Wittig, language is not an easy material. As evinced by her insistence on the labor and brute force that goes into stripping language of its sedimented social meaning to allow it to mean otherwise (something that happens uniquely in a literary context),[20] it is a fundamentally intractable material.

Garréta, by insisting on the materiality of concrete and shit in *Dans l'béton,* primes her reader to be attentive to the materiality that is found in the text itself. The descriptions of concrete and shit are certainly evocative and seek to operate on a physical register, but the actual material at hand is that of language, and it is no coincidence that the materials through which she would have the materiality of language refracted are themselves intractable. Shit is hard to work with; concrete is hard to work with—and so too with language. Language, like shit and concrete, is intractable, and we seem not to have the time in our late capitalist lives (marked by scarcity of time and resources) to work with it, to do the work that Wittig, and following Wittig, Garréta, do in making it resist the flattening social order into which we are born and raised. And yet it is precisely this intractable material of language—whose intractable materiality is illustrated through shit and concrete's intractable materiality—that constitutes a social contract that, to use Wittig's terms, cannot be consented to anymore, that must be reworked, intractability be damned.

A Shitty Social Contract

Laure Murat has described Garréta as follows: "In France today, only Anne F. Garréta . . . can boast not only of being Monique Wittig's spiritual heir but of pursuing her task of pushing even further the limits of language when it comes to gender—this is no small challenge."[21] This is no small challenge because what is at stake is the entire social contract itself in its currently inegalitarian manifestation, which, if we follow Garréta as Wittig's spiritual heir, is what both authors write against in their literary projects. Wittig, in her essay "On the Social

Contract," formulates the social contract in terms that resonate with the project of *Dans l'béton* as I have worked through it here:

> For to a writer language offers a very concrete matter to grasp hold of. It seems to me that the very first, the permanent, and the final social contract is language. The basic agreement between human beings, indeed what makes them human and makes them social, is language. . . . Now when I say let us break off the heterosexual contract per se . . . I did not mean that we must break off the social contract per se, because that would be absurd. For we must break it off as heterosexual. Leaning upon a philosophical examination of what a well-established social contract could do for us, I want to confront the historical conditions and conflicts that can lead us to end the obligations that bind us without our consent while we are not enjoying a reciprocal commitment that would be the necessary condition of our freedom, to paraphrase Rousseau.[22]

The problem, as Wittig lays it out, is not the existence of a social contract—to abolish the social contract would be to abolish sociality would be to abolish humanity—but the existence of an oppressive social contract that imposes inequality on what should be an equal humankind, as demonstrated exemplarily by heterosexuality as a compulsory social, economic, and political formation that subordinates women to men.[23]

If Wittig finds Jean-Jacques Rousseau a rich figure for thinking with despite his reputed misogyny, it is because of a denaturalizing, emancipatory kernel she finds in Rousseau's thought,[24] which enables her to gloss his essay on the social contract, writing:

> Clearly, in what Rousseau says, it is the real present existence of the social contract that is particularly stimulating for me—whatever its origin, it exists here and now, and as such it is apt to be understood and acted upon. Each contractor has to reaffirm the contract in new terms for the contract to be in existence.
>
> Only then does it become an instrumental notion in the sense that the contractors are reminded by the term itself that they should reexamine their conditions. Society was not made once

and for all. The social contract will yield to our action, to our words.[25]

Rousseau's formulation of a historicized rather than a natural or an essential social contract permits Wittig to conceive of the social contract as fundamentally malleable. If something is malleable, it means that it is made of a material that can be worked on and shaped. This is all Wittig needs to imagine a radically different social contract, one that might be made through fleeing the oppressive social contract that is society as we know it in order to be in a position in which to rework language rather than be worked by it.

The sense of possibility that the social contract's malleability engenders is what is behind Wittig's lyrical description of the social contract in *Le Chantier littéraire*, her doctoral thesis for the École des Hautes Études en Sciences Sociales (EHESS), or School for Advanced Studies in the Social Sciences: "Language exists as a paradise made from visible, audible, palpable, savory words."[26] The social contract is language in its materiality and none other than the writer is better positioned to know, intimately, this materiality. Garréta takes this to heart and by rolling up her sleeves and plunging into the shit and concrete that show us what kind of a material language is, creates, in the space of her novel, a fugitive space, a space that undoes the social contract as we know it and articulates the desire for a different kind of shared language, one that would build social structures besides those heterosexual and racist ones that currently shape the social landscape.

For Wittig, as for Garréta, the critique of heterosexuality is always a critique more broadly of the ontological mutilation of humankind that follows from naturalizing difference to justify oppression. Where heterosexuality naturalizes sexual difference, racism naturalizes racial difference. What Garréta targets, then, in *Dans l'béton*, by targeting the twin structures of heterosexual kinship and racism, is a social contract that exists only to tie humans to each other in and through violence. And as *Dans l'béton* demonstrates, the violence of the pre-existing social contract must be counteracted by the kind of violence that shit and concrete, as analogues of language, allow the decentered subject of the narrator to wield. The novel is thus a primer in turning the everyday material of language into a weapon.

Garréta, in channeling the experience of language through the experience of shit and concrete, insists on the difficulty of working with such intractable materials. To deal with language, as with shit and concrete, is work. With language, that is, with the social contract, we can either take on the exertion of working on it or passively allow ourselves to be worked on by it. The twinned materials of shit and concrete dramatize this choice in presenting us with a vivid set of consequences. We can either allow language to cover us, encasing us in the world as it has always been (what happens to Angélique with concrete), or to blind us (what happens to the racist forces Angélique and the narrator combat), or, as Garréta suggests, work with it to do something completely different. In this light, the linguistic experimentation that obtains throughout *Dans l'béton*, seen in the highly unorthodox orthography in the passages cited, far from being preciosity, or a twenty-first-century imitation of Queneau's néo-français, is an example of what happens when we dare to work with and against language, rather than simply be in it. Garréta's narrator, in producing the text, adopts the position Wittig takes when confronted with the charge that this is "mere utopia": "Then I will stay with Socrates's view and also Glaucon's: If ultimately we are denied a new social order, which therefore can exist only in words, I will find it in myself."[27] Even if there is, perish the thought, no egress out of a social order that reproduces (through) inequality, the self can always become a fugitive space—a lesson that suggests that Garréta, just as much as she is Wittig's spiritual heir, might also be Genet's, writing against society in order to be in it.

) 6 (

DANIEL PENNAC'S
EXCREMENTAL POETICS

Literature for All

***

In the last chapter, we saw how Garréta, via Wittig, treats language as the social contract, as an intractable material that, like shit, must be worked on, weaponized, resisted. Garréta targets heterosexual kinship and racism, with language (as worked on in literature) the means by which to effect such a concerted campaign. In this chapter, I extend that logic beyond language to treat literature itself as an object that can be worked on, weaponized, its sedimentation into rarefied and exclusive cultural capital, resisted. I want now to show how that kind of political energy, through excremental literature—through literary excrement—can also be turned against literature itself, as seen in Daniel Pennac's novel *Journal d'un corps* (*Diary of a Body*) (2012), which manifests an excremental poetics that is a literary politics.

Journal d'un corps, which ties together scatological and literary forms of production, foregrounds the fecal—its stunning originary scene centers around a humiliating and public bout of diarrhea[1]—but the work's reception was marked by a collective refusal to recognize the fecal. As its title indicates, Pennac's work is the diary of a body, an attempt at writing an entire life that lovingly follows the evolution of the narrator's body from youth to death, through sickness and health.

What distinguishes it from "regular" diaries is its evacuation of the emotional and the sentimental—or so the narrator claims[2]—in order to trace one's life through an unflinching attention to the body and its processes. The idea is that by focusing on the corporeal over the psychological or emotional, we can get a different sort of life-writing.

The novel received mixed reviews from the mainstream press. For example, Amélie Grossman-Etoh for *L'Express* described it as "an almost perfect novel," while Éric Naulleau for *Paris Match* dismissed it, writing that "a good idea doesn't necessarily make for a good book."[3] Across the board, the work's reviewers passed over the originary scene, choosing to ignore the narrative's fecal roots. The one reviewer to evoke this scene, *Le Figaro*'s Patrick Grainville, scrubbed it clean, focusing instead on emotional content devoid of fecal matter.[4] Grainville's sanitization of this scene and the other reviewers' silence around it, while certainly more polite than the scatological reading I propose to undertake, are unable to account for *Journal d'un corp*'s literary, aesthetic impetus—one that has a profoundly political impact.

If we concentrate explicitly on the fecal matter that has been disposed of in the critical discourse around this work, Pennac's work reveals itself to be more than a moving meditation on corporeality and mortality, more than a making visible of the geriatric body, more than an insistence on the metamorphoses of a body that we attempt to shield from the ravages of time through exercise, surgery, and an array of pharmaceutical products. *Journal d'un corps* is more than life-writing, more than a writing of the body. It is all these things, but the scatological originary scene is also an articulation of an excremental poetics, an aesthetic vision that sees the fecal not only as a potent and efficient way of theorizing literary creation, but as a literary material that democratizes literature, opening up this cultural field in order to make it accessible to all. The fecal, in other words, is mobilized to level differences and transcend them through this shit from which none of us can escape.

I want to revisit again Roland Barthes's assertion that, "when written, shit does not have an odor."[5] Pennac, in writing the originary scene of diarrhea that transforms into the narrator's logorrhea, does his best to restore to shit its odor (like Céline before him).[6] To play on the double-meaning of *sentir* in French as both smelling and feeling, while Pennac might not succeed in having us smell the narrator's liquid feces, he certainly does his best to make us feel it, to feel what it was like for the narrator to be so terrified as a young boy that he would be unable to hold in the contents of his intestines.

Pennac writes a preliminary sequence of two framing narratives, or pre-texts, that the reader has to go through before we reach the originary fecal scene. The book opens with a foreword to the reader signed by D.P. (ostensibly Daniel Pennac), who explains to the reader that his "dear, old, inimitable, and very exasperating, friend Lison" (5; 9)—where Lison's name is a play on the imperative "Lisons" (Let's read)—shared with him the book that we are going to read in the form of a pile of notebooks bequeathed to Lison by her recently deceased father. D.P., blown away by what he reads, consults his friend Postel, who was the deceased's doctor, whose reaction is immediate: "Publish it! Do not hesitate. Send this to your publisher and get it published!" (5; 10). Despite D.P.'s ambivalence about anonymously publishing the diaries of the fairly well-known figure Lison's father is made out to be, he follows Postel's advice and does so.

After this foreword, we move on to the second pre-text: a letter from Lison's father explaining the existence of the diary and why he is bequeathing it to her instead of to her brother, Bruno. This posthumous letter is then followed by our first foray into the diary itself. Instead of reading the first diary entry, chronologically speaking, dated September 28, 1936, when the narrator was twelve years, eleven months, and eighteen days old, which simply reads, "I won't be afraid anymore," repeated five times in incantatory fashion (21; 27), the first entry the reader sees is instead a much later one, dated December 28, 1987, when the narrator was sixty-four years, two months, and eighteen days old. Why does Pennac depart from chronology and prevent the reader from having the same experience that D.P. would himself have had of reading the notebooks from beginning to end? If D.P. was left "totally dumbfounded" after such a reading (5; 9), why not allow us to have that experience as well? Plucking this entry

out of a much later notebook and transplanting it to the beginning
has the consequence of emphasizing the fecal origins of this text: it
places the entire work under an excremental sign so that we might
never forget its fecality, even as the diary moves away from the fecal
to other corporeal phenomena such as nasal polyps, flatulence, the
descent of the testicles, baldness, yawning, and dermatitis.

This first entry centers the fecal as a way of accounting not only
for this particular text's origins and the process by which it is made,
but for writing in general. The entry takes the form of a defecation diptych. We move from the narrator's measured description of
his granddaughter's soiling herself out of fear, delivered to us in a
contained past tense, to the narrator's visceral description, or rather,
reenactment, in the present tense, of when, as a young boy, he shits
himself out of fear. This is the episode responsible for the diary's
existence, as it is to conquer the fear that left him shitless that the
narrator, aged twelve, takes pen to paper. If this 1987 entry had been
kept in its place, readers would enter this "diary of a body" with no
sense of the fear that compelled the text into existence, and no sense
of the feces that gave fear such a palpable form. In other words, this
originary scene demonstrates excremental formalism, showing how
shit is an effective and efficient medium for representation, a material
that succeeds in structuring and holding up an entire text. By assuming a diptych form, with the narrator's traumatic experience succeed-
ing his granddaughter's, the entry takes us from an instance of feces
as the object of representation to feces as the means and condition
of possibility of representation. In what follows, I examine this first
entry, paying close attention to the second fecal scene for the ways it
articulates an excremental poetics that takes us beyond the confines
of Pennac's text to larger questions of why we write, what it is to
write, and why writing matters.

The first panel of the defecation diptych features the narrator's
granddaughter, Fanny (pun likely intended), as the defecator. The
narrator's grandson, Grégoire, and his friend Philippe terrify six-
year-old Fanny by telling her that they are going to reenact Joan of
Arc's trial. Fanny is at first delighted to play the role of Joan, this

saint whose praises Grégoire and Philippe had been singing, assuring her of heaven's many advantages. She soon discovers that this entails being burned alive, thrown into the giant bonfire that the narrator's wife had ordered the boys to make to get rid of old furniture. Terrified, she runs screaming to her grandfather, who attempts to console his granddaughter only to discover that she has soiled herself: "I took her on my knee and felt that she was damp. More than that, even: she had soiled her pants out of sheer terror" (13; 18). The process of shitting oneself has been reduced to two neat sentences. Returning to Barthes, this excrement indeed does not smell—it is not even named. We are to infer its presence through the "more than that," which implies that Fanny had done more than simply wet herself. If the narrator is able to feel (and smell, as he proceeds to bathe Fanny) his granddaughter's fear-induced feces, we are left at a remove. While the narrator writes in the first person, prompting readerly identification, there is no description of his olfactory and tactile encounter with Fanny's feces to identify with. If we are to have a close encounter of the fecal kind, it is up to our imagination to provide it. However, because this first fecal episode takes up so little space on the page and moves on quickly to the second fecal episode from the narrator's past, we do not have the time, as readers, to fill in the details that Pennac leaves out.

The second panel of the defecation diptych follows smoothly from the first. As Fanny, sitting in the bathtub, is recounting to her grandfather what had frightened her so, the narrator is transported back to the originary scene of trauma and to the present tense: "And so I find myself back at the time when this diary was first created. September 1936. I am twelve years old, almost thirteen, a Boy Scout" (14; 18). What follows is a painstakingly detailed re-creation of where, when, and how the narrator shit himself out of fear, crammed into a single paragraph that runs over five consecutive pages, the text flowing like diarrhea. Like Fanny, the narrator, a young boy scout, is playing a game—in this case, Capture the Flag. The narrator has been captured, his flag taken from him, and his captors tie him to a tree and leave him there. All alone in the woods as the other scouts continue to play, the narrator, who insists that he is grown up—"I am a Boy Scout, and this is important, I am no longer a Wolf Cub, I am not a little boy, I am big, I am a grown-up" (14; 18)—waits calmly until he spies an ant colony nearby and sees that not one, but two ants have begun to crawl up his foot. The sight of the second ant triggers the narrator's raw panic that the ants will devour him alive: screaming and yelling in fear, he has diarrhea. After the narrator's bowels have been fully evacuated, the narrator returns to the past tense, to a more controlled and measured attitude, to describe the aftermath of this event: the scout leader, a Father Chapelier, hoses the narrator down while he is still in his uniform, upbraiding him for having shamed the scouts in front of hikers, accusing him of having fun at the hikers' expense. The narrator's mother, who we learn from the rest of the diary is frigid, monstrous, and "the only person to whom I didn't call out" (17; 23), picks up the narrator, who is sent home early from scout camp. Finally, in a brief paragraph, the sixty-four-year-old narrator recalls that his twelve-year-old self started the diary the next day, thus explaining how this fecal episode constitutes the originary scene from which the text emerges.

At the dense center of the five-page-long paragraph is the following passage, which I will cite at length. This passage treats the sequence of fear and defecation and constitutes a tightly written articulation of an excremental poetics:

> It is no longer a question of being bitten; I am going to be completely covered with ants, eaten alive. My imagination does not represent the thing in all its detail, I don't tell myself that the ants are going to climb up my legs, devour my penis and anus or enter me through my eye sockets, my ears, my nostrils, that they will eat me from the inside out, winding their way through my intestines and sinuses; I don't see myself as a human anthill tied to this pine tree and vomiting through my dead mouth columns of worker ants busily transporting me crumb by crumb into the terrifying belly swarming upon itself three meters from me; I don't imagine these tortures, but they are all there in the howl of terror I let out now, eyes closed, mouth immense. It is a cry for help that must sheathe

the entire forest, and the world beyond—a stridency in which my
voice breaks into a thousand shards, and it is my whole body
that screams through the voice of the little boy I have once again
become. My sphincters scream as immoderately as my mouth, my
insides run down my legs, I can feel it as it happens; my shorts are
filling up and I am dripping. Diarrhea mixes with resin, and this
increases my terror because, I tell myself, the odor will intoxicate
the ants and attract other animals, and my lungs dissolve in my
cries for help. I am covered in tears, drool, snot, resin and shit.
(15–16; 20–21)

This complex passage poses the questions of writing as excrement,
of writing as representation, and posits feces as the site for thinking the *propre* (proper), in both the sense of cleanliness (*propreté*) and
of property (*propriété*), where the *propre,* and its antonym, the *impropre* (improper), are crucial to thinking through our own relation to
literature.

Before we get to the narrator's shit, the fecal is gestured toward in
the fantasy of being devoured by ants and other animals that precedes
bowel evacuation. The fantasy is marked by a regular evocation of
pairs of body parts that center the gastrointestinal tract: "my penis
and anus . . . my intestines and sinuses." In the first pairing, the anus
is not figured as an orifice, like "my eye sockets, my ears, my nostrils"
through which the ants might breach and enter his body. It is not
figured as a passageway or an intermediary but as a central object
unto itself. It is as important as the genitals—the penis—around which
human history has been cast as a phallic enterprise of domination. In
the second pairing, the sinuses, which border our brain, are paired
with the intestines, which contain the feces. The fecal, before it has
made its explosive appearance as diarrhea, is already being aligned
with a porosity and contiguity between world and brain, world and
self, world and writing—without the brain, there is no sense of self
and no possibility for writing.[7]

In this nightmarish fantasy, even as Pennac turns his narrator
away from a contemplation of imminent bodily destruction to the
ants themselves, the ants are placed under a gastrointestinal sign: he

likens the ant to vomit and the ant colony to a stomach, so that his own digestive system in crisis is prefigured by the vision of an external digestive system. Seeing the ant-colony-as-digestive-organ roiling and the ants-as-vomit flowing from his fantasized dead mouth triggers the flow of the narrator's excrement. He produces and becomes what he imagines: the brain's image becomes a physical reality. The narrator sees reality, has an imaginative response to it that transforms it, and proceeds to represent this transformed reality through his own body, fecally. This set of steps parallels the process of writing, where the writer, who lives in the same reality as does the reader, transforms reality through his imagination and proceeds to represent this transformed reality through writing, a process that implicates his body, as all writing is embodied: the body sits up, the hands hold the pen or type on the keyboard, the eyes register what has just been written, the brain silently registers the sounds of the words and produces the thoughts that are transcribed in addition to coordinating the neurological signals that allow the body to make the physical gestures necessary for writing.

For Pennac's narrator, the metaphorical analogue to writing is excremental. This pairing of feces with writing forces us to think writing through the fecal, to think writing as excrement. While other bodily fluids and products are evoked in the passage, such as tears, snot, and saliva, such secretions are not taken up as ways of figuring writing: the fact of being expressed by the body does not then impart to them some sort of expressive and representational status.[8] For that, Pennac insists on the fecal: when he writes, "My sphincters scream as immoderately as my mouth," he unites mouth with anus and brings them into relation by using the verb *hurler* (to scream) for both. The mouth, through which the narrator's voice emerges, cries out, as does the sphincter, through which feces erupt. Given the anus as mouth, the feces constitute then a voice, which is regularly evoked metonymically to stand in for a writer's style, for what characterizes the singularity of a writer's oeuvre, making it recognizable as a corpus, visible as a literary body.

This establishment of feces as voice and the fecal as the literary is reinforced by Pennac's opting for diarrhea as the fecal material of this originary scene. What we are contending with as readers is not a solid, finished text that can stand on its own because it has a distinct form, but rather with a text-in-progress, akin to liquid feces that have not yet been fully processed. For this originary scene to elucidate a poetics, it is necessary for the feces implicated to be liquid, to speak to process rather than product.

The relation between liquid feces and ink, diarrhea and the writing process, is reinforced by its difference from the return of feces later in the text, when Pennac's narrator contemplates stains left behind in the toilet bowl by a solid bowel movement (129–30; 176–77). The feces here, observed and recorded when the narrator is an adult, evoke none of the humiliation and psychic distress of the originary scene, and serve as a metaphor for how *Journal d'un corps* is structured: each diary entry is like a bowel movement that can be inspected, revealing the particular state of the body, a manifestation of its health (or lack thereof). Here, the feces are contained, sanitized, lending themselves to the sort of attention we can accord to each entry, wherein we attend to each entry for its narrative content rather than for the process by which it was produced. Thus, while we can posit an analogy between feces (in general) and writing, when it comes to theorizing a poetics within Pennac's framework, our focus needs to be diarrheal: it is diarrhea that serves as the entry into the writing life for the narrator, while the solid feces become a way of measuring time, of accounting for the repetitious and quotidian nature of the effort required to produce a text.

The young narrator's diarrhea, which acts not so much as a coming to writing but as a violent propulsion into writing, is not due to bacteria or a virus, but is instead psychologically induced. *Journal d'un corps* is a story of being desperately afraid of fear: "I won't be afraid anymore, I won't be afraid anymore." In the context of a text that serves as an extended reflection on aging, on the ineluctably mortal quality of corporeality, the primordial fear is a fear of death. The young narrator feared he would die, his body destroyed by ants, and he shit himself. And in order to master his fear, to conquer it, to be governed no longer by an imminent death that would wrest away control of his mind and body, he begins to write. This originary fecal scene asserts that we write because we fear death: writing leaves behind some literary trace that might have an afterlife.

Fecality and the Diary Form

The question of poetics is a question of form, and in Pennac's case, the form in which his excremental poetics is contained is the diary. If Pennac posits writing as an attempt to leave behind a trace, to thwart the erasure of death, that motive does not in and of itself explain why Pennac makes the originary scene discussed above culminate in a novel that takes the form of the diary, sectioned into entries that fragment the text more thoroughly than the chapters that typically make up a novel. If we consent to the idea that the fabrication of fiction (itself a word that etymologically signals creation, as witnessed in its root, *fingere,* which means "to fashion or form") implicates the question of form, then we must investigate the particular form—the diary—and its relation to the fecal.

The novel's masquerading as a diary can be mapped onto the fecal, where the (ideally) quotidian regularity of expressing feces from the bowels is tied to the (ideally) quotidian regularity of expressing oneself through the writing of a diary. Pennac is not the first writer to use the diary form to write the body and the self, placing it under a distinctly excremental sign. Hervé Guibert regularly chronicled the deterioration of his body from HIV and then AIDS through such autofictional and autobiographical texts as *À l'ami qui ne m'a pas sauvé la vie* (*To the Friend Who Did Not Save My Life*), *Le Protocole compassionnel* (*The Compassion Protocol*), and *Le Mausolée des amants* (*The Mausoleum of Lovers*).[9] This work serves as a useful point of comparison that helps make sense of why both Pennac and Guibert make their diaries distinctly diarrheic ones.

Guibert tracks the ceaseless movement of his body toward death and, like Pennac's narrator, is driven by fear of death—a death that announced itself all too clearly and precociously—into literary production. Guibert, like Pennac's narrator, meticulously records the evolution of his body, committing his body to the page, and again, like Pennac's narrator, opts for the diary form to do so. As with *Journal d'un corps,* Guibert's corpus is traversed by a distinctly scatological thread, where the fecal figures as an object of interest, even obsession, and this from before Guibert's HIV diagnosis. Even a text from Guibert's juvenilia, such as *La Mort propagande* (*Propaganda Death*), combines the will to keep a diary of the body and to foreground the fecal:

> This period when I started to photograph my excretions. Diarrhea, defecation, violent spatters of shit on the toilet's white porcelain, tiny bursts and squirts, to reproduce them. To enumerate them: defecation #1, #2, to tally them up. As the toilet isn't flushed, they've increased, accumulated. . . . I stayed there for hours, kneeling as at an altar, with all the more interest since these wonders are wholly mine. I adored them like holy relics intoxicating me, sacramental wines infused with decay. What an aroma! . . . Secret laboratory with frozen, white walls that I tainted, my eyes half-shut, arrested by the pleasure of liquid, burning shit ruining my anus before bathing our bellies. I came in all dressed up, brought out my undone, contorted, raving body.[10]

Because it dates from before Guibert's HIV infection, this vivid description of genuflection before a fecal altar is distinct from the narratives we find in AIDS or Holocaust writing—the two literary contexts in which feces, especially of the violent, diarrheic sort, figure most commonly—and is inscribed instead within the frame of the everyday.

The young Guibert's diarrheic ecstasy, while figured as a kind of limit-experience through transcendent and mystical language, is also clearly figured as a willed experience, as seen in the lines following this passage, where Guibert recounts the foods he would regularly consume to provoke diarrhea: "I set off these violent evacuations, swallowing various fats, prunes, pig testicles" (33; 189). The repeated, carefully recorded nature of his encounter with his feces parallels the repeated, carefully recorded nature of a diary. Already in Guibert's juvenilia, the fecal is privileged as a site of spectacular representation (the object that must be captured), of knowledge (toilet bowl as laboratory), of selfhood (the wonder of recognizing the shit as his), and of temporality (the quotidian repetition of diarrhea; the accumulation of shit in the toilet a way of measuring time), making his body something both to inhabit and to be expelled from, where excrement makes it possible to have an out-of-body experience because of how much one is *in* said body.

All of these aspects figure in Guibert's AIDS writing and are developed and intensified through his increasing closeness to death, his seropositivity placing him in a truncated temporality rather than the open temporality he inhabited when he published *La Mort propagande*: at twenty-two, death would have been a distant horizon. As Catherine Mavrikakis points out in her articulation of Guibert's excremental poetics, if Guibert so often represents his fecal production (in diary entries, as seen in *Le Mausolée des amants,* and on film, as seen in the documentary *La Pudeur ou l'impudeur* [*Modesty or Immodesty*] directed by Guibert in 1992), it is because fecal matter is the best form and material for his literary legacy:

> Guibert's work, imaginary waste, secretion of the mouth or turd,
> is built then like a tomb that preserves inside all that is already on
> the order of the rotten, toxic, decomposed. It is this mausoleum,
> filled with shit and spit of all kinds, that Guibert delivers up to
> his readers in order to have them see the violence of AIDS and
> of existence enacted on his body. To strip himself naked, while
> offering the reader or viewer a well-thought interiority that's like a
> mummified turd, a sublime gob of spit, grandiose filth—this is the
> insane project Hervé Guibert yoked himself to.[11]

Excrement is both an effective way of representing the waste of a life and of a body that AIDS provokes, and the perfect medium for self-writing. While Pennac treats diarrhea as an exceptional event that informs and colors the rest of the text, Guibert writes of his diarrhea over and over again, so that the reader cannot avoid it and is contaminated or marked by it. Through the diary format, Guibert turns diarrhea into a banal experience, where the reader's eventual numbness to the continual "violent spatters of shit" is itself testament to "the violence of AIDS and of existence enacted on his body."

If Guibert turns to the diary format rather than the more conventional *récit* (narrative) or *roman* (novel), I would suggest that it is because those other forms cannot fully convey the shocking banality of dying in the way that the diary—perhaps the most banal genre of writing—is able to through the experience it provides of repetition and duration. How better to evoke the horror of a death sentence and the systematic, progressive degradation of one's body than through a diary, where each respective entry is like a clock counting down, each percussive, punctuating tick marking the closing of the laughably small interval that separates one from nothingness? And how better to express the inexorable, moribund, regular rhythm of dying than through the regular rhythm of defecation?

There is thus an implacable logic to Guibert's diaries being so diarrheic, to his investment in excremental form and material. In *Journal d'un corps,* Pennac shares with Guibert an investment in form (diary) and material (diarrhea), but Pennac's excremental logic and poetics depart from Guibert's in his decision to place the diary within the framework of fiction. Through comparison with Guibert's corpus, which cannily ties together self-writing and the project of writing (against) death, the consequences of Pennac's opting for the diary form in *Journal d'un corps,* but one that is fictional, become clearer.

Valerie Raoul, in her study of the fictional diary/journal, observes that writing is present on two levels in the fictional diary: on one level is the author who writes the novel, and on the other, the narrator who produces a journal.[12] The distance between these two levels is created by fiction, and, in Pennac's case, this distance permits his narrator's feces not to figure as an extension of the authorial body because we do not link Pennac's authorial identity with the biographical content of the narrative. However, in Guibert's case, we are all too aware that the descriptions of diarrhea are "real" (in *La Pudeur et l'impudeur,* the viewer watches Guibert rush to the toilet to expel diarrhea) and attach that diarrhea immediately to the biographical person of Guibert.[13]

In *Journal d'un corps,* because we do not link Pennac's authorial identity with his biographical one, as we do with Guibert, the body we read of, and the narrative produced by such attention to that body, is automatically a generalized one, which, in not belonging to a "real" individual, arguably serves more easily as a site of collective experience. For Pennac, unlike Guibert, this project of writing against death is not about writing his own self or about creating a legacy that might be tied to it. Of course, autofictional and autobiographical texts can also produce strong readerly experience and identification, but without the biographical subject of the author acting as an alluring referent for the text being produced, any readerly identification with Pennac's narrator bypasses identification with "a real person" endowed with a self. Any such identification is instead with an experience of language. Pennac's turn to a fictional diary as opposed to a "real" one thus makes literature about the *demos* rather than the *autos,* using the fecal to do so.

Quoting Wolfgang Iser, Raoul writes that "fiction is 'form without reality'; it exists only through the text."[14] Feces, in contrast, are form with reality. Their reality grabs hold of our bodies through the text. The visceral reaction we have to scatological texts is the activation of our own body's memory of defecation. It appears to me that autofictional writing such as Guibert's allows for a short-circuiting of such a triggering of our memory, where the biographical and real status of the author's own well-documented body contains the feces he writes to his individual body, allowing his to be the body that defecates while we are the bodies that read about it. In Pennac's case, however, the fecal appears to endow the "empty" form of his fiction with too-real substance and targets our readerly bodies as the only real guts present in the text. Written, shit might not smell, but we can feel it, remember it, and know all too well what it is, and this knowledge is one shared by all.

Pennac's singular, originary shit, in its necessarily diarrheic form, constitutes a malodorous ink that responds to the "good mother's milk . . . white ink"[15] of Hélène Cixous's *écriture féminine,* by proposing, in the place of an ink sourced from a female, maternal, lactating body, a brown ink that all bodies can produce.[16] Who among us has not experienced diarrhea? Who among us does not defecate, does not carry this waste within us? We can see this will toward universality also in the fact that the narrator identifies with and has his memory triggered by his granddaughter, not his grandson. This experience of fear-induced fecal production, which in turn inspires narrative production (Fanny narrates to her grandfather what happened; he narrates to his reader what happened), is one that transcends age and sex.

The idea of fecal matter as a difference-leveling substance is not new and it is certainly not a twentieth-century discovery. The psychoanalyst Janine Chasseguet-Smirgel attributes to the Marquis de Sade an excremental poetics as well, where the proliferation of excrement in his corpus, which is always tied to its misuse and misplacement (as with coprophagy), is the expression of Sade's will to level all differences, as enacted in his many scenes of incest, where incest becomes a way of destroying the distinction between the categories of parent and child, for instance. The transgression commonly attributed to Sade is thus in the service of dismantling reality in order to create a new one:

> More generally speaking, pleasure, linked to transgression, is supported by the fantasy of possession, and in breaking the barriers that separate man from woman, child from adult, mother from son, daughter from father, brother from sister, erogenous zones from each other, and, in murder, a body's molecules from each other, pleasure *destroys reality and, through this very act, creates a new one, that of the anal universe, where all differences are abolished.* This universe is, essentially, that of *sacrilege,* since everything—and, in particular, what is taboo, forbidden, sacred—is engulfed in a gigantic grinding machine—the digestive tube—that disintegrates molecules to make the mass thus obtained into excrement.[17]

Pennac's universalism is hardly Sadean. Instead of overturning civilization and putting into place a new social disorder where the only principle is that of transgression, Pennac's fecal universalism is a positive counterweight to Sade's negative, sacrilegious one. The fecal, instead of being placed under the sign of transgression and disorder, is treated instead as fertilizer that would nourish a new kind of civic spirit and renew, through literature, an *esprit de corps* that takes the *corps* (body) literally and frames it, productively, as a defecating one. Pennac does not sanitize the fecal by applying a high-culture gloss on it. Instead, he shows that what is *propre* to literature is in fact *impropre*: a truly democratic culture requires moving away from the *propr(i)eté* of the canon toward a readerly and writerly culture that is decidedly *impropre*.

The *Propre* and the *Impropre*

Feces are marked by a seemingly contradictory relationship to the *propre*, where, in order to be *propre*, in the sense of *proper*, we must empty our bowels (to be constipated, or to feel the buildup of fecal matter in our rectum placing increasing pressure on our sphincter, is hardly *propre*); but the moment our feces pass from inside us, where they are invisible but keenly felt, to outside us, where they are felt no longer but are keenly visible, they become improper and unclean. In French, *propre* (meaning both *clean* and *proper*) grounds both *propreté* (cleanliness, and by extension, propriety) and *propriété* (property), a shared conceptual foundation that has important consequences. As Dominique Laporte argues in *History of Shit*, the ideologies of propriety and property are linked.[18] According to Laporte, the notion of *propriété* originates in the fecal, in early modern waste management practices imposed by the king, which required individuals to recognize and distinguish their own feces from their neighbors' in order to dispose of them. Bound up in practices of *propreté* was the necessity of claiming one's feces as one's own, attributing to them the status of *propriété*. The sense of *propriété*, however, lends our feces some amount of *propreté*, relatively speaking, as the sight of our own shit does not provoke the same amount of disgust as the sight of someone else's. The tension that inheres in feces, which are poised precariously between *propreté* and *propriété*, challenging our conceptualizations of both, is mirrored by the representational tension we find in *Journal d'un corps*, where the most efficacious representation is one that negates itself, and where the represented object is displaced from its representation.

In the originary scene, the visceral representations of fear and destruction are all under the sign of negation: "Mon imagination *ne* me représente *pas* la chose dans son détail, je *ne* me dis *pas* . . . je *ne* me vois *pas* . . . je *ne* me représente *pas*" (My imagination does *not* represent the thing in all its detail, I *don't* tell myself . . . I *don't* see myself . . . I *don't* imagine) (21; my emphases). The narrator insists that he is not figuring or representing these things, that they are outside the field of representation, and yet "ils sont tous dans le hurlement de terreur que je pousse maintenant" (they are all there in the howl of terror I let out now) (21). Representation, which is a capacity we normally attribute to the mind or imagination as a conceptual operation, is instead displaced from these usual sites onto the body, which turns into a wordless, fecal cry. Similarly, the first entry of the diary (chronologically speaking), with its incantatory repetition of "je n'aurai plus peur" (I won't be afraid anymore), sidesteps representation and opts not to represent. By delivering up the bodily, fecal scene representing the invoked fear *before* he gives us access to the denial of representation enacted by the first entry, Pennac creates a strong tension between representation and its refusal by displacing representation, both chronologically and sequentially: the first chronological entry displaces representation by refusing to represent, whereas the first entry that we read displaces chronology, imposing a writerly, literary time instead that has the authorial/editorial voice taking precedence over the narrative one.

Pennac mobilizes this tension and displacement in order to place literature itself between *propreté* and *propriété*. The interval between narrative and authorial voices that is opened by a fictional diary poses the question of the literary, of who writes what, of what it means to attribute a voice to an author, to allow a person to own a voice, a text, a parcel of language and a way of using it. This literary question, like the fecal one, is bound up with the question of *propriété*, where *propriété* is a way of drawing and reinforcing the boundaries without which possession and property would be meaningless. *Propriété* is deeply caught up in the notions of internality and externality, and the originary scene, with its negative and displaced representation, insists on this. Just as the internalized feces are both *propre* and not (*propre* for being invisible; *impropre* for being waste matter that ought to be evacuated), as are the externalized feces (*propre* for being waste that has successfully been evacuated from our organism; *impropre* for being visible), so too does Pennac figure writing as paradoxically *(im)propre*. It is *impropre* in the etymological sense of this word insofar as the narrator refuses to claim the written representation as his, as *propre* to him ("je ne me représente pas," "je ne me dis pas," and "je ne me vois pas" are all ways of saying: this is not my representation, I am not the one who represents) and it is *propre* insofar as his body, which is undeniably and irrevocably his, is what comes to represent those things ("c'est tout *mon* corps qui hurle"; it is *my* whole body that screams). Furthermore, the rejected, *impropre* representation is *propre* in that the fantasy is imagined, lacking the materiality that is the necessary substrate for *malpropreté* (uncleanliness), which is itself tied to *impropriété* (impropriety), and the *propre* corporeal representation is *impropre* for being fecal, and not just fecal, but diarrheic.

This conflictual equilibrium between the *propre* and the *impropre* manifests itself in the passage as a troubling of the boundaries separating inside from outside as seen in the indistinction the narrator experiences between his body and his environment: "Diarrhea mixes with resin . . . I am covered in tears, drool, snot, resin and shit" (21). He is covered not only in himself and his own fluids, but in the tree's resin. This liquid excreted by the tree that holds him up is joined with the liquids that were formerly in him but are now outside him. The sense of *propriété*–if he is covered in the tree and the tree is covered in him, can one really maintain the boundaries that would normally distinguish boy from tree?–that would normally be present disappears when *propreté* does. It is significant that such a blurring of boundaries occurs through the transposition of what was previously inside to the outside: writing is the creation of a textual representation of a world that occurs through a process connecting the writer's mind to the text he produces, excreting thoughts into form, bridging interiority and exteriority. Excrement, in the narrator's case, is what is best able to figure the process of literary representation wherein the internal and the external are rendered accessible at the same time in a continual drawing and blurring of boundaries.

Boundary trouble is inherently *impropre,* a transgression of both *propreté* and *propriété,* and while Pennac's disregard for a literature of *propreté* can be easily seen in his foregrounding of the fecal, I want to turn to his vision of literature as one of *impropriété.* Rather than introducing the fecal into this text only to sanitize it by transforming its excrementality into literariness, Pennac takes advantage of the fecal to make the slippage between *propriété* and *propreté,* rejecting both. Pennac's excremental poetics, his vision of an excremental literature, is intimately tied to his desire to both democratize literature and to dirty it.

Shit for All, Literature for All

Pennac's 1992 essay *Comme un roman* (*Better Than Life*; literally, *Like a Novel*), lauded as a celebration of literature (deemed then, as now, to be in a state of crisis and attrition), can be seen as laying the groundwork for the fecal vision of *Journal d'un corps.* In *Comme un roman,* Pennac formulates a readerly Bill of Rights, which claims for readers rights such as "1. The Right to Not Read 2. The Right to Skip Pages . . . 5. The Right to Read Anything."[19] *Comme un roman* responds to the decline of the novel in an increasingly audiovisual society by claiming for literature the right to be free from *propriété.* Pennac calls for the democratization of literature so that it is no longer the property of elite arbiters of culture, to be distributed to readers according to their individual abilities and their access to a particular education. Literature, in this manifesto, should be a public good, there to be enjoyed by all however they want to. The only way to restore to literature its value is to be unafraid to handle it, treating it not as some precious artifact but as an everyday object. And in the case of *Journal d'un corps,* this everyday object is one that is traversed by feces, flatulence, saliva, sperm, urine, nasal polyps, nosebleeds—bodily products usually placed under the sign of shame or embarrassment, deemed anything

204 * DANIEL PENNAC'S EXCREMENTAL POETICS

but *propres,* but that all comes with the territory of having a body and inhabiting it every day. We can see further proof of Pennac's desire to liberate the text in the index that accompanies the novel, which, by mapping out the dizzying array of corporeal phenomena that the diary tracks, serves to enable the reader to skip pages and read out of order, following their desire and curiosity instead of succumbing to the pressure of linearity.[20] For Pennac, to liberate literature, refusing *propriété,* entails opening up literature to the *impropre* in both how we read and what we write.

Journal d'un corps calls attention to its own literariness, its construction, by calling attention to its fecal, *impropre* nature. It shows how what terrifies us gives us the material and the motivation for creation. By making this literary material fecal, a material we all have access to, Pennac's excremental poetics is a declaration of literary universalism: literature of and for all in the same way that defecation is a reality shared by all. No matter the various differences that have been codified into identity categories that sort humanity into hierarchies of race, sex, sexuality, class, or able-bodiedness: none of these is able to escape our fecal nature, and our feces cannot solidify or impose identity as these identity categories do. Our feces are not a part of us in the same way that our heart or bones or stomach are integrated parts of us, or the way our race, sex, sexuality, class, and able-bodiedness are considered parts of who we are.

Our gastrointestinal tract, and hence the feces traversing it, despite being perceived as inside us, is actually the presence of the outside in us: it is a tube that connects our mouth to our anus and makes us into a complicated donut. Pennac writes for the leaky, fecal donuts that we all are. What we have in *Journal d'un corps* is not so much writing the body, where the body is transformed into a textual experience, but the body elucidating what literature is through the narrator's excremental situation. The body claims that it is always already a textual experience in and through the fecal matter expressed. There is the body that is written, and then there is the body that writes: in *Journal d'un corps,* this first body is built on the second, which exercises a diarrheic poetics that turns the outside—the world—which is curiously, wondrously contained by our insides, into a model for writing. It is a vision for how we transform the world and represent it, for how we turn the world we take in into the world outside us, leaving traces behind for and in a world that will remain when we are no longer.

Returning to the originary scene, when the young narrator's sphincters cry out at the same time as his mouth cries out, what is represented is raw fear, in all its abjection and intensity. As readers, we transform this fear into something else just as the narrator's body transformed his fear into feces. What the fecal cry represents as a literary experience is not fear, but rather, freedom—a freedom that is not *propre* because it belongs to us all. Reading *Journal d'un corps* for its excremental poetics, we are presented with a challenge: first, to overcome our conditioned blindness to the scatological, which we assume because we aspire to be *propre*; and then, to embrace the literary lack of *propreté* to resist and undo our compulsion to transform literature into *propriété*. The challenge is a daunting one indeed, but one that contains the potential to join readers together in a joyous Célinian "caca communism."[21]

) CONCLUSION (

CACA COMMUNISM

***

Because it is not as you think, that only death matters. To live,
something you don't know about because it is susceptible to rot—to
live while rotting matters quite a bit. A harsh way to live: a way to
live the essential.

—Clarice Lispector, "Report on the Thing"

I have argued elsewhere that the excrementality of the French canon
is the means by which it might end the canon, that it figures an imperative to end the canon.[1] If shit levels difference and distinction and
the canon is the epitome of difference and distinction, then wouldn't
it follow that shit would, by nature, tend toward the abolition of the
canon? In the course of writing and revising this book, however, I've
come to reconsider that position.

Just as with the nation-state—which the canon serves,[2] as a durable manifestation of a national tradition that is so clearly, in the case
of a nation like France, also an imperialist one—the canon is rightfully
an object of critique. We ought to be critical of the exclusionary nature of the canon, of its capacity to efface and delegitimate cultural
production by minoritarian, marginal subjects. We ought to be critical of the way the canon has a kind of stranglehold on culture and on
the ways we think about culture. But in dwelling with the canonical
texts that make up *Cacaphonies'* corpus, I've come to also appreciate
the canon not as a hierarchical site of power, which it undeniably is,

but as a site of assembly, of community, as an experience that can be shared. The canon, against the ephemerality of trends in public opinion and taste, seems to have the capacity to perdure, to last beyond the never long enough interval of a lifetime. In other words, the canon is a kind of consolation for the fact that we end. It promises that some part of us—the experience and pleasure of reading, and, if we are authors, the creation of a text—will outlast us. The canon, in this regard, becomes a collective will and testament that we bequeath to the generations that follow and that testifies to the people we were when we are no longer.

Just as life is a kind of freedom that interrupts death and nonexistence and carves out a space within mortality for us to inhabit, so too does shit interrupt literature, carving out a space within the canon for the kind of egalitarianism—of caca communism—that is at odds with its inherently inegalitarian nature. Shit, by continually undermining the canon from within, holds open the possibility of freedom within the canon, of an unbounded experience of literary community or belonging that transcends time. Shit anchors the abstracted value of literature in the concrete experience of corporeality that produces it. Shit grounds literature by reminding us that to be human is to be embodied, to be subjected to the strictures of time and materiality, living always at risk of precarity.

Shit, in other words, is what makes literature human. But the kind of humanity that shit calls our attention to unceasingly is not the self-centering, destructive *Anthropos* of the Anthropocene or the appropriative human that makes of abstract universalism both an alibi and foundation for hierarchy. Rather, it is a concrete, corporeal humanity that situates its own ephemeral and precarious life within the larger ecological, planetary framework of fragility and interrelation constituted by a continual cycle between life and death.

This is what accounts for the constant tension between the canon and the shit it contains. The canon is literature trying to attain the status of the eternal, whereas shit is the resounding refusal of the eternal, a continual reminder of the impossibility of attaining the eternal. Shit can never be forever as shit is transformation and movement.

What starts out as food is processed into shit, is transformed from whatever it was into shit. And shit itself cannot remain shit, as it too breaks down and is transformed, its decomposing what enables something else to be composed.

The canon, while a dynamic object, as it is continually being formed, is one that would like to pass itself off as already fully formed. The canon needs shit in a way that shit does not need the canon. Shit is shit without the canon, but without shit, the canon risks ossifying into something lifeless: into an abstract humanism that, as with the abstract universalism that humanism, as an Enlightenment value, is so closely tied to, is the site of a constitutive exclusion. Shit injects into the canon a vital and urgent call to movement and transformation, to generation. Shit, as the transgressive material it is taken to be, reminds literature of its capacity to transgress.

Literature is a bit like the housecat: despite being domesticated through scholarship, criticism, and readerly narratives that, through their reproduction, attain the status of doxa and convention, literature remains a wild, unmasterable thing. This, I submit, is why we find shit from the beginning of French literature to its current manifestation— because literature, against the ceaseless attempts made to master it, needs to and desires to be continually reminded of its untameable, uncontainable potential. The canon's fecality is the presence of that potential. When literature taps into this potential that shit renders sensible, it invites caca communism as the modality by which it ought to be engaged with.

Literary caca communism, then, rather than end the canon and redistribute prestige so that works would be valued equally—a leveling of the distinction between authors or between texts—is a call to democratize literature so that it might be lived by everybody, just as fecality is an experience lived by every body. Recalling the utopian vision of the Communards, literature, then, as elucidated by the concrete fecal universalism that permeates it, would be a communal luxury: the canon for all.[3]

Rather than reject the canon, we can adopt Aimé Césaire's position toward it. Césaire loved the French language, refusing to be subjugated by it despite its being an instrument of colonization. Instead, he saw in a canonical figure like Stéphane Mallarmé an inspiration for transforming French: no matter if French didn't make room for him, he would make French his. Rather than reject French language and culture as being the tools and patrimony of the oppressor, Césaire insisted on inflecting it: "I am not a prisoner of the French language! . . . if I loved Mallarmé so much, it is because he showed me . . . that language is ultimately arbitrary. . . . my aim was to inflect French, to *transform* it to express, let's say, 'this me, this black-me, this creole-me, this Martinican-me, this Antillean-me.'"[4] Césaire, then, like Monique Wittig, who also rejects a narrative of being excluded from culture (going so far as to posit that the narrative of women's exclusion from the canon itself functions to "turn the canon into a male edifice"), would respond to Audre Lorde's oft-cited declaration that "the master's tools will never dismantle the master's house" by affirming that if tools can build something up, then tools can certainly take something down.[5] But to be sure, those tools would probably have to be wielded, precisely, by someone other than the master, given the obvious interest the master has in having a house (or more precisely, in others not having a house, or in having a bigger house than others). But that is indeed what Césaire and Wittig did as minoritarian subjects writing in French, digesting French language and culture and turning them into the materials with which to construct their own literary homes. The shit we find continually throughout the canon is an invitation, then, to do likewise: to make of French—of language, in general—a literary home, either by writing one's way into it, or by reading one's way into it. Wherever shit is found in the canon is a reminder that literature is a living thing, that the canon is, in effect, a literary body, one that, like any other body, can be moved, molded, transformed.

This utopian call for a communal appropriation and possession of the canon is not meant to downplay the very real and potent mechanisms of exclusions and inequality that are played out in and by the canon. The process by which certain texts are canonized is itself an inegalitarian one, and, in the French context, continues to favor texts produced by white, male authors. However, the democratic, universalizing energy of shit is in productive tension with the inegalitarian nature of the canon as it has been and is. This tension is what carries the capacity to transform the canon into a public good, detaching it from the constraints and coercion it currently signifies. Refusing to sanitize and deodorize our literary imaginary can produce a democratized relation to literature, one that is grounded in the corporeal universalism that is our fecality. If this corporeal, fecal universalism is allowed to be foregrounded, rather than occluded or denied, covered by the cloak of decorum and the blindness and silence that decorum demands, then it cannot help but have consequences for the canon of the future. Attending to the shit our present canon calls on us to hear requires, for those who hold it, abdicating the privilege of abstract universalism to enact instead a caca communism that takes seriously what the conjunction of *commun* and the suffix *-ism* points to: the art, process, and practice of a commonality that makes shit—and the literature that *Cacaphonies'* authors treat as shit—every body's destiny, every body's property.

ACKNOWLEDGMENTS

In the spring of 2018, Fox News and other right-wing media caught wind of a graduate seminar I was teaching on scatological French literature, and I became the target of unwelcome attention. While it was an unpleasant experience, it also came with the silver lining of learning that I had the full support of my colleagues and students at Harvard. I am grateful to Mariano Siskind, Joe Blackmore, Janet Beizer, Robin Kelsey, Heather Lantz, and Rachael Dane for their help in navigating a difficult situation. I am especially grateful to the students of "Cacaphonies" for their thoughtful engagement with our excremental texts that semester. I feel fortunate to call Romance Languages and Literatures and WGS my intellectual homes at Harvard: my colleagues' support for and encouragement of this project from its inception have helped me forge ahead and see things through to the end. I am grateful to my colleagues in the French section—Janet Beizer, Tom and Verena Conley, Virginie Greene, Sylvaine Guyot, Alice Jardine, Françoise Lionnet, and Kathy Richman—for looking so kindly on my insistence on casting the shared object of our study and teaching in a fecal light. The Radcliffe Institute of Advanced Studies very generously funded an exploratory seminar, "Close Encounters of the Fecal Kind," where a brilliant interdisciplinary group of fecal-minded folks—Warwick Anderson, Karen Chin, Dalie Giroux, David Howell, Nicholas Kawa, Lior Lobel, Alison Moore, and Susan Signe Morrison—expanded my fecal horizons. I am also grateful for the generous support I received from Harvard's Anne and

Jim Rothenberg Fund for Humanities Research as well as the Dean's Competitive Fund for Promising Scholarship.

This has been a project that has met with a fair amount of skepticism and resistance. I am grateful to Yannick Chevalier, Rebecca Colesworthy, Julie Elsky, Alice Kaplan, Michèle Longino, Brian Martin, Durba Mitra, Taylor Moore, Laure Murat, Roxanne Panchasi, Kashia Pieprzak, Maurie Samuels, Helen Solterer, and Olivier Wagner for their belief in *Cacaphonies*' worth. My thanks also go to Grace An, Maxime Blanchard, Bruno Penteado, Emma Wilson, and Lucas Wood for expressing enthusiasm for the project and providing venues for sharing this work publicly.

Conversations and exchanges with Nancy Armstrong and Leonard Tennenhouse, Howard Bloch, Morgane Cadieu, Bruno Chaouat, Rey Chow, Quentin Deluermoz, Anne Garréta, Lucas Hollister, Lynne Huffer, Joy Kim, Agathe Novak-Lechevalier, Debarati Sanyal, and Christy Wampole have helped me work through ideas and given me food for thought. I am grateful to Hannah Freed-Thall, Vivian Huang, Durba Mitra, and Annette Lienau for their insightful reading and commenting on parts of the manuscript at various stages. And to the many people who, over the past few years, have kept their fecal feelers out for me, sending me the fecal tidbits they come across: thank you for helping to fertilize my thinking.

Odile Harter was of invaluable help in showing me how to navigate the embarrassment of riches that is the Harvard Libraries' extensive collections. Endless thanks to the Libraries for getting me literally everything I asked for. My thanks also to Anne Ratnoff for her research assistance at the beginning stages of the project, when I needed it most.

I would like to thank the members of my working group—David Atherton, Sarah Dimick, Annette Lienau, Nicole Sütterlin, Naomi Weiss, Saul Zaritt—for their solidarity and companionship; knowing that we are writing and reading together even as we are writing and reading apart has been a comfort.

My deepest thanks to Leah Pennywark, for taking a chance on this book and believing in it, and to Anne Carter, Eric Lundgren,

ACKNOWLEDGMENTS * 215

Rachel Moeller, and Mike Stoffel—it has been a pleasure to work with the University of Minnesota Press. My endless gratitude to the manuscript's readers: Thangam Ravindranathan's feedback was generative and her enthusiastic response and affirmation that fecality is indeed a rich site for confirming what only literature can know helped sustain me during the troughs of my writing. Words cannot begin to capture my indebtedness to Lynne Huffer, who is the most careful, incisive, and generous reader, with an almost unsettling capacity to pinpoint what a work's core argument or concept is. Rewriting and revising have been a source of awe, as each time I've responded to and worked through one of Lynne's comments, things have just clicked into place, her feedback a continual set of epiphanies. I am so grateful she saw through what the manuscript was to the book it could be.

Thanks also to Mark Mastromarino, who makes poetry of indexes, and to Nicholas Taylor for his meticulous copyediting.

And thank you to my parents, whose matter-of-factness around fecality made it possible for me to see all the shit in this literature that others could not or would not see. Their refusing the fecal taboo has made this book possible.

Last but not least, my thanks to those who have lived with this book as much as I have. My thanks to Minou and Zazie, the best cats a human could ask for, and beautiful reminders of what it means to be a creature, to be embodied. Thanks also to Dua Lipa and *Future Nostalgia* for providing me the soundtrack for my writing. Finally, my thanks to Hannah Frydman, whose name appears here for the first time but could have appeared in every single paragraph and line before this. Hannah is my first and last reader (with many readings in between), skeptic and sounding board, illuminating interlocutor, and community. Thank you for giving me so much shit.

NOTES

Introduction

1. Latour, *We Have Never Been Modern.*

2. Even as we become increasingly cyborgized, no amount of integrating tech into our fleshly bodies can do away with the continual production and elimination of fecal matter.

3. Enders, *Gut.* This reinvestment in the gut can also be seen in humanistic scholarship outside waste studies, as evidenced by Wilson, *Gut Feminism,* which seeks to center the gut as a thinking organ in feminist theory as a way to reconcile feminist theory with biology.

4. The anthropologist Robin Nagle (New York City's Department of Sanitation's anthropologist-in-residence) founded the website Discard Studies.com, dedicated to "social studies of waste, pollution, and externalities," and opts for the term "discard studies" over "waste studies." As her collaborator, Max Liboiron, explains it, "The crux of the argument is that most people already have an idea of what 'waste' is, yet the main thrust of this genre of research is to denaturalize and offer critical alternatives to popular and normative notions of waste. Thus, we use 'discard studies' instead of 'waste studies' to ensure that the categories of what is systematically left out, devalued, left behind, ruined, and externalized are left open" ("Why 'Discard Studies'?"). It is precisely around exclusion that I opt out of "discard studies" to refer to "waste studies" instead, because "discard studies" leaves out the process of defecation that produces the human waste we call shit. Shit is waste, it is not a discard.

5. Anthropologists such as Brenda Chalfin, Nicholas Kawa, and Sophia Stamatopoulou-Robbins have been working on the waste front lines,

examining waste practices in Ghana, the American Midwest, and Palestine. See Chalfin, "Public Things, Excremental Politics"; Kawa, "Mend to the Metabolic Rift?"; and Stamatopoulou-Robbins, *Waste Siege*.

6. See Douglas, *Purity and Danger*; Bauman, *Wasted Lives*; Hawkins, *Ethics of Waste*; and Thompson, *Rubbish Theory*. Waste studies has also found a companion field in the material turn that has taken place in the humanities as a counterreaction to the dominance of post-structuralism as a theoretical paradigm. Under the broad and heterogeneous aegis of New Materialisms, thinkers such as Jane Bennett and Bruno Latour have helped create a new, noninstrumentalizing sensibility attuned to things as having an agency of their own, with Bennett calling on us to recognize the "vital materialism" of things, and Latour using the term "actant" to expand our notion of activity and agency beyond the human. See Bennett, *Vibrant Matter*, 17; and Latour, *Reassembling the Social*, 54.

7. See Morrison, *Excrement in the Late Middle Ages*; Guynn, *Pure Filth*; Persels and Ganim, *Fecal Matters*; and Stockton, *Playing Dirty*, for studies of medieval and early modern shit. Rachele Dini is a leading voice in this literary turn toward waste as the founder of LiteraryWaste.com, a network of literary scholars that cuts across the usual demarcations of national tradition and period that organize literary studies to demonstrate (as the organization states on its homepage) "that the literary representation of waste across media is as important as the conceptualisation of waste by sociologists, economists, anthropologists, and psychologists." See Dini, *Consumerism, Waste, and Re-Use*; Schmidt, *Poetics of Waste*; Kramer, *Scatology and Civility*; and Morrison, *Literature of Waste*, for recent examples of literary waste studies concerned with modern waste. While much of this work is not on shit, per se, its openness to fecality as a form of waste maintains excremental possibility and invites work to be done on fecal matter.

8. Morrison, *Excrement in the Late Middle Ages*, 154.

9. Morrison, in her work on medieval excrement, goes even further in defending the use of *shit* over its more polite alternatives, citing Boccaccio's remarks in *The Decameron* on the well-ordered mind's incapacity to be corrupted by language to argue that "if you find my book unpleasant, it can only mean your mind is corrupt" (17).

10. Bataille, *Story of the Eye*, 114–15. The bracketed notes are the translator's.

11. Bataille, *Blue of Noon*, 15. Translation modified to translate *fesse* as *ass* rather than *crotch*.

12. Jean-François Louette notes that this magazine was probably based on *La Révolution surréaliste*. See Louette, "Notes," in Bataille, *Romans et récits*, 1089n40.

13. Bataille, in his writing on Sade, performs this dematerialization and abstraction, as when he quotes a coprophagic scene from Sade not to discuss the shit-eating in its materiality, but as an example of appropriation as a process that produces homogeneity. See Bataille, "The Use Value of D.A.F. Sade," in *Visions of Excess*, 95. In his second version of "The Use Value of D.A.F. Sade" (not translated into English), Bataille describes the way a reaction such as laughter to the excremental strips it of its materiality, turning it into an ideological and abstract object: "[Excretion] becomes ideological insofar as the excremental object of spasmodic contractions is merely an image and not a specific quantity of sperm, urine, blood, or excrement." Bataille, "La valeur de l'usage de D.A.F. de Sade (2)," in *Œuvres complètes*, 71. Here and elsewhere, if no English-language source is cited, a translation is mine.

14. Louette, "Notes," in Bataille, *Romans et récits*, 1097–98n115.

15. Louis Aragon, cited in Bataille, 1098n115.

16. Casually, as an aside, Bataille links *scatologie* to *hétérologie* in a footnote, defining *scatologie* as the "double of an abstract term like *heterology*." Georges Bataille, "Dossier de la polémique avec André Breton," in *Œuvres complètes*, 62. In his "Dossier 'Hétérologie,'" scatology is nowhere to be found despite being heterology's double. Bataille, *Œuvres complètes*, 165–202. It's elsewhere, in a succinct section on "Appropriation and Excretion," that Bataille ties the actually scatological to the heterological by identifying fecal matter, along with sperm and menstrual blood, as being a "(heterogeneous) *foreign body*." Bataille, "Use Value of D.A.F. Sade," in *Œuvres complètes*, 94.

17. Bataille, *Accursed Share*, 28–29. While Bataille conceives of the sun in terms of anality in "Solar Anus" and "Jesuve," doing so privileges the sun as the basis of comparison to which the anal is made subordinate. The sun is the starting point, the anus a metaphor or analogy deployed in service of the sun. Moreover, anality does not equal fecality: the anus is the orifice through which feces most often pass but it is not constitutively fecal (as demonstrated in individuals with colostomies who defecate via a stoma). Even in these most anal of Bataille's texts, shit remains offstage. In "Solar Anus," we can see Bataille's penchant for metaphor in his reading of volcanoes as the earth's anus and magma as excrement. See Bataille, "Solar Anus," in *Visions of Excess*, 8. Excrement and the anus are not taken on their own terms; they are used to recast geological phenomena. Even in the text's explosive closing, which

evokes the "intact anus" (9) of the eighteen-year-old girl the narrator wishes to violate, shit—that is to say, fecal matter, the real stuff that comes out of our bodies as opposed to the metaphorical layer that Bataille turns shit into—is absent. In describing said intact anus, Bataille turns not to the shit that one might find there but to the sun. In a brilliantly solar flourish, Bataille transforms the anus from a lowly conduit for fecal matter into something cosmic: "The solar annulus is the intact anus of her body at eighteen years to which nothing sufficiently blinding can be compared except the sun, even though the anus is night" (9). In "Jesuve," Bataille evokes "the shit-smeared and obscene anuses of certain apes" but does so to focus on the anal over the fecal, describing with verve "these filthy protuberances, dazzlingly colored excremental skulls, sometimes dappled, going from shocking pink to an extraordinarily horrible, pearly violet." See Bataille, "Jesuve," in *Visions of Excess*, 75. None of that descriptive energy is used to describe the shit that smears these anuses and makes them excremental, to describe their color, their odor, their consistency, their materiality—shit, for Bataille, is peripheral in relation to anality. The text discusses the evolution of ape anus to human anus as entailing the development of buttocks, wherein the anus "secluded itself deep within flesh" (77), thereby effacing the shit smears characterizing ape anality.

18. See, for example, Hussey, *Beast at Heaven's Gate*; Crowley, "*Postface à la transgression*"; Surkis, "No Fun and Games"; Patry, *L'Interdit, la transgression*; and Guerlac, *Literary Polemics*.

19. See Noys, "Georges Bataille's Base Materialism," for an elaboration of base materialism that places it in relation to the other forms of materialism Bataille is engaging with. For more on Bataille's aesthetic vision, grounded in the *informe*, see Krauss, "'Informe' without Conclusion," as well as the catalog for the exhibit at the Centre Pompidou on formlessness curated by Krauss and Yve-Alain Bois, *Formless*.

20. Bataille, "Formless," in *Visions of Excess*, 31. Where Bataille turns to formlessness to thwart hierarchy, *Cacaphonies*' writers demonstrate that we have simply to turn away from abstracted forms—not form in general—in order to do so.

21. Bataille, 31.

22. Freud, "Character and Anal Erotism," in *Standard Edition*, vol. 9, 167–76.

23. Freud, "From the History of an Infantile Neurosis," in *Standard Edition*, vol. 17, 80.

24. See Freud, "Character and Anal Erotism," 169–70; and Freud, "Three Essays on the Theory of Sexuality," in *Standard Edition,* vol. 7, 184–86.

25. See Chare, *Auschwitz and Afterimages,* which charges most uses of Kristevan abjection as focusing on the physical phenomena deemed abject at the expense of forgetting the importance of literature and literary style for Kristeva's thought.

26. This is not to say that literary critical work done on scatological texts hews to a strictly psychoanalytic analysis. Susan Signe Morrison in her work on Chaucer draws on Deleuze, Jed Esty in his work on post-independence African literature is primarily invested in postcolonial theory, Gary Mole in his work on Holocaust fiction attends to historical and anthropological perspectives and engages with the Frankfurt school. But by and large, even works that transcend a psychoanalytic framework do not bypass the requisite engagement with Freud and/or Kristeva, which are expected references precisely because of the dominance psychoanalysis has as a theoretical account of fecality. See Morrison, *Excrement in the Middle Ages*; Esty, "Excremental Postcolonialism"; and Mole, "Scatology, Chopped Liver."

27. See especially chapter 1 of Hunt, *Inventing Human Rights.* See also Keen, *Empathy and the Novel.* Popular journalism also abounds with articles and essays on literature's capacity to teach us to be human through instilling empathy. See Bury, "Reading Literary Fiction"; Hammond, "Does Reading Make Us Better"; and Penguin Random House, "How Fiction Teaches Us."

28. This is the subject of my first book, *Unbecoming Language,* which examines Nathalie Sarraute, Monique Wittig, and Anne Garréta's works for their wielding of an unbecoming language that, far from shoring up the identitarian subject, is used to erode the self and combat the difference that is foundational to the hierarchy that arises concomitantly with identities.

29. *Cacaphonies* avoids making the kind of argument about national character that we find in a text like Alan Dundes's *Life Is Like a Chicken Coop Ladder,* which argues that Germans are obsessed with shit.

30. Even if this is nothing but urban legend, it is one that is commonly recounted, whereas Anglophones do not routinely speak of "How do you do?" or "How is it going" as having excremental origins. What matters is less the accuracy of this narrative and more the fact that it is solidly anchored in the popular imaginary.

31. Elias, *Civilizing Process,* 109–21. Elias himself has been properly conditioned insofar as he uses the euphemism "natural functions" to speak of defecation.

32. *Étron* is defined in the *Trésor de la langue française* as "matière fécale (de l'homme ou de certains animaux) consistante et moulée" (fecal matter [from humans and certain animals] that is substantial and molded) and *crotte* as "fiente globuleuse plus ou moins dure de certains animaux et, *p. ext.,* tout excrément solide (animal et humain)" (globular excrement from certain animals that is more or less hard and, by extension, any solid excrement [animal and human]). *Étron* is thus concerned more with shape and *crotte* with solidity.

33. The late eighteenth century is also situated as the beginning of the modern, following the French Revolution, but I would identify the late eighteenth century as being simply the beginning of the long nineteenth.

34. See Alain Corbin's classic *The Foul and the Fragrant* for an account of the progressive deodorization of the French imaginary that took place from 1750 through the nineteenth century (the period of the urbanization of modernity, namely, Haussmannization), which constituted a wide cultural shift away from a quotidian lived in proximity to excrement and waste toward a "purer" sensorial regimen. Turning to the following century, Kristin Ross and Roland Barthes take up the twentieth-century obsession with cleanliness, with Ross tying the twentieth century's departure from an outdated nineteenth-century set of hygienic norms to decolonization and increasing Americanization, and Barthes tying it to the transformation of the bourgeoisie with the advent of an industrial, multinational capitalism operating through technological advances unknown to the nineteenth century. Ross, *Fast Cars, Clean Bodies*; Barthes, *Mythologies*.

35. As a call for papers on the excremental nineteenth century puts it, "En dehors des textes à vocation comique, le XIXe siècle interdit l'excrémentiel en régime littéraire, qu'il s'agisse des censeurs au nom de la morale, ou des auteurs au nom de la beauté" (Outside of comic texts, the nineteenth century excludes excrementality in the literary domain, either through censors acting on behalf of morality, or authors acting in the name of beauty). See https://www.fabula.org/actualites/l-excrementiel-au-xixe-siecle_96859.php.

36. Even if the culture of this moment may have departed from its Rabelaisian predecessors, the scholarship on nineteenth-century French studies has, in recent years, demonstrated a keen interest in the century in its corporeality, in particular, along digestive lines. See, for example, Mathias and Moore, *Gut Feeling and Digestive Health*; and Janet Beizer's monograph in process on food studies and consumption. And as mentioned in the prior note, at the time of writing (2020), Marie-Ange Fougère is editing a volume,

L'Excrémentiel au XIXe siècle (*The Excremental in the Nineteenth Century*), to be published by Du Lérot.

37. For more on early modern fecality's intertwining of corporeality and concept, see Persels and Ganim, *Fecal Matters*; and Guynn, *Pure Filth.*

38. See Kalifa, *Les Bas-fonds,* 42–51, for an overview of this systematic association of society's undesirables with excrementality.

39. Bonneuil and Fressoz, *L'Événement anthropocène,* 214.

40. Bonneuil and Fressoz, 215.

41. Mbembe, *Necropolitics,* 2.

42. Wittig, *Straight Mind.*

43. McSweeney, *Necropastoral,* 3.

44. "The Necropastoral is not an 'alternative' version of reality but it is a place where the farcical and outrageous horrors of Anthropocenic 'life' are made visible as Death." McSweeney, "What Is the Necropastoral?"

45. See Chaouat, "Ce que chier veut dire," for an excellent elaboration of the Nazis' lethal excremental logic.

46. French universalism isn't a uniquely post-revolutionary invention, as Naomi Schor demonstrates in tracing universalism back to its religious, Catholic roots, but its codification into the basis of citizenship is a post-revolutionary development. See Schor, "Crisis of French Universalism," 44.

47. This tension between particular identity and universality is the continual thorn in universalism's side, and remains in a perpetual state of conflictual irresolution. For a thinker like Ernesto Laclau, this tension cannot be resolved and is universalism's constitutive paradox. For him, this situation is not a negative one, as it is what he considers to be the structural impossibility of universalism that makes democracy possible. See Laclau, "Universalism, Particularism."

48. Samuels, *Right to Difference,* 9–10.

49. Schor, "Crisis of French Universalism," 64.

50. Scott, *Parité!,* 5.

51. Scott, 5.

52. Hartman, *Scenes of Subjection,* 153–54.

53. Schor, "Crisis of French Universalism," 47.

54. Césaire, "Letter to Maurice Thorez," 152.

55. Scott, *Parité!,* 56–57. See chapter 3 for an attentive account of the *paritaristes'* argumentation for an anatomical dualism that would not fall into the concreteness of sexual difference.

56. To this day, despite the *parité* law having been adopted two decades

ago, the number of women in the French legislature falls well short of the 50 percent aimed for by the *paritaristes*. The 2017 elections saw women make up a record 38.7 percent in the Assemblée nationale and 31.6 percent in the Sénat. See Brunner and Maurin, *Rapport sur les inégalités*.

57. Butler, *Frames of War*, 32.

58. Butler, 30.

59. Bernard Frechtman's translation of this essay flushes out some of the fecality implied in the original title, by translating it as "What Remains of a Rembrandt Torn into Four Equal Pieces and Flushed Down the Toilet," a translation that adds a flush that doesn't exist in the original, which has the pieces of the Rembrandt being stuffed (*foutu*) in the *chiottes,* or shitter. Charlotte Mandell's later translation, "What Remains of a Rembrandt Torn into Little Squares All the Same Size and Shot Down the Toilet," also evokes flushing, referring to the disappearance of a Rembrandt rather than its being obscenely displayed like a turd someone has not flushed down.

60. Genet, trans. Mandell, "What Remains of a Rembrandt," 92. Genet later elaborates that this universal identity is not simply that "every man is like every other" but that "every man is all other men" (96).

61. "Beneath his crumpled, rough, dingy clothes, his body must have been dirty and wrinkled. His mouth was soft and protected by a badly trimmed moustache" (93).

62. While periodization is always fraught, just as the nineteenth century is widely considered to extend beyond the strict delineation of the hundred-year century, I consider literature to still be in a long twentieth century, insofar as there are no real formal innovations or movements that mark a significant departure from all the literary developments of the twentieth century—the century where everything became possible, literarily. The turning point between the nineteenth and twentieth centuries is often taken to be World War One (see Rabaté, *1913*), but I take Céline rather than Marcel Proust to be the beginning of twentieth-century literature: not literature produced during the war, but the first formally innovative writing of the war.

63. Marin, *Food for Thought*, 101–2.

64. Marin, 102.

65. Marin, 111.

66. Yes, corn kernels pass through undigested, but if chewed properly, they too turn into shit, indistinguishable from whatever other foods were eaten with the corn.

67. Rousseau, quoted in Derrida, *Of Grammatology*, 7.

1. Céline

1. The author Philippe Sollers describes the problem of Céline as follows: "One is obligated to treat him as a 'great writer,' he's a monster that's all the more active the more one rejects or censors him, he eludes his admirers along with his adversaries, no academy can confine him, no academic discourse define him, he flees, he tricks, he exceeds, he is the devil in 'Pléiade' (like Sade), he is crime in liberty, the printing of the inadmissible, a nightmare for eternity" (*Céline*, 72).

2. A variation of this can be seen in the writer André Gide's defense of Céline's anti-Semitic ravings in "Les Juifs, Céline et Maritain," a review of the anti-Semitic pamphlet *Bagatelles pours un massacre,* arguing that his anti-Semitism is not to be taken seriously at all as it is all a joke for Céline. While Gide's response does not condemn the pamphleteer to elevate the novelist, it effectively elevates Céline as a literary creator—it's his literary writing that is his real work, while the anti-Semitic stuff isn't serious—and maintains a division between the literary and the political by downplaying the latter in favor of the former.

3. This third approach is the most common one as temporal distance from World War II and its massacre of Jews affords a critical distance that enables critics to think together Céline the writer and Céline the pamphleteer. As David Carroll puts it simply, "[Céline's] antimimetic poetics and anti-Semitism, and his poetic and political visions, were inextricably linked together and . . . no critic can afford to ignore the one in order to either praise or condemn the other" (*French Literary Fascism,* 194).

4. An entire book has been published dedicated to exploring the impact of that single word, *ça.* See Kanony, *Céline?*

5. See Godard, *Henri Godard présente "Mort à crédit"*; and Godard, *À travers Céline.*

6. As mentioned earlier, for most critics, Céline's poetics originate from the same source as his politics—a continuity that Julia Kristeva would place under a psychoanalytic sign, so that their unified nature tracks back to the unconscious—and cannot be separated. I find such arguments convincing, but the will to keep Céline's anti-Semitism foregrounded, on the same plane as his literary writing, leads to the occlusion of things that are as present as his anti-Semitism, such as his excrementality. I am not denying the anti-Semitism, but rather allowing the excremental to be foregrounded, to see what kind of a reading ensues from this shift in focus, in depth of field.

7. This is not to say that the psychical isn't itself physical or material,

but that the focus shifts from an immediate or seemingly unmediated experience of the material and physical to a position invested instead in signification and narrative, if we consider psychoanalysis as being, at its core, the production of narrative by analysand and analyst to write a person into comprehensible being. We can see more banal psychoanalytic readings of Céline in Knapp, *Céline,* which passes over the materiality of excrement to explain it away as a sign of narcissism and of enmity for society, or as a manifestation of the effect withholding and rigid parents have on their developing child.

8. Barthes, *Sade, Fourier, Loyola,* 137.

9. See Kaplan, *Reproductions of Banality,* 108–9; and the introduction to Roussin, Schaffner, and Tettamanzi, *Céline à l'épreuve.*

10. Kaplan, *Reproductions of Banality,* 110.

11. Barthes, *Sade, Fourier, Loyola,* 137.

12. Certainly, excrementality and modernism are not a particularly surprising combination, and traditional accounts of French literature do not claim the total absence of the fecal from its modern texts: the scatological dimension of writers like Céline and Samuel Beckett, for instance, are not secrets. However, the scatology of twentieth-century key texts is treated as incidental, with the literary innovation of their authors being situated elsewhere, such as in the fragmentation of subjectivity, whereas the scatological dimension of premodern and early modern texts are framed as being more essential than is the case for their modern counterparts.

13. *Bagatelles pour un massacre* was not Céline's first political pamphlet: *Mea Culpa,* published the previous year, 1936, was his first, but this earlier work of political writing, which described his disappointment in humanity after a visit to the USSR led him to see communism as destined to fail because of humanity's inherent egoism, had none of the fascist, right-wing, anti-Semitic ideology that would characterize *Bagatelles pour un massacre, L'École des cadavres,* and *Les Beaux Draps.*

14. Céline, *Death on the Installment Plan,* 47; Céline, *Romans I,* 544. In subsequent parenthetical references, the first page number is from the English translation, the second from the original French. I occasionally amend Ralph Manheim's translation.

15. Céline is attached to his narrator having some concrete memory of the past century, and has Ferdinand born two years before he was, in 1892. The two extra years that Ferdinand gains positions him as a more reliable narrator than Céline for remembering the past century.

16. For more on Céline's nostalgia, melancholy, and identification with

a nineteenth century that he did not actually know, see Sugiura, "Perte et deuil," which maps Céline's sense of loss and a "Célinian poetic of melancholy" (200) onto Ferdinand as a character continually grieving the people and the time he has lost.

17. For those unfamiliar with the imperfect subjunctive, it is an extraordinarily refined and literary tense. There is no grammatical equivalent in English, but as far as equivalent registers go, speaking in the imperfect subjunctive tense would be similar to speaking like the King James Version of the Bible.

18. Céline uses ellipses frequently in his writing. Any ellipses I insert will be done so in brackets to distinguish from his ellipses.

19. As Rachele Dini puts it, evocatively, "Where dirt is matter out of place, waste is matter out of time" (*Consumerism, Waste, and Re-Use*, 5).

20. The number of pages depends on what edition of *Mort à crédit* one is reading. In the translation, it is twenty-one pages, whereas in the Pléiade edition, it is twenty-three pages, and in the bulkier Folio edition, thirty-two pages. I give page numbers here in order to communicate a sense of duration, to show how Céline moves away from the excremental for a considerable amount of time before returning, as he will, over and over, to Ferdinand's shit.

21. In the French, given that *faisait* can also mean to defecate, in addition to acting, this quotation can also be read as indicating Ferdinand's shared excrementality with the dog.

22. For more on Céline's ambivalence toward the maternal, see Renard, *Céline*. Granted, there are other kinds of psychoanalytic readings of Céline, such as Kristeva's, which focuses more on what Céline does with language, or Isabelle Blondiaux's, which also focuses on Céline's writing, treating it, rather than the man, as being psychotic, or Jean-Charles Huchet's, which takes up instead the question of perverse sexuality. See Kristeva, *Powers of Horror*; Blondiaux, *Une écriture psychotique*; and Huchet, "La Clinique littéraire de Céline." The psychoanalytically-oriented critics who treat Céline's excrementality tend to engage in a straightforward type of criticism where an excremental scene is taken to symbolize some aspect of Ferdinand or Céline's psyche.

23. Ferdman, "'I Had to Wear Pampers'"; Holmes, "Slanted Toilet."

24. See chapter 6 of Walker, *Consumer Chronicles*, for a discussion of *Mort à crédit* as a socioeconomic history relating the demise of small shopkeepers like Céline's and Ferdinand's mothers in a new industrial age of mass production.

25. See Thompson, "Time, Work-Discipline," for a discussion of the important role watches played in inculcating workers into the rhythms of capitalist time.

26. Céline, *L. F. Céline*, 71, 75. Godard insists on the weight that mortality casts on Céline throughout his various works on the author, and Céline's obsession with death has led Pierre-Marie Miroux to consecrate a lengthy monograph to the subject. See Godard, *Henri Godard présente "Mort à crédit"*; Godard, *À travers Céline*; Godard, *Poétique de Céline*; Miroux, *Matière et lumière*.

27. For more on the bivalent nature of shit, see chapter 4 of Miroux, which casts shit as both imprisoning and liberating.

28. See Steiner, "Cry Havoc"; Kaplan, *Reproductions of Banality*; Wolf, *Le Peuple dans le roman français*; and Benjamin, "Present Social Situation."

29. *Bagatelles pour un massacre* is filled with anti-Semitic and homophobic vitriol directed at Proust, whose polished language and lyricism are antipodal to Céline's.

30. While Auguste enthusiastically goes to the World Exposition of 1900, Caroline dies that year, not having to contend with the fearsome technologies promised by the twentieth. See Sugiura, "Perte et deuil," for more on Caroline as a figure representing the refusal of industrialization.

31. Despite a shared antipathy toward capitalism and the inequity it produces, Céline would never adhere to France's Communist Party and, after a visit to the USSR, wrote his first pamphlet, *Mea Culpa*, as a critique of communism, seeing in it no solution to the woes of capitalism.

32. For instance, some women see dealing with other people's waste as more abject than selling sex, despite the stigmatized nature of sex work, and choose to do the latter rather than have a lower-paying job as a cleaning woman where they are forced to scrub toilets covered with someone else's feces. Bienaimé, "Le Prix du sexe."

33. As Dominique Laporte argues, private property and personal identity are a product of shit, of the reflexive question "Is this shit mine or someone else's?" that follows any confrontation with shit (*History of Shit*, 28–31).

34. Kaplan elegantly describes the way "this moment of loss [bodily elimination] is also the great moment of leveling—the ultimate basis of human sociability" (*Reproductions of Banality*, 110).

35. Céline, *Voyage au bout de la nuit*, 252. I have opted for my own translation over Ralph Manheim's "a joyous shitting communism," which loses both the alliteration of *caca* with *communism* and replaces *caca*, a noun that serves as an adjective, with the present participle of *to shit*. Céline, *Journey to the End of the Night*, 169.

36. I have forced students to read this passage out loud together in class, which required them to overcome their evident disgust.

37. Godard sees the body in this intense passage, where passengers are literally covered in their insides, anticipating its future: "In expelling outside himself a part of himself that is an object of repulsion, the body merely anticipates what it is itself called on to become: putrefaction" (*Henri Godard présente "Mort à crédit,"* 47). Roussin, in contrast, sees the scene's proliferating vomit as mirroring Céline's logorrheic way of narrating, where Céline's writerly impetus is the will to say everything, to vomit up everything. Against the backdrop of World War I, this "everything" that needs to be purged is the language of heroism, of patriotism, that sent so many men to their deaths, with the corporeal act of vomiting itself the only adequate expression of the horror of life in the trenches ("Tout dire," 260).

38. Naturalism, as conceived by Zola, combined Balzac's desire to capture the world as precisely as possible with the scientific positivism that marked the latter half of the nineteenth century. Zola envisioned the novel as a kind of laboratory or scientific experiment that could demonstrate the effects of certain conditions on a test subject, showing how environmental or hereditary factors could produce, for example, an alcoholic.

39. Céline, "Hommage à Zola."

40. Céline, 90.

41. See Earle, "*Les Deux Cents Familles,*" for a discussion of how Céline's sense of authenticity is grounded in emotion. Given the equation of emotion with the gut as a center of such feeling, it is little surprise that Céline would be invested in both the excremental and the emotional.

42. Manheim translates *culottes* as *pants*, which I've amended to *underwear*: by the time of the novel's writing, *pantalon* had replaced *culottes* to mean *pants*, with *culottes* now referring to undergarments. He also translates *tinette* here as *bowl* rather than as the waste receptacle beneath the toilet, which attenuates the strong material association between *tinette* and shit.

43. The idea of shit in Céline being used to call attention to process and transformation is reinforced by key moments of development in the novel being accompanied by dramatic scatological scenes. When he receives his *certificat d'études* (certificate of studies), Ferdinand and all his classmates shit themselves (134; 633). Their transformation from uneducated to educated is marked by a collective defecation. At another point later on in the novel, when Ferdinand beats his father so severely he nearly dies (316–18; 822–24)—a passage that has been oft-cited as exemplifying the Oedipal complex at work in Céline's writing—this moment of physical violence is

followed by Ferdinand's defecating uncontrollably: "I've got a spasm in my asshole . . . I shit in my pants" (318; 824). Critics have observed how this is a key scene narratively as it marks the end of the first part of the novel and is the point at which Ferdinand leaves home for good, replacing his biological father with the father figure of the scientist–inventor–conman Courtial des Pereires. That is, the scene marks the transformation of Ferdinand from the son to Ferdinand the fatherless. Such a significant transition is marked by the abundant production of fecal matter.

44. But, as noted earlier, this reinforcement of boundaries, which is experienced by all, as defecation is experienced by all, ultimately winds up gathering everyone together into a catastrophic commonality of caca.

45. We see a glimpse of this when Céline has Ferdinand describe how Clémence's prolonged constipation of eight days becomes Auguste's obsession and source of fear (129; 628). While Ferdinand suffers from the opposite problem as Clémence, defecating too easily, his defecation, like her constipation, poses a problem that cannot be easily solved.

46. See Whorton, *Inner Hygiene*, which discusses the widely held belief that constipation is fatal because our fecal matter is viewed as poisoning us if it remains inside us. Céline also held constipation in horror as something to be avoided at all costs. For him, shit was something that needed to circulate and he would receive an enema every day after the age of forty-one (see Kanony, *Céline?*, 157–59). We can see this fear of constipation given literary form in the fecal ravings of a postwar text like *Féerie pour une autre fois* (*Fable for Another Time*). See Hainge, "Language of Suffering," for a discussion of how such ravings constitute a writing of pain exceeding the language of suffering to make language itself suffer.

47. See Godard, *À travers Céline*, 171–73; Miroux, *Matière et lumière,* especially part 2.

48. Godard, *Henri Godard présente "Mort à crédit,"* 97.

49. Kaplan, *Reproductions of Banality*, 114.

50. *Féerique* can be translated roughly into English as *magical*, but is associated in French, etymologically and conceptually, with the *fée*, or fairy—those diaphanous creatures who inhabit matter so much more lightly than we humans.

51. Godard, *À travers Céline*, 171–73; Miroux, *Matière et lumière*, 67.

52. Miroux, 72.

53. For a critique of modern waste management, see Rockefeller, "Civilization and Sludge"; and Yorifuji and Fujita, *Au cœur du caca.*

54. See Hoffmann, *Les Paradoxes de la postérité,* for a discussion of this death-defying function that we attribute to writing.

55. If you look at a dictionary like *Le Trésor de la langue française,* much of the vulgar vocabulary that Céline uses is illustrated in the dictionary's definitions with quotations from his works. And the Pléiade edition of his novels includes a lengthy and much needed glossary of Céline's invented language.

56. Monique Wittig, in *Le Chantier littéraire,* insists on writing as labor and on language as matter, advancing thus a conception of literature as a profoundly material enterprise. As Wittig writes, comparing the nature of language to the nature of light, which is both wave and particle, "In the same way, the nature of language is double, participating at the same time in abstraction, in conceptual thought insofar as it is opposed to the real and to the material, [acting as] the signified to the signifier, the figurative to the proper, and participating in the material order through words and their geographical and sonic space. This is why it is possible to affirm that language participates in the real, that it is in fact just as real as the referent to which one opposes it, just as real as social relations and as physical reality since it is part of both" (45–46). Wittig also describes language as "visible, audible, palpable, and tasteable" (61). See chapter 2 of my *Unbecoming Language* for a discussion of how Wittig's unique brand of materialism is able to bridge the gap that often exists between the so-called linguistic and new materialist turns in theory.

57. Even in a theoretical movement as invested in attending to disregarded or neglected forms of materiality as new materialisms, we can see the facility with which language is erected as the immaterial poststructuralist strawman, the relic of a wanton fetishization of representation and mediation, against which new materialisms react to save the metaphysical day.

58. See Watts, "Postmodern Céline."

59. Godard, "Notice," in Céline, *Romans I,* 1402. Notice how his critics carefully avoid reproducing Céline's language, insisting instead on demonstrating their cultivation by remaining in more proper registers. Original emphases.

60. Godard, *Henri Godard présente "Mort à crédit,"* 144–45. Original emphases.

61. Céline, *Bagatelles pour un massacre,* 172. See Kaplan, *Reproductions of Banality,* 111–16, for an excellent discussion of how Céline brings literature back to life by insisting on an excremental, base corporeality.

62. See Heining et al., "Disgusting Smells."

63. It is interesting that, while, in 1936, Céline's contemporaries could

not but obsess about the scatological nature of his work, literary scholarship and criticism in the latter part of the twentieth century and in the twenty-first century sidestep shit in both his and others' work, deftly avoiding it to take up other considerations instead.

2. Beckett

1. See Fehsenfeld and Overbeck, *Letters of Samuel Beckett,* 19, 42, 383.

2. See O'Hara, *Samuel Beckett's Hidden Drives*; Wasser, *Work of Difference*; Bryden, *Beckett and Animals*; Bates, *Beckett's Art of Salvage*; Dini, *Consumerism, Waste, and Re-Use*; Broadway, "Holes, Orifices, and Porous Subjectivity"; Christensen, "'Tis My Muse'"; Anderton, *Beckett's Creatures*; Barron, *Against Reason*; Tucker, *Samuel Beckett and Arnold Geulincx*.

3. For a classic critique of Beckett as an apolitical writer, see Lukács's "Ideology of Modernism" in *Realism in Our Time*. See Morin, *Beckett's Political Imagination,* for a reading that maps Beckett's political activity onto his writing and recuperates his writing as political; and Weisberg, *Chronicles of Disorder,* for a reading that tries to think outside the political/apolitical binary to instead articulate Beckett's conceptualization of the political as singular.

4. Rabaté, "Beckett et la poésie de la zone," 75.

5. Rabaté, 77.

6. See La Durantaye, *Beckett's Art of Mismaking,* 68; and Rabaté, *Think, Pig!,* especially chapter 13, "The Morality of Form—A French Story."

7. See Katz, "Beckett's Absent Paris," for an analysis of Beckett through the influence of *Mort à crédit* that argues for Céline's major contribution to Beckett being not of register or tone, but of a form of address.

8. La Durantaye, *Beckett's Art of Mismaking,* 15.

9. Others have found in *Molloy* rich fodder for thinking through questions of excrementality. Andrew Christensen devotes an essay to elaborating four dimensions of the novel's scatology: Beckett's use of excrement as a metaphor for language as excess; psychoanalytical theories of defecation that link it to creativity; excrement as a means to critique religion satirically; and excrement as a site of existential anxiety. Will Broadway reads Beckett's obsessive orificiality—his fascination with the anus and its excrement—as a way of combatting the usual anatomical hierarchy that subordinates the anus to the mouth that is its analogue and establishing the porous body and its attendant subjectivity as radically permeable and open. See Christensen, "'Tis My Muse'"; and Broadway, "Holes, Orifices, and Porous Subjectivity."

10. Ruby Cohn does an admirable job summarizing the novel's plot and

its peripatetic narrators' adventures, which, when articulated with the sort of lucidity Cohn displays, demonstrates just how absurd *Molloy* is. See Cohn, *Beckett Canon*, 161–65.

11. Though Minuit inserts a note in *Nouvelles et textes pour rien* specifying that the *nouvelles* date from 1945, "L'Expulsé" was first published in 1946, in the journal *Fontaine*.

12. Beckett, *Stories and Texts for Nothing*, 14; Beckett, *Nouvelles et textes pour rien*, 21–22. Cf. Céline, *Romans I*, 566, where Céline describes Ferdinand's fecal crust. Interestingly, in Beckett's translation into English of this passage, he excises the *croustillant* (crusty/crunchy) that makes clearest the Célinian intertext and places both writers' narrators in a shared fecal crustiness, something that speaks to a certain material as well as temporal relation to shit (shit needs time to dry to become crusty).

13. When Molloy describes his relationship with his deaf and, for all intents, mute mother, he describes her as recognizing him through his smell ("She knew it was me, by my smell"; 22; 22), which is not a particularly pleasant one, as he admits when alluding to how terrible his mother's weekly visitor, a woman, smelled: "I smelt a terrible smell. It must have come from the bowels. Odour of antiquity. Oh I'm not criticizing her, I don't diffuse the perfumes of Araby myself" (24; 24). Interestingly, in the English translation by Patrick Bowles in collaboration with Beckett, woman, *femme*, is translated as *hotel cleaner*, removing all of the ambiguity that we get in the original French version about what sort of a woman the visitor was. Here, as elsewhere, the first page number refers to the translation, the second to the edition in the original French.

14. I've modified Bowles's translation of "Mimétique malgré lui" as "Chameleon in spite of himself." Given the literary stakes of mimesis (something that can hardly be said of chameleons, *pace* chameleons), I've chosen to translate this phrase more literally.

15. Other readings deploy the scene toward more specific ends: Andrew Christensen takes Molloy's "I hardly fart at all" at face value to suggest that the scatology in *Molloy* is minimal compared to the more material and in-your-face scatological works found in the visual arts, such as Piero Manzoni's cans of shit for "Merda d'artista"; Will Broadway interprets the scene in exactly the opposite way to argue for how it illustrates how pervasive and long-lasting Beckett's scatology is: "Although he now dismisses the problem [of farting] as unremarkable, he has remarked on it at such length that a foul odor lingers"; and Ulrike Maude treats the obsessive fart counting as

symptomatic of Tourette's syndrome and its frequent accompaniment by obsessive-compulsive disorder. Christensen, "'Tis My Muse,'" 94; Broadway, "Holes, Orifices, and Porous Subjectivity," 88; Maude, "'Stirring beyond Coming and Going,'" 161.

16. We can see the choice to name the *Times Literary Supplement* as a critique of a literary establishment that, far from serving as the incubator and guardian of literary culture, serves to stultify and suffocate it, quashing the innovation that literature depends on for its life.

17. By mapping the layer onto the seasons, Beckett introduces the question of time, which fart-counting puts into relief, so that one could see Molloy relaying a phenomenology of time, where the fart as a means of experiencing the passage of time becomes, more largely, the means of establishing a self.

18. Certainly, the compression of an entire winter into a sentence raises questions as to the exact nature of Molloy's winter body. Are we to think that during the winter, this season of hibernation, Molloy's body also hibernates so that his bodily functions shut down and he doesn't defecate or urinate all winter long? Or are we to understand the declaration of the *Supplement*'s solidity and non-porosity, capable of withstanding *tout épreuve,* to mean being able to withstand bodily functions? And lest we speculate that the paper only wraps the trunk, leaving his nether regions free, Molloy's declaration that the paper is able to resist his farts makes it clear that the paper wraps his buttocks as well. The toilet paper / newspaper wrapping, as a detail, poses an interpretive challenge, one that cannot be read outside a scatological frame, as the paper, in this passage, is a material that exists in relation to and because of the scatological material—either solid or gas—it is meant to receive. But regardless of how much Molloy's body evacuates or doesn't during the winter period, even if his defecation is suspended for the complete time, there is no way that his wrapping would be able to remain clean by any standard after that much continual contact.

19. Both Céline and Beckett write this ecological fact into their texts. In *Mort à crédit*, Céline has Ferdinand collecting pigeon shit as fertilizer for Courtial des Pereire's agricultural projects, and in *Watt* (1942), Beckett has Watt distributing Knott's feces in the garden as fertilizer.

20. This foray into a Cartesian privileging of mind over body is, as we'll see, a temporary one. In scholarship that tracks Beckett's complex relation to philosophy, the influence of Descartes has been abundantly commented on, and the dominant narrative is of Beckett's Cartesianism constituting an

earlier stage of his intellectual development, with his later exposure to philosophers like Arnold Geulincx and Arthur Schopenhauer displacing his
initial Cartesian sensibilities. See Calder, *Philosophy of Samuel Beckett*; Rabaté,
Think, Pig!; Tucker, *Samuel Beckett and Arnold Geulincx*; and Cordingley, "Beckett's Ignorance."

21. "Have contemporary philosophers had any influence on your
thought?–I never read philosophers.

"Why not?–I never understand anything they write.

"All the same, people have wondered if the existentialists' problem of being may afford a key to your works.–There's no key or problem. I wouldn't
have had any reason to write my novels if I could have expressed their subject in philosophic terms." Beckett to Gabriel D'Aubarède, quoted in Graver
and Federman, *Samuel Beckett*, 217.

22. Molloy's assertion that he's hardly a farter appears ridiculous on its
face, given that a healthy person farts on average twenty times a day–a number Molloy reaches in seventy-five minutes. But if we take the regular and
regimented nature of this flatulence as a way of measuring time, then Molloy's claim to hardly fart at all becomes a poignant recognition of how short
life is: one can fart millions of times in one's lifetime (if Molloy is accorded
a lifespan of seventy-five years and if we suspend the fart-count for the eight
hours of sleep an average person has a night–even though one continues to
fart in slumber–and count at the rate of four farts every fifteen minutes, that
amounts to 7.008 million farts total) and it still won't be enough.

23. Bersani, "Is the Rectum a Grave?"

24. Critics have remarked on Molloy's anality, such as his assertion that
he was born from his mother's anus, and his anal sexuality, wherein vagina
and anus lose their distinction and wherein Molloy sticks his finger up his
own anus. See Broadway, "Holes, Orifices, and Porous Subjectivity"; Macaskill, "Logic of Coprophilia"; Miller and Souter, *Beckett and Bion*; Stewart,
Sex and Aesthetics; and chapter 7, "Beckett's Kantian Critiques," in Rabaté,
Think, Pig!

25. Tajiri, "Review," 279.

26. Much of the more recent work on Beckett and philosophy has
drawn on the archives, in particular his "Philosophy Notes," an extensive set
of notes taken by Beckett as he studied philosophy on his own in the British
Museum's reading room during the summer of 1932.

27. Dirk Van Hulle glosses this excision, among others in Beckett's oeuvre, to make the point that such excisions leave behind "textual scars" that

remind the reader not to take the published text as a polished, final product
("Textual Scars," 307–8).

28. O'Reilly, "*Molloy,* Part II."

29. O'Reilly.

30. O'Reilly.

31. O'Reilly.

32. O'Hara, *Samuel Beckett's Hidden Drives.*

33. Taken together, Ballyba provides a setting that is materially
excremental—the whole region stinks to the high heavens of shit and is covered in it—while Shitba provides a setting that is nomenclaturally excremental. Together, you get both the representation and the object of representation, the shit and the language that names the shit—both sides of the mimetic
operation.

34. In this case, what has been described as the sublimation of the fecal
in Beckett's later works, where we get less shit and more mud, isn't so much
an instance of Beckett outgrowing or moving beyond shit, but trusting that
his reader, who is by now sufficiently acquainted with the excremental core
of his writing, is able to mine the shit for themselves, able to see the mud and
dirt for what they stand for.

35. Guiley, *Encyclopedia of Magic and Alchemy,* 94.

36. See especially chapter 5, "The Grotesque Image of the Body," in
Bakhtin, *Rabelais.*

37. See chapter 6, "The Material Bodily Lower Stratum," in Bakhtin.

38. Boulter, "'Wordshit, Bury Me,'" 3.

39. Bataille develops this idea throughout his work, notably in *The Accursed Share* and "The Notion of Expenditure" in *Visions of Excess,* 116–29.

40. Boulter, "'Wordshit, Bury Me,'" 16.

41. Boulter, 17.

42. Cohn, *Beckett Canon,* 168.

43. Cohn, 168.

44. Gershon, *Second Brain.*

45. Hadhazy, "Think Twice." This connection between mood and gut
and the gut's capacity to think has been examined in depth by Elizabeth Wilson, who turns away from the brain to focus on the enteric nervous system,
examining, for example, the impact of antidepressants on eating disorders
through their action on the gut. See Wilson, *Gut Feminism.*

46. In the context of the gut, the occult nature of this ontological sabbath
takes on added meaning, insofar as shit is itself occult, shut off from view

or exposure. And joy, in the context of philosophy, is occulted, cast aside for weightier metaphysical, ontological, or ethical questions, shunted to the realm of pop philosophy or to theology.

47. Beckett, *Unnamable*, 134; Beckett, *Proust*, 93. For more on Beckett's conceptualization of life as pensum, see Louar, "Beckett's Bodies in the Trilogy."

48. And there are sometimes defecatory instances where one feels like one couldn't possibly defecate any further, and yet the abdomen keeps contracting and the body keeps expelling yet more feces—a fecal staging of "I can't go on. I'll go on."

3. Fecal Freedom

1. As political theorist Hanna Pitkin points out, "Speakers of English have a unique opportunity: They get to choose between 'liberty' and 'freedom.' No other European language, ancient or modern, offers such a choice" ("Are Freedom and Liberty Twins?," 523). In rendering *liberté* in English, I opt for *freedom* in part because Sartre's translators have opted for *freedom* as well but also because conceptually, it captures what fecality maps onto, following Hannah Arendt's insistence on the distinction between liberty and freedom (*On Revolution*, 29). I concur with Pitkin's gloss of the distinction wherein freedom "is more likely to be holistic, to mean a total condition or state of being, while liberty is more likely to be plural and piecemeal. Second, freedom is more likely than liberty to be something psychic, inner, and integral to the self. . . . Liberty seems to connote something more formal, rational, and limited than freedom" (542–43).

2. As the story goes, Sartre reads Genet and immediately takes Genet under his wing (a feeling of closeness that will be reciprocated in Genet's dedication of his first novel, *Notre-Dame-Des-Fleurs*, to Sartre and Beauvoir); Sartre promotes Genet and, along with Cocteau, helps keep Genet out of prison; Sartre writes and publishes *Saint Genet*, a work that effectively kills Genet's creativity as he stops writing for years, having felt petrified, deadened by Sartre's analysis; Genet stops talking to Sartre; Sartre's reading of Genet is overthrown by Derrida's *Glas*, which has aged better in most circles than the terribly sincere existentialism of Sartre's magnum opus.

3. Bauer, "Pretexts for Texts," 93.

4. "Undesirable *in his very being*, he is not that woman's son but her excrement"; "Are not Evil, the criminal and Genet himself the excrement of society?"; "Genet *is* excrement, and it is as such that he asserts himself." Sartre, *Saint Genet*, 8, 109, 170.

5. Certainly, Sartre hardly has a monopoly on Genet criticism, as Mairéad Hanrahan points out in her review of Loren Ringer's *"Saint Genet" Decanonized,* which she charges with overstating the influence of Sartre in Genet studies, pointing to Derridean and Deleuzian approaches to Genet. Be that as it may, Derrida's *Glas* is itself a reaction to *Saint Genet* and any non-Sartrean reading of Genet cannot skirt the fact of having to come after Sartre, who serves as an inevitable flashpoint and foil against whom one cannot help but be in relation. Hanrahan, "Review."

6. As Genet said, in an interview with Madeline Gobeil, "Sartre stripped me bare without mercy. . . . I finally allowed him to publish it because my concern has always been to take responsibility for what I give rise to. But it took me a while to recover. I was almost unable to continue writing. I could have continued to develop novels mechanically. I could have tried to write pornographic novels in a kind of automatism. Sartre's book created a void that allowed a sort of psychological deterioration to set in. . . . For six years I lived in this miserable state" (Genet, *Declared Enemy,* 12).

7. For more on Genet's relation to the French canon as its bad boy, see Amin, *Disturbing Attachments,* 3–4.

8. Bersani, *Homos,* 152.

9. See Busch, *Power of Consciousness,* which tracks freedom as a unifying concept for Sartre's work and thought that evolves, in distinction to readings of Sartre that treat freedom as a stable and fixed concept.

10. The anti-relational thread of queer theory was notably solidified as a conceptual object when the 2005 MLA convention held a panel, "The Antisocial Thesis in Queer Theory," following the publication of Lee Edelman's *No Future: Queer Theory and the Death Drive.* In this discussion, whose follow-up was published in *PMLA* (see Caserio et al., "Antisocial Thesis in Queer Theory"), queer theory's antisocial thread was traced back to Leo Bersani's anti-relational position articulated in Bersani's *Homos.* The queer antisocial thesis in effect claimed queer theory's position as one of opposition to the normativity of the dominant social order—not so much anti-relational as anti-what-heteronormative-society-deems-to-be-proper-relationality.

11. The kind of literary and intellectual exchange and mutual influence the two writers had on each other emerged out of the friendship they developed following their meeting each other in 1944. See chapter 11 in White, *Genet.*

12. Rybalka, "Sartre," 132.

13. For a good summary of Sartre's continued identification with op-

pressed groups and the connection between his politics and his philosophy, see Detmer, *Sartre Explained*.

14. As Annie Cohen-Solal puts it, quoting Sartre, "Philosophy is for him at once a tool for self-comprehension and a tool for literary production, what he would confirm himself years later. 'The moment I understood what philosophy was, it seemed normal to me to require it of the writer'" (*Jean-Paul Sartre*, 38).

15. "It's this realization of the total gratuity of existence that founds all Sartrean philosophy of liberty, the assumption by the for-itself of its fundamental contingency and the choosing of authenticity" (Tomès, "Petit lexique sartrien," 186).

16. Sartre describes the text that would eventually become *La Nausée* as such in a letter to Beauvoir. See Sartre, *Œuvres romanesques*, 1660.

17. "I would like them to remember *Nausea*, one or two plays, *No Exit* and *The Devil and the Good Lord*, and then my two philosophical works, more particularly the second one, *Critique of Dialectical Reason*. Then my essay on Genet, *Saint Genet*. . . . If these are remembered, that would be quite an achievement, and I don't ask for more." Sartre, quoted in Max Charlesworth, *Existentialists*, 154.

18. See Flynn, *Sartre*, 137–61, for a discussion of *La Nausée* as a paradigmatic philosophical novel. *La Nausée* is often read through *L'Être et le néant*, in which the latter is the philosophical explication of the former, but there is a compelling case to be made for taking *La Nausée* on its own. See, for example, a reading that cautions against reading the novel as a demonstration of Sartre's philosophy: Hewitt, "'Looking for Annie.'"

19. Gerald Prince gives an account of the exemplariness of *La Nausée* as a text that lends itself to a proliferation of reading frameworks, or closures. Prince reminds the reader that the text's meaning "is the untotalizable sum of its closures" ("*La Nausée*," 190). In other words, it is completely understandable why critics would disproportionately focus on *La Nausée* as a text that begs to be read.

20. Sartre, in his autobiography *Les Mots* (*The Words*), describes his younger self as "fake to the marrow of my bones and hoodwinked" (252). See also Lacapra, *Preface to Sartre*, 95.

21. A process pushed along by Simone de Beauvoir, who played a pivotal role in encouraging him to produce fiction.

22. Morin, "Thinking Things," 44.

23. Falzon, "Sartre and Meaningful Existence," 115.

24. Sartre, *Nausea*, 126–27; Sartre, *La Nausée*, 181. In subsequent parenthetical references, the first page number is from the English translation, the second from the original French.

25. As Kôichirô Fujita puts it, "Excrement is much more slippery than you think. I had thought poop would have more or less the consistency of papier-mâché, but in fact, it's closer to that of a wet bar of soap" (Yorifuji and Fujita, *Au cœur du caca*, 4). Having manually unclogged a toilet, I can confirm this. This texture of sliminess is one that recurs throughout Sartre's writing. For an interesting reading that ties Sartre's preoccupation with this texture to Nathalie Sarraute's and draws out each writer's project's philosophical resonances, see Willging, "Partners in Slime."

26. Mauriac, "L'Excrémentialisme"; Raymond Las Vergnas, cited in Idt, *"Le Mur,"* 148.

27. Camus, *"Le Mur."*

28. Harvey, "Jean-Paul Sartre's 'L'Enfance d'un chef,'" 207, 209.

29. Sartre, *The Wall*, 86; Sartre, *L'Enfance d'un Chef*, 11–12.

30. Louette, "'L'enfance d'un chef,'" 370.

31. I've modified Lloyd Alexander's translation here of "étron diabolique," which renders "diabolique" as "imitation" rather than "diabolical"—a bewildering choice.

32. While the feces pointed to in the beginning's fecal drama are not actually produced, the idea of them is that of a solid turd: what Lucien's mother urges him to push out is a normal, solid bowel movement.

33. For more on Lucien's absolute passivity, expressed via imitation, see Idt, *"Le Mur,"* 51–54. This moment of self-delusion presages the novella's sardonic ending, where a now radicalized fascist, anti-Semitic Lucien, after having violently assaulted a Jew, gazes at his "pretty, headstrong little face that was not yet terrible" (270; 130) and says to himself, in the text's last line, "Je vais laisser pousser ma moustache" (130); "I'll grow a moustache" (270). Louette comments on Lucien's mustache, "Thus the truth of this mustache is revealed to be: a turd on a face" by pointing to the verb *pousser* (to push, to grow) as a link: the first instance of the verb *pousser* was used for Lucien's potty training, and this last instance of the verb, used for the mustache, casts it under a fecal light. Louette, "'L'enfance d'un chef ,'" 380. Lucien thinks his declaration of letting his mustache grow is an expression of his will, an active decision on his part, but his decision is completely dependent on his own body's rhythms, over which he has no real control. This "decision" is about as much an expression of his will as Lucien's decision to take off his pajamas himself.

34. As Lucien grows, he goes through several stages of willing himself to conform to models he encounters: the effete homosexual model, the strong masculine fascist model, et cetera.

35. In this, we could see Sartre anticipating Beauvoir's elaboration, in *The Second Sex,* of the way embodiment can lead to the bad faith position of immanence, wherein women, through the accident of their physical bodies, are led to believe that they do not have the same transcendent freedom that allows them to project themselves into the world as do men.

36. We can see the embodiment of refusal to accept contingency in those individuals who are so disgusted by their excrementality that they will themselves into a lethal constipation—they would rather die than deal with shit. See Sims, "Teenage Girl Dies."

37. I have found no indications in my research that Genet engaged intellectually and literarily with Sartre before their first meeting each other in 1944.

38. White, *Genet,* 270–71.

39. Cohen-Solal, *Jean-Paul Sartre,* 65–66.

40. Genet, *Miracle de la rose,* 348. Genet and Céline thus both could be situated literarily in the *tinette.*

41. Gene Plunka puts it succinctly: "Genet glorified the abject as a transcendence from the gaze of the oppressor—for him, a type of sainthood" ("Review of *The Body Abject,*" 124).

42. Genet, *Our Lady of the Flowers,* 184; Genet, *Notre-Dame-des-Fleurs,* 184.

43. "Mon imagination est plongée dans l'abject, mais sur ce point-là, elle est noble, elle est pure. Je me refuse à l'imposture; et s'il m'est arrivé d'exagérer en poussant héros et aventures vers l'horrible ou vers l'obscène, c'est dans le sens de la vérité." Interview with Robert Poulet (*Bulletin de Paris,* September 19, 1956), cited in Lozier, *De l'abject au sublime,* 111.

44. Hartman, "Homage to *Glas,*" 358.

45. The original reads, "Elles [les latrines] sont humaines" (They are human). Frechtman adds the emphatic "alone" in his translation, an editorializing choice that indicates his conviction of Genet's strong tying together of the excremental with the human.

46. For more on *Notre-Dame-des-Fleurs* as a working through and conceptualization of fantasy, see Lucey, "Genet's *Notre-Dame-Des-Fleurs,*" 80.

47. We can see this problematization of identity along excremental and material axes described in a flashback to Culafroy's/Divine's childhood where Genet describes Culafroy's relation to his excrement: "When they were still warm, he took a tender delight in their odor, but he spurned

them with indifference—at times with horror—when they had too long since ceased to be part of himself" (238; 262). When Culafroy's turds are fresh, still giving off a strong odor, that odor is able to transport him, to take him elsewhere, give him access, we can imagine, to the treasures that Genet evokes elsewhere. When the turds lose their odor and are nothing but form and material, they are repulsive because they are no longer him. There's an equivalence being established here between odor and identity, and the simple form and matter of the turd by itself is not enough to hold Culafroy's identity, or rather, to Culafroy's fantasy of being something else. La matière Genet, the *matière* that his books are made of, must bring together the odorous and the material to be able to participate in both the orders of the real and the imagined.

48. We can surmise this from the fact that Genet did not resist or protest Cocteau's and Sartre's efforts to keep him from having to serve a life sentence in prison for his recidivism.

49. This idea of Genet transforming himself into literature, into shit, will be even more clearly expressed in a later work like *Les Pompes funèbres* in its famous rimming scene, where Genet performs analingus on his lover Jean, avidly devouring the fecal matter clinging to Jean's anus and fantasizing about eating all of Jean by starting at the anus. As Bersani describes the scene, "Thus Genet eating Jean inside Jean could himself become the expeller of Jean's waste or, more accurately, the expeller of Jean *as* waste. (Or perhaps Jean would expel *him* as waste . . .)" (*Homos*, 157–58). The rimming scene thus expresses a Genetian poetics, where Jean the writer eats Jean's shit and Jean-as-shit to expel Jean the text as waste—to shit him out as poetry. Just as there is the convergence/identity of names—Jean Jean—so too is the boundary between shit and the body that produces it dissolved. For Genet, the difference between poetry and shit doesn't exist.

50. We can also frame this choice as Genet's choosing matter—*la matière Genet*—over immateriality—*le pet (fart) Genet*. Mairéad Hanrahan describes Genet as having an abiding interest in materiality—in conveying the materiality of an aesthetic object (*Lire Genet*, 18).

51. Derrida, *Glas*, 20.

52. Magedera, "'Seing' Genet, Citation and Mourning," 30. For more on the fundamental importance of undecidability for *Glas* and Derrida's understanding of Genet, see Hanrahan, "Double Signature"; and Spitzer, *Derrida, Myth*, 92–120.

53. As Derrida writes, "The flower is *(de)part(ed)*. It holds, from its being-

(de)part(ed), the force of a transcendental excrescence that only makes it seem such (transcendental) and that no longer even has to be deflowered. Practical deconstruction of the transcendental effect is at work in the structure of the flower" (*Glas,* 14).

54. See chapter 3 of Lucey, *Someone,* which demonstrates the way Genet accounts for the rigidly structured and highly codified nature of sexuality only to throw it off balance, demonstrating how sexuality exceeds our capacity to constrain it linguistically.

55. Sartre, *Saint Genet,* 448.

56. "À la fois l'orifice extrêmement important servant à évacuer les déchets produits par notre usine intestinale, à savoir l'anus, mais aussi ce qui l'entoure, le 'cul' ou postérieur." See "Avoir du cul."

57. Beauvoir, *Prime of Life,* 459.

58. Robert Harvey, in his essay treating the Sartre–Genet–Derrida triangle, attends not only to each man's relation to Genet, but with each other, writing that Sartre and Derrida are "Genet's caressed, cherished couple linked, as vines climbing the Bacchic thyrsus, in a sort of *affolement*: Darling and Divine" ("Genet's Open Enemies," 106). If we continue to map out their relation onto *Notre-Dame-des-Fleurs,* this would make Genet the Notre-Dame to Sartre's Darling—two enmeshed characters locked together in a homoerotic fraternal friendship in which they embrace but never penetrate each other (see Lucey, "Genet's *Notre-Dame-Des-Fleurs,*" 84–86). There is no physical penetration, but I would argue that there is a mutual penetration with freedom.

59. In this regard, the dynamics of Genet and Sartre's relationship resonate with Lauren Berlant's reading of))< >((as demonstrating the impossibility of pure or sustained relationality, wherein the emoji shows that "people can be together only if they're also apart in some way" (Berlant and Edelman, *Sex,* 27). The < > (freedom) is precisely what brings Genet and Sartre together and separates them, the interval that measures their intimacy and their distance.

4. To Wipe the Other

1. It was only in 2019 that Gary finally entered Gallimard's prestigious La Pléiade collection, a gesture that accords to Gary a sure legacy and the status of classic. For a discussion of Gary's Pléiadization, see Bloch-Lainé, "'Je me suis toujours été un autre.'"

2. If I use the term "fictions" to describe even the purportedly

autobiographical or true narratives included in this collection, it's because *La Douleur,* in classic Durassian style, blurs the distinction between fact and fiction, history and fabulation, truth and reality—a move that puts the entire collection under the sign of fiction. While the generic identity of this work can be contested, what is certain is its aim of communicating the *douleur,* or suffering and pain, of war in all its dimensions. While the first part of *La Douleur* is described as a found text and the second part comprises three narratives that Duras claims in prefatory notes as being true accounts, it is entirely up in the air as to what truth is to Duras. See Crowley, *Duras,* especially chapter 4, for a discussion of the implications of Duras's relation to the real in *La Douleur* and the ambiguity of the text's status. For more on the messiness of *La Douleur*'s generic identities and for an account of what might motivate Duras to engage in such genre-blurring, see Plottel, "Memory, Fiction and History."

3. Duras, *La Douleur,* 12; Duras, *The War,* 3–4. See chapter 4 in James, *Documentary Imagination,* for a discussion of this topos of the found manuscript and its documentary status wherein the documentary memory produced by the text is different from the memory produced by experience, making then of memory something profoundly other.

4. Alison James comments on Duras's disavowal, noting that "Duras does not actually deny having written the text, but simply cannot remember or even imagine having done so" (183). Duras's denial, then, is not on the level of facts, but rather, on the level of recognition: she cannot recognize herself in the text just as she cannot recognize Antelme's shit as human.

5. Barbara Bray makes the bizarre choice of translating "elle," which refers to "la mort," as "the excretion," completely erasing the equation Duras makes of shit with death.

6. Duras emphasizes *dix-sept,* or seventeen, as the number of days that Antelme's shit stayed inhuman. It's possible that Duras settled on the number because of the similarity between the pronunciations of *dix-sept* and *disette,* or scarcity, dearth: *dix-sept* days spent in an experience of extreme *disette.*

7. My emphases.

8. Indeed, the translation fails even before one opens the book: the title, *The War: A Memoir,* not only refuses to place the book under the sign of an affect—*douleur,* suffering, or pain—as does the original, but slaps on a generic identification, *memoir,* that Duras leaves open.

9. See the introduction for more on the *informe.*

10. As Duras describes the first encounter between Antelme upon his

return and the doctor they call to save him, "He didn't understand. And then he realized: the form wasn't dead yet, it was hovering between life and death, and he, the doctor, had been called in to try to keep it alive" (55; 70).

11. See Chaouat, "Ce que chier veut dire," which reads excrement as the physical reality of the Holocaust, a sign of the depths of the Nazi atrocity that systematically dehumanized Jews and others and turned them into "corps-déchets" (waste-bodies). For Chaouat, excrement is the referent and sign of an experience that challenges representation and asks how to say the unsayable. See also Chaouat, "'La mort ne recèle pas tant de mystère.'"

12. Bruno Chaouat is one of the rare critics to treat Duras's shit writing as important to the project of representing the all too human inhumanity of the Holocaust, and explicitly poses the question of a necessary relation between the excremental and the literary. See Chaouat, "Ce que chier veut dire," 162.

13. Winston, *Postcolonial Duras,* 148.

14. Winston, 149.

15. Another way of framing what I'm calling nonhuman humanism—a humanism in which the nonhuman is deeply embedded—is as "residual humanism," the term Martin Crowley coins to describe Robert Antelme's conception of the human as "something which remains within and against its attempted abolition" wherein the human is what remains, stubbornly, despite attempts at annihilating it, mirroring shit in its residuality (Crowley, *Robert Antelme,* 25).

16. I am reading Duras through the particular ethical lens of care. For a discussion of Duras that takes up the question of ethics more broadly speaking, see Crowley, *Duras,* which explores the question of ethics in Duras's entire literary oeuvre.

17. If taken outside its dominant feminist perspective, the origin of care ethics has also been traced back earlier to the Scottish Enlightenment (see Tronto, *Moral Boundaries*) and, even earlier, to Socrates (Friedman, "Care and Context"). Joan Tronto has also identified Heidegger as a moral philosopher concerned with care (*Moral Boundaries,* 208n1). For a useful introduction to care ethics, see Brugère, *Care Ethics.* Fabienne Brugère, as a French thinker, is at a productive distance from care ethics' distinctly American origins.

18. Noddings, *Caring,* 175. I am citing from the second edition and it is interesting to note the replacement of "feminine" in the title with "relational," a move made by Noddings to insist on the universality of care as a

246 * NOTES TO CHAPTER 4

relational question, but one that she still sees as being anchored in women's experience. See "Preface to the 2013 edition" in *Caring*.

19. See chapter 1 of Gilligan, *In a Different Voice*, especially pp. 7–13.

20. Gilligan, *In a Different Voice*, 18–19.

21. As Gilligan puts it, "This ethic, which reflects a cumulative knowledge of human relationships, evolves around a central insight, that self and other are interdependent" (74). See also Brugère's description of care as "a relational ethics structured by the attention people give to others" (*Care Ethics*, 9).

22. Tronto, *Moral Boundaries*, 125. I am interested in applying the universality of instinct to intra-human relations in ways that would treat the human as nonhuman (as animal). For an exploration of human–nonhuman relations from a feminist care ethics perspective, see Donovan and Adams, *Feminist Care Tradition*.

23. See Kantrowitz, "Why Men Leave"; and Noor, "Men Who Leave."

24. Tronto, like Duras, is attuned to the material dimensions of caregiving, but her evocation of dressing someone's wound, for instance (Tronto, *Who Cares?*, 4), serves a primarily contextual and descriptive function, illustrating rather than conceptualizing care, as Duras does.

25. Stiegler, *Neganthropocene*, 215.

26. It is worth pointing out that *La Douleur* was published in the 1980s, during the AIDS crisis, when those who were either suffering from AIDS or caring for those who had AIDS would come to have an intimate experience of excrement as central to the act of care.

27. Maurice Blanchot famously refers to the Holocaust as a dis-aster, or *dés-astre*—a separation from the star—placing the Holocaust under the dark sign of a starless cosmos (*L'Écriture du désastre*).

28. Plottel, "Memory, Fiction and History," 55.

29. See Mehlman, "Holocaust Comedies of 'Emile Ajar'"; and the introduction to Bellos, *Romain Gary*.

30. For more on the elaborate nature of the hoax, see Miller, *Impostors*.

31. See Bellos, *Romain Gary*; Melcer-Padon, "Romain Gary"; Roumette, "'La hausse des cris'"; Rosse, *Romain Gary*; Gelas, *Romain Gary*; Chaudier, "'Dieu ait son cul'"; Miller, *Impostors*; and Hangouët, *Romain Gary*.

32. The one work to attend to Gary's excrementality is Pépin, *Aspects du corps*, which compiles the manifold ways that Gary represents corporeality in profane and vulgar terms in order to argue for its importance in Gary's writing.

33. Gary, *Life before Us*, 4–5; Gary, *La Vie devant soi*, 14–15. I amend Ralph Manheim's English translations occasionally.

34. See Pépin, *Aspects du corps*, 54–55, for a discussion of Momo's shitting as an instance of a corporeal language that would be better able to represent Momo's suffering than proper language.

35. In literature, Jonathan Littell's *Les Bienveillantes*, Daniel Zimmermann's *L'Anus du monde*, and Michel Vinaver's *Par-dessus bord* insist on the excremental dimension of the Holocaust. For a classic scholarly discussion of the excrementality of the concentrationary universe, see Des Pres, *The Survivor*, especially the chapter "Excremental Assault."

36. We can see here a foreshadowing of what Momo's relation to Madame Rosa will become: she will, in effect, in her incontinence and senility, be reduced to a giant set of buttocks, his interactions with her marked primarily by his wiping her when she soils herself.

37. See Lévinas, *Éthique et infini*.

38. See Gorrara, "Bearing Witness"; and Kritzman, "Duras' War." Gorrara's name is misspelled in the article as Gorarra.

5. Fighting Words

1. See my *Unbecoming Language* for a discussion of how Garréta's affiliation with the Oulipo has led to her work being read in the same apolitical light under which the Oulipo is generally cast.

2. Rose, "Zazie dans le BTP"; Loret, "Anne F. Garréta"; Artus, "Anne F. Garréta"; Pachet, "Casser des murs."

3. Wittig, "Trojan Horse," in *Straight Mind*, 68–75.

4. See *Unbecoming Language* for a discussion of Garréta's previous works and their Wittigian influence.

5. Pachet, "Casser des murs," 21.

6. Garréta, *Dans l'béton*, 9; Garréta, *In Concrete*, 11. I will occasionally modify Emma Ramadan's translation.

7. Wittig, *Le Chantier littéraire*, 46.

8. Kim, "Riddle of Racial Difference."

9. These are not the only structures under attack in the novel. As the incipit's invocation of *pédés* (fags) might suggest, a persistent if intermittent queerness is at play in the text, where *pédé* circulates as a false epithet and identity marker that floats lingeringly in the atmosphere without landing on or attaching to those subjects who might be considered to be "really" or authentically queer.

10. Portland is a reference to a type to cement.

11. Garréta further undermines the father's functionality as patriarch by implying that he might not even be heterosexual, as he inherits from "un pédé, un vrai" (a fag, a real one) (126; 129). The father insists he never knew about his friend's homosexuality (128; 131), his ignorance a way of distancing himself from the specter of queerness.

12. The mother is excluded from this model, likely because she is too closely aligned with the father as his spouse and the means through which he is able to reproduce himself, to be a proper ally.

13. This resonates strongly with feminist philosopher Sally Haslanger's assertion that "providing our children the social bases for alternative family schemas [to the natural nuclear family] may not be only permissible, but morally good; it may even be a moral duty to combat bionormativity" (*Resisting Reality*, 180).

14. *Intersectionnalité*, adopted from American *intersectionality*, has become firmly established as a feminist imperative, as it has in the States. Even a "féministe historique" (historic feminist) like Christine Delphy, a major figure of the MLF (Mouvement de Liberátion des Femmes), calls for intersectional analyses of oppression. Bienaimé, "Qui sont les autres?" And the notion of race as a construct has been assimilated by the political establishment, compelling French president Emmanuel Macron and his administration to try to push through an amendment to France's constitution to remove the word *race*, which seems to naturalize race, instead of acknowledging the social process of *racisation*. Saada, "'Without Distinction of . . . Sex.'"

15. "Jaune sire" is tricky to translate as Garréta here is playing with the resemblance between *jeune* (young) and *jaune* (literally, yellow, but also a term for a scab, for a right-aligned member of the proletariat unwilling to go on strike, unlike red workers). I have tried to communicate something of this combination by combining *callow* with *callous* to convey this sense of youth combined with lack of solidarity. Ramadan chooses to translate "jaune sire médisant" and its variation "jaunâtre sire" (98) in a number of different ways: "glanderous yellow creep" (99) and "jaundiced jamoke" (101). Neither *creep* nor *jamoke*, however, evokes class distinction the way "sire" does. While my translation loses the sense of yellowness found in the original, I think it's important to convey the way class figures in this passage as an important site of distinction.

16. See Okin, *Justice, Gender, and the Family,* for a strong critique of the notion that the heterosexual nuclear family has any natural foundation.

17. A case in point is the anti-gay marriage Manif pour Tous movement, which casts the necessity of the heterosexual nuclear family in psychoanalytic terms. The discourse around the nuclear family is a recent one and differs from the sorts of natalist narratives originating in the Third Republic. The nuclear family shifts the focus away from one of demographics and population growth (although it obviously is implicated in them) to one that is psychologizing. See Robcis, *Law of Kinship*, for a demonstration of how this psychologizing bent comes into being through the vulgarization of Claude Lévi-Strauss and Jacques Lacan, of structuralism and psychoanalysis, from which emerges the idea of the psychic necessity of a heterosexual parental structure for proper development.

18. Dorlin, *La Matrice de la race*, examines the relatively recent history of the construction of race as biological fact; Haslanger, *Resisting Reality*, examines what it means, philosophically and politically, for race and gender to be social constructs.

19. See hooks, *Feminist Theory*, for a persuasive argument casting the family unit as an efficient mechanism for reproducing ideologies of oppression and domination.

20. Wittig, *Le Chantier littéraire*, 96–97.

21. "Aujourd'hui, en France, seule Anne F. Garréta . . . peut non seulement se vanter d'être l'héritière spirituelle de Monique Wittig mais de poursuivre sa tâche, en repoussant encore les limites de la langue dans le travail du genre—et la gageure n'est pas mince" (Murat, "Un siècle de littérature lesbienne," 45).

22. Wittig, *Straight Mind*, 34–35.

23. Wittig's critique of the heterosexual social contract spans from the ancients, from Aristotle, all the way to Lévi-Strauss. Wittig's critique of Lévi-Strauss's theory of the exchange of women as foundational to his formulation of kinship thus reinforces Garréta's attacks on heterosexual filiation—Garréta as a reader of both Wittig and Rousseau, would certainly be aware of Wittig's implicit critique of kinship.

24. See Burton, "On the Origin," for an extended discussion of Wittig's engagement with Rousseau.

25. Wittig, *Straight Mind*, 38.

26. Wittig, *Le Chantier littéraire*, 61.

27. Wittig, *Straight Mind*, 45. The reference to Socrates and to Glaucon is to the following dialogue from Plato's *Republic*, quoted by Wittig as follows:

GLAUCON: But the city whose foundation we have been describing has its being only in words; there is no spot on earth where it exists.

SOCRATES: No; but it is laid up in heaven as a pattern for him who wills to see, and seeing, to found that city in himself. Whether it exists anywhere, or ever will exist, is no matter. (36–37)

6. Daniel Pennac's Excremental Poetics

1. I refer to this scene as an originary scene because it explains the origins of the diary-writing that winds up being the *journal* evoked in the title.

2. Pennac, *Diary of a Body*, 25–26; Pennac, *Journal d'un corps*, 33. I modify Alyson Waters's translation occasionally.

3. Grossmann-Etoh, "*Journal d'un corps*"; Naulleau, "Le Coup de gueule de Naulleau."

4. Grainville, "Daniel Pennac."

5. Barthes, *Sade, Fourier, Loyola*, 137.

6. See chapter 1 for a discussion of how Céline rejects a deodorized version of written shit.

7. While instances of the blood–brain barrier being crossed, as with sinus infections that spread to the brain, are rare, what is important for my argument is not the frequency with which such interaction between the nasal passageway and brain occurs, but the fact that it can occur.

8. In this respect, Pennac differs from Camille Laurens, for instance, who likens writing to secretion rather than excretion, treating language as "a secretion that allows us to tell a secret" ("Qui dit ça?," 29).

9. Guibert, *À l'ami*; Guibert, *Le Protocole compassionnel*; Guibert, *Le Mausolée des amants*.

10. Guibert, *Written in Invisible Ink*, 33; Guibert, *La Mort propagande*, 88–89.

11. Mavrikakis, "La Sépulcre de merde," 32.

12. Raoul, *French Fictional Journal*, 3–4.

13. Camille Laurens argues that what makes autofiction interesting is "this manner of engaging the writing body's subject" and cites Guibert as an autofictional archetype ("Qui dit ça?," 28).

14. Iser, *Die Appellstruktur der Texte*, 10; cited in Raoul, *French Fictional Journal*, 7.

15. Cixous, "Laugh of the Medusa," 881.

16. In this regard, Pennac's alignment with fecality keeps him from mak-

ing the parturient swerve that Louis Marin makes, as discussed in the introduction, when it comes to conceptualizing creation and generation, opting
to place these things under the sign of the fecal rather than under the sign of
the feminine (as the site of the maternal).

17. Chasseguet-Smirgel, "L'Univers sadique-anal," 200; original emphases.

18. Laporte, *History of Shit*, 30. Michel Serres also identifies a "stercoraceous or excremental origin of property rights" (*Natural Contract*, 33).

19. Pennac, *Comme un roman*, back cover; Pennac, *Better Than Life*, table
of contents. Each right is developed in the section "Le qu'en lira-t-on, ou les
droits imprescriptibles du lecteur," 147–75; "The Reader's Bill of Rights,"
175–207.

20. The text does not name the indexer, but we might reasonably assume that it is Pennac, given that Gallimard does not usually index the
novels it publishes. Interestingly, the originary scene is not indexed under
"Défécation" (Defecation) or "Diarrhée" (Diarrhea), but under "Peur"
(Fear). Indexing the originary scene to fear, the motor for writing, rather
than to the explicitly fecal, makes the greater statement that the fecal here
is not just fecal, able to be indexed according to what type of feces we are
dealing with: a standard, generalized defecation, or the more extraordinary
defecation of diarrhea. The fecal is not just fecal because it is literary, constitutive of the drive to create.

21. Céline, *Voyage au bout de la nuit*, 252.

Conclusion

1. Kim, "Return to Culture."

2. As Toni Morrison puts it forcefully, "Canon building is empire
building. Canon defense is national defense" (*Source of Self-Regard*, 169).

3. For an analysis of the Paris Commune and its contemporary resonances, see Ross, *Communal Luxury*.

4. Leiner, "Entretien avec Aimé Césaire," cited in Wilder, *Freedom Time*,
34. Gary Wilder eloquently describes Césaire's inflectional position: "Césaire's critical strategy regarding language, culture, *and* politics is condensed
in his will to 'inflect' rather than reject; to bend, refigure, and refunction
French was inseparable from his ambition to expand, explode, and elevate
France" (34).

5. Wittig, cited in Jardine and Menke, *Shifting Scenes*, 193; Lorde, *Sister
Outsider*, 102.

BIBLIOGRAPHY

Amin, Kadji. *Disturbing Attachments: Genet, Modern Pederasty, and Queer History*. Durham, N.C.: Duke University Press, 2017.

Anderton, Joseph. *Beckett's Creatures: Art of Failure after the Holocaust*. New York: Bloomsbury Publishing, 2016.

Arendt, Hannah. *On Revolution*. New York: Penguin, 1990.

Artus, Hubert. "Anne F. Garréta queer et béton." *Causette,* October 1, 2017.

"Avoir du cul / Avoir du pot / Avoir du bol." *Expressio.fr*. https://www.expressio .fr/expressions/avoir-du-cul-avoir-du-pot-avoir-du-bol.

Bakhtin, Mikhail. *Rabelais and His World*. Translated by Helene Iswolsky. Bloomington: Indiana University Press, 1984.

Barron, Anthony. *Against Reason: Schopenhauer, Beckett and the Aesthetics of Irreducibility*. Stuttgart: Ibidem-Verlag, 2017.

Barthes, Roland. *Mythologies*. Paris: Seuil, 1957.

Barthes, Roland. *Sade, Fourier, Loyola*. Translated by Richard Miller. Berkeley: University of California Press, 1989.

Bataille, Georges. *The Accursed Share: An Essay on General Economy*. Translated by Robert Hurley. New York: Zone Books, 1988.

Bataille, Georges. *Blue of Noon*. Translated by Harry Matthews. London: M. Boyars, 1986.

Bataille, Georges. *Œuvres complètes*. Vol. 2. Edited by Denis Hollier. Paris: Gallimard, 1970.

Bataille, Georges. *Romans et récits*. Bibliothèque de la Pléiade. Paris: Gallimard, 2004.

Bataille, Georges. *Story of the Eye*. Translated by Joachim Neugroschel. New York: Urizen Books, 1977.

Bataille, Georges. *Visions of Excess: Selected Writings, 1927–1939*. Edited by

Allan Stoekl. Translated by Allan Stoekl, Carl Lovitt, and Donald Leslie Jr. Minneapolis: University of Minnesota Press, 1985.

Bates, Julie. *Beckett's Art of Salvage: Writing and Material Imagination, 1932–1987*. Cambridge: Cambridge University Press, 2017.

Bauer, George H. "Pretexts for Texts: Sartre and Barthes before Genet and Camus." *L'Esprit créateur* 27, no. 3 (1987): 89–99.

Bauman, Zygmunt. *Wasted Lives: Modernity and Its Outcasts*. Cambridge: Polity Press, 2004.

Beauvoir, Simone de. *The Prime of Life*. Translated by Peter Green. Cleveland: World Publishing Company, 1962.

Beckett, Samuel. *Molloy*. Translated by Patrick Bowles in collaboration with Beckett. New York: Grove Press, 1955.

Beckett, Samuel. *Molloy*. Paris: Minuit, 1988.

Beckett, Samuel. *Nouvelles et textes pour rien*. Paris: Minuit, 1955.

Beckett, Samuel. *Proust*. London: J. Calder, 1965.

Beckett, Samuel. *Stories and Texts for Nothing*. New York: Grove Press, 1967.

Beckett, Samuel. *The Unnamable*. London: Faber & Faber, 2010.

Bellos, David. *Romain Gary: A Tall Story*. London: Harvill Secker, 2010.

Benjamin, Walter. "The Present Social Situation of the French Writer." In *Selected Writings, Volume 2, Part 2: 1931–1934*, 744–67. Edited by Michael W. Jennings, Howard Eiland, and Gary Smith. Translated by Rodney Livingstone and Others. Cambridge, Mass.: Belknap Press, 1999.

Bennett, Jane. *Vibrant Matter: A Political Ecology of Things*. Durham, N.C.: Duke University Press, 2010.

Berlant, Lauren, and Lee Edelman. *Sex, or the Unbearable*. Durham, N.C.: Duke University Press, 2013.

Bersani, Leo. *Homos*. Cambridge, Mass.: Harvard University Press, 1996.

Bersani, Leo. "Is the Rectum a Grave?" *October* 43 (1987): 197–222.

Bienaimé, Charlotte. "Qui sont les autres? Christine Delphy, Épisode 5." *À voix nue*, January 18, 2019. https://www.franceculture.fr/emissions/a-voix -nue/christine-delphy-55-qui-sont-les-autres.

Bienaimé, Charlotte. "Le Prix du sexe: Prostitution, quel est le problème?" *Un podcast à soi*, February 6, 2019. https://www.arteradio.com/son/6166 0960/le_prix_du_sexe_15.

Blanchot, Maurice. *L'Écriture du désastre*. Paris: Gallimard, 1980.

Bloch-Lainé, Virginie. "'Je me suis toujours été un autre'—à propos de Romain Gary dans la Pléiade." *Analyse Opinion Critique*, May 16, 2019. https://aoc.media/critique/2019/08/15/je-me-suis-toujours-ete-un-autre-a -propos-de-romain-gary-dans-la-pleiade/.

Blondiaux, Isabelle. *Une écriture psychotique: Louis-Ferdinand Céline.* Paris: A. G. Nizet, 1985.

Bois, Yve-Alain, and Rosalind Krauss. *Formless: A User's Guide.* New York: Zone Books, 1997.

Bonneuil, Christophe, and Jean-Baptiste Fressoz. *L'Événement anthropocène: La Terre, l'histoire et nous.* Paris: Seuil, 2013.

Boulter, Jonathan. "'Wordshit, Bury Me': The Waste of Narrative in Samuel Beckett's *Texts for Nothing.*" *Journal of Beckett Studies* 11, no. 2 (January 2002): 1–19.

Broadway, Will. "Holes, Orifices, and Porous Subjectivity in Beckett's *Molloy.*" *Journal of Beckett Studies* 27, no. 1 (April 2018): 83–94.

Brugère, Fabienne. *Care Ethics: The Introduction of Care as a Political Category.* Translated by Brian Heffernan. Leuven: Peeters, 2018.

Brunner, Anne, and Louis Maurin. *Rapport sur les inégalités en France, édition 2021.* Tours: L'Observatoire des inégalités, 2021. https://www.inegalites .fr/paritefemmeshommespolitique.

Bryden, Mary, ed. *Beckett and Animals.* Cambridge: Cambridge University Press, 2013.

Burton, William. "On the Origin and End of Sex: Language, Science and Social Construction in Jean-Jacques Rousseau and Monique Wittig." PhD diss., Columbia University, 2020.

Bury, Liz. "Reading Literary Fiction Improves Empathy, Study Finds." *The Guardian,* October 8, 2013. https://www.theguardian.com/books/books blog/2013/oct/08/literary-fiction-improves-empathy-study.

Busch, Thomas W. *The Power of Consciousness and the Force of Circumstances in Sartre's Philosophy.* Bloomington: Indiana University Press, 1989.

Butler, Judith. *Frames of War: When Is Life Grievable?* New York: Verso, 2009.

Calder, John. *The Philosophy of Samuel Beckett.* Surrey: Alma Books, 2001.

Camus, Albert. "*Le Mur* de Jean-Paul Sartre." *Alger Républicain,* October 20, 1938.

Carroll, David. *French Literary Fascism: Nationalism, Anti-Semitism, and the Ideology of Culture.* Princeton, N.J.: Princeton University Press, 1998.

Caserio, Robert L., et al. "The Antisocial Thesis in Queer Theory." *PMLA* 121, no. 3 (2006): 819–28.

Céline, Louis-Ferdinand. *Bagatelles pour un massacre.* Paris: Denoël, 1937.

Céline, Louis-Ferdinand. *Death on the Installment Plan.* Translated by Ralph Manheim. New York: New Directions Publishing, 1966.

Céline, Louis-Ferdinand. "Hommage à Zola." *Études françaises* 39, no. 2 (2003): 87–91. First published 1936.

Céline, Louis-Ferdinand. *Journey to the End of the Night.* Translated by Ralph Manheim. 1983. Reprint, New York: New Directions Publishing, 2006.

Céline, Louis-Ferdinand. *L. F. Céline.* Edited by Michel Beausejour, Dominique de Roux, and Michel Thélia. Paris: L'Herne, 1972.

Céline, Louis-Ferdinand. *"Mea Culpa" suivi de "La Vie et l'œuvre de Semmelweis."* Paris: Denoël et Steele, 1973.

Céline, Louis-Ferdinand. *Romans I.* Bibliothèque de la Pléiade. Paris: Gallimard, 1981.

Céline, Louis-Ferdinand. *Voyage au bout de la nuit.* Folio. Paris: Gallimard, 2011.

Césaire, Aimé. "Letter to Maurice Thorez." Translated by Chike Jeffers. *Social Text* 28, no. 2 (2010): 145–52.

Chalfin, Brenda. "Public Things, Excremental Politics, and the Infrastructure of Bare Life in Ghana's City of Tema." *American Ethnologist* 41, no. 1 (2014): 92–109.

Chaouat, Bruno. "Ce que chier veut dire (Les *ultima excreta* de Robert Antelme)." *Revue des sciences humaines* 261 (2001): 147–62.

Chaouat, Bruno. "'La mort ne recèle pas tant de mystère': Robert Antelme's Defaced Humanism." *L'Esprit créateur* 40, no. 1 (2000): 88–99.

Chare, Nicholas. *Auschwitz and Afterimages: Abjection, Witnessing and Representation.* London: I.B. Tauris, 2011.

Charlesworth, Max. *The Existentialists and Jean-Paul Sartre.* London: George Prior, 1976.

Chasseguet-Smirgel, Janine. "L'Univers sadique-anal et la perversion." In *Éthique et esthétique de la perversion*, 183–213. Seyssel: Editions du Champ Vallon, 1984.

Chaudier, Stéphane. "'Dieu ait son cul': Le style de Momo-Rosa." *Europe*, nos. 1022–23 (2014): 145–62.

Christensen, Andrew G. "'Tis My Muse Will Have It So': Four Dimensions of Scatology in Molloy." *Journal of Modern Literature* 40, no. 4 (October 2017): 90–104.

Cixous, Hélène. "The Laugh of the Medusa." Translated by Keith Cohen and Paula Cohen. *Signs* 1, no. 4 (1976): 875–93.

Cohen-Solal, Annie. *Jean-Paul Sartre.* Que sais-je? Paris: Presses universitaires de France, 2005.

Cohn, Ruby. *A Beckett Canon.* Ann Arbor: University of Michigan Press, 2001.

Corbin, Alain. *The Foul and the Fragrant: Odor and the French Social Imagination.* Cambridge, Mass.: Harvard University Press, 1986.

Cordingley, Anthony. "Beckett's Ignorance: Miracles/Memory, Pascal/Proust." *Journal of Modern Literature* 33, no. 4 (2010): 129–52.

Crowley, Martin. *Duras, Writing, and the Ethical: Making the Broken Whole.* Oxford: Oxford University Press, 2000.

Crowley, Martin. "*Postface à la transgression,* or: Trash, Nullity, and Dubious Literary Resistance." *Dalhousie French Studies* 88 (2009): 99–109.

Crowley, Martin. *Robert Antelme: Humanity, Community, Testimony.* Oxford: Legenda, 2003.

Derrida, Jacques. *Glas.* Translated by John P. Leavey and Richard Rand. Lincoln: University of Nebraska Press, 1986.

Derrida, Jacques. *Of Grammatology.* Translated by Gayatri Chakravorty Spivak. Baltimore: Johns Hopkins University Press, 1998.

Des Pres, Terrence. *The Survivor: An Anatomy of Life in the Death Camps.* New York: Oxford University Press, 1976.

Detmer, David. *Sartre Explained: From Bad Faith to Authenticity.* Chicago: Open Court, 2008.

Dini, Rachele. *Consumerism, Waste, and Re-Use in Twentieth-Century Fiction: Legacies of the Avant Garde.* New York: Palgrave Macmillan, 2016.

Donovan, Josephine, and Carol Adams, eds. *The Feminist Care Tradition in Animal Ethics: A Reader.* New York: Columbia University Press, 2007.

Dorlin, Elsa. *La Matrice de la race: Généalogie sexuelle et coloniale de la nation française.* Paris: La Découverte, 2006.

Douglas, Mary. *Purity and Danger: An Analysis of Concepts of Pollution and Taboo.* New York: Routledge, 1966.

Dundes, Alan. *Life Is Like a Chicken Coop Ladder: A Portrait of German Culture through Folklore.* New York: Columbia University Press, 1984.

Duras, Marguerite. *La Douleur.* Folio. Paris: Gallimard, 1993.

Duras, Marguerite. *War: A Memoir.* Translated by Barbara Bray. New York: Pantheon Books, 1986.

Earle, Jason. "*Les Deux Cents Familles*: A Conspiracy Theory of the Avant-Garde." *Romanic Review* 104, nos. 3–4 (2013): 333–52.

Elias, Norbert. *The Civilizing Process: Sociogenetic and Psychogenetic Investigations.* Malden, Mass.: Blackwell Publishing, 1994.

Enders, Giulia. *Gut: The Inside Story of Our Body's Most Underrated Organ.* Vancouver: Greystone Books, 2015.

Esty, Jed. "Excremental Postcolonialism." *Contemporary Literature* 40, no. 1 (1999): 22–59.

Falzon, Chris. "Sartre and Meaningful Existence." In *Sartre's Nausea: Text, Context, Intertext,* edited by Alistair Rolls and Elizabeth Rechniewski, 105–20. Amsterdam: Rodopi, 2006.

Fehsenfeld, Martha Dow, and Lois More Overbeck, eds. *The Letters of Samuel Beckett, Vol. 1: 1929–1940.* Cambridge: Cambridge University Press, 2009.

Ferdman, Roberto A. "'I Had to Wear Pampers': The Cruel Reality the People Who Bring You Cheap Chicken Allegedly Endure." *Washington Post,* May 11, 2016. https://www.washingtonpost.com/news/wonk/wp/2016/05/11/i-had-to-wear-pampers-many-poultry-industry-workers-allegedly-cant-even-take-bathroom-breaks/.

Flynn, Thomas R. *Sartre: A Philosophical Biography.* Cambridge: Cambridge University Press, 2014.

Freud, Sigmund. *The Standard Edition of the Complete Psychological Works of Sigmund Freud.* Vol. 7. Edited by James Strachey. London: Hogarth Press, 1953.

Freud, Sigmund. *The Standard Edition of the Complete Psychological Works of Sigmund Freud.* Vol. 9. Edited by James Strachey. London: Hogarth Press, 1959.

Freud, Sigmund. *The Standard Edition of the Complete Psychological Works of Sigmund Freud.* Vol. 17. Edited by James Strachey. London: Hogarth Press, 1955.

Friedman, Marilyn. "Care and Context in Moral Reasoning." In *Women and Moral Theory,* edited by Eva Kittay and Diana Meyers, 190–204. Totowa, N.J.: Rowman and Littlefield, 1987.

Garréta, Anne. *Dans l'béton.* Paris: Grasset, 2017.

Garréta, Anne. *In Concrete.* Translated by Emma Ramadan. Dallas: Deep Vellum Publishing, 2021.

Garréta, Anne. *Sphinx.* Paris: Grasset, 1986.

Gary, Romain. *La Vie devant soi.* Folio. Paris: Gallimard, 1982.

Gary, Romain. *The Life before Us.* Translated by Ralph Manheim. New York: New Directions, 1986.

Gelas, Nicolas. *Romain Gary ou l'humanisme en fiction.* Paris: L'Harmattan, 2012.

Genet, Jean. *The Declared Enemy: Texts and Interviews.* Translated by Jeff Fort. Stanford, Calif.: Stanford University Press, 2004.

Genet, Jean. *Miracle de la rose.* Folio. Paris: Gallimard, 2005.

Genet, Jean. *Notre-Dame-des-Fleurs.* Folio. Paris: Gallimard, 1976.

Genet, Jean. *Our Lady of the Flowers.* Translated by Bernard Frechtman. New York: Grove Press, 1963.

Genet, Jean. *What Remains of a Rembrandt Torn into Four Equal Pieces and Flushed Down the Toilet.* Translated by Bernard Frechtman. New York: Hanuman Books, 1988.

Genet, Jean. "What Remains of a Rembrandt Torn into Little Squares All the Same Size and Shot Down the Toilet." Translated by Charlotte Mandell. In *Fragments of the Artwork*, 91–102. Stanford, Calif.: Stanford University Press, 2003.

Gershon, Michael. *The Second Brain: A Groundbreaking New Understanding of Nervous Disorders of the Stomach and Intestine.* New York: HarperCollins, 2019.

Gide, André. "Les Juifs, Céline et Maritain." *Nouvelle Revue Française,* no. 295 (April 1, 1938): 630–36.

Gilligan, Carol. *In a Different Voice: Psychological Theory and Women's Development.* Cambridge, Mass.: Harvard University Press, 1982.

Godard, Henri. *À travers Céline, la littérature.* Paris: Gallimard, 2014.

Godard, Henri. *Henri Godard présente "Mort à crédit" de Louis-Ferdinand Céline.* Folio. Paris: Gallimard, 1996.

Godard, Henri. *Poétique de Céline.* Paris: Gallimard, 1985.

Gorrara, Claire. "Bearing Witness in Robert Antelme's *L'Espèce humaine* and Marguerite Duras's *La Douleur.*" *Women in French Studies* 5 (1997): 243–52.

Grainville, Patrick. "Daniel Pennac: *Journal d'un corps.*" *Le Figaro,* February 15, 2012.

Graver, Lawrence, and Raymond Federman, eds. *Samuel Beckett: The Critical Heritage.* London: Routledge, 1979.

Grossmann-Etoh, Amelie. "*Journal d'un corps*: 'Un roman presque parfait.'" *L'Express,* April 23, 2012.

Guerlac, Suzanne. *Literary Polemics: Bataille, Sartre, Valéry, Breton.* Stanford, Calif.: Stanford University Press, 1997.

Guibert, Hervé. *À l'ami qui ne m'a pas sauvé la vie.* Paris: Gallimard, 1992.

Guibert, Hervé. *"La Mort propaganda" et autres textes de jeunesse.* Paris: Régine Deforges, 1991.

Guibert, Hervé. *Le Mausolée des amants: Journal, 1976–1991.* Paris: Gallimard, 2003.

Guibert, Hervé. *Le Protocole compassionnel.* Paris: Gallimard, 1993.

Guibert, Hervé. *Written in Invisible Ink: Selected Stories.* Translated by Jeffrey Zuckerman. South Pasadena, Calif.: Semiotext(e), 2020.

Guiley, Rosemary. *The Encyclopedia of Magic and Alchemy*. New York: Infobase Publishing, 2006.

Guynn, Noah. *Pure Filth: Ethics, Politics, and Religion in Early French Farce*. Philadelphia: University of Pennsylvania Press, 2019.

Hadhazy, Adam. "Think Twice: How the Gut's 'Second Brain' Influences Mood and Well-Being." *Scientific American*, February 12, 2010. https://www.scientificamerican.com/article/gut-second-brain/.

Hainge, Greg. "The Language of Suffering: The Place of Pain in Louis-Ferdinand Céline's 'Féerie pour une autre fois' I." *L'Esprit créateur* 45, no. 3 (2005): 18–28.

Hammond, Claudia. "Does Reading Fiction Make Us Better People?" *BBC*, June 2, 2019. https://www.bbc.com/future/article/20190523-does-reading-fiction-make-us-better-people.

Hangouët, Jean-François. *Romain Gary: À la traversée des frontières*. Paris: Gallimard, 2007.

Hanrahan, Mairéad. "Double Signature." *Paragraph* 39, no. 2 (2016): 165–86.

Hanrahan, Mairéad. *Lire Genet: Une poétique de la différence*. Montreal: Presses de l'Université de Montréal, 1997.

Hanrahan, Mairéad. "Review: 'Saint Genet' Decanonized: The Ludic Body in 'Querelle.'" *French Studies* 57, no. 3 (July 2003): 420–21.

Hartman, Geoffrey. "Homage to *Glas*." *Critical Inquiry* 33, no. 2 (2007): 344–61.

Hartman, Saidiya. *Scenes of Subjection: Terror, Slavery, and Self-Making in Nineteenth-Century America*. New York: Oxford University Press, 1997.

Harvey, C. J. "Jean-Paul Sartre's 'L'Enfance d'un chef': The Longing for Obscenity." *Romance Notes* 23, no. 3 (1983): 204–9.

Harvey, Robert. "Genet's Open Enemies: Sartre and Derrida." *Yale French Studies*, no. 91 (1997): 103–16.

Haslanger, Sally. *Resisting Reality: Social Construction and Social Critique*. New York: Oxford University Press, 2012.

Hawkins, Gay. *The Ethics of Waste*. Oxford: Rowman and Littlefield, 2006.

Heining, Maike, Andrew W. Young, Glavkos Ioannou, Chris M. Andrew, Michael J. Brammer, Jeffrey A. Gray, and Mary L. Phillips. "Disgusting Smells Activate Human Anterior Insula and Ventral Striatum." *Annals of the New York Academy of Sciences* 1000 (December 2003): 380–84.

Hewitt, Nicholas. "'Looking for Annie': Sartre's *La Nausée* and the Inter-War Years." *Journal of European Studies* 12, no. 46 (1982): 96–112.

Hoffmann, Benjamin. *Les Paradoxes de la postérité*. Paris: Minuit, 2019.

Holmes, Aaron. "This Slanted Toilet Was Designed to Increase Productivity and Decrease Smartphone Use by Being Painful to Sit on for More Than 5 Minutes, and People Are Horrified." *Business Insider*, December 18, 2019. https://www.businessinsider.com/slanted-toilet-design-decrease-phone-social-media-use-bathroom-breaks-2019-12.

hooks, bell. *Feminist Theory: From Margin to Center*. New York: Routledge, 2014.

Huchet, Jean-Charles. "La Clinique littéraire de Céline: *Mort à crédit*." *Littérature* 90, no. 2 (1993): 74–87.

Hunt, Lynn. *Inventing Human Rights*. New York: Norton, 2008.

Hussey, Andrew, ed. *The Beast at Heaven's Gate: Georges Bataille and the Art of Transgression*. Amsterdam: Rodopi, 2006.

Idt, Geneviève. *"Le Mur" de Jean-Paul Sartre: Techniques et contexte d'une provocation*. Paris: Librairie Larousse, 1972.

Iser, Wolfgang. *Die Appellstruktur der Texte*. Konstanz: Universitätsverlag, 1970.

James, Alison. *The Documentary Imagination in Twentieth-Century French Literature: Writing with Facts*. Oxford: Oxford University Press, 2020.

Jardine, Alice, and Anne Menke, eds. *Shifting Scenes: Interviews on Women, Writing, and Politics in Post-68 France*. New York: Columbia University Press, 1991.

Kalifa, Dominique. *Les Bas-fonds: Histoire d'un imaginaire*. Paris: Seuil, 2013.

Kanony, Serge. *Céline? C'est ça! . . .* Paris: Le Petit Célinien, 2012.

Kantrowitz, Barbara. "Why Men Leave When Cancer Arrives." *Newsweek*, November 15, 2009. https://www.newsweek.com/why-men-leave-when-cancer-arrives-76637.

Kaplan, Alice. *Reproductions of Banality: Fascism, Literature, and French Intellectual Life*. Minneapolis: University of Minnesota Press, 1986.

Katz, Danièle. "Beckett's Absent Paris." *Études Anglaises* 59, no. 1 (2006): 7–17.

Kawa, Nicholas. "A Mend to the Metabolic Rift? The Promises (and Potential Pitfalls) of Biosolids Application on American Soils." In *Thinking with Soils*, edited by Juan Francisco Salazar, Céline Granjou, Matthew Kearnes, Anna Krzywoszynska, and Manuel Tironi, 141–56. London: Bloomsbury, 2020.

Keen, Suzanne. *Empathy and the Novel*. New York: Oxford University Press, 2010.

Kim, Annabel. "A Return to Culture: Literature as Ecology." *Contemporary French and Francophone Studies: Sites* 25, no. 1 (2021): 85–94.

Kim, Annabel. "The Riddle of Racial Difference in Anne Garréta's *Sphinx.*" *Diacritics* 45, no. 1 (2017): 4–22.

Kim, Annabel. *Unbecoming Language: Anti-Identitarian French Feminist Fictions.* Columbus: Ohio State University Press, 2018.

Knapp, Bettina. *Céline: Man of Hate.* Tuscaloosa: University of Alabama Press, 1974.

Kramer, Reinhold. *Scatology and Civility in the English–Canadian Novel.* Toronto: University of Toronto Press, 1997.

Krauss, Rosalind. "'Informe' without Conclusion." *October* 78 (1996): 89–105.

Kristeva, Julia. *Powers of Horror: An Essay on Abjection.* Translated by Leon Roudiez. New York: Columbia University Press, 1982.

Kritzman, Lawrence. "Duras' War." *L'Esprit créateur* 33, no. 1 (1993): 63–73.

Lacapra, Dominick. *A Preface to Sartre.* Ithaca, N.Y.: Cornell University Press, 1978.

Laclau, Ernesto. "Universalism, Particularism, and the Question of Identity." *October* 61 (Summer 1992): 83–90.

La Durantaye, Leland de. *Beckett's Art of Mismaking.* Cambridge, Mass.: Harvard University Press, 2016.

Laporte, Dominique. *History of Shit.* Translated by Rodolphe el-Khoury and Nadia Benabid. Cambridge, Mass.: MIT Press, 2000.

Latour, Bruno. *Reassembling the Social: An Introduction to Actor-Network Theory.* Oxford: Oxford University Press, 2005.

Latour, Bruno. *We Have Never Been Modern.* Cambridge, Mass.: Harvard University Press, 1993.

Laurens, Camille. "Qui dit ça?" In *Autofiction(s): Colloque de Cerisy, 2008,* edited by Claude Burgelin, Isabelle Grelle, and Roger-Yves Roche, 25–34. Lyon: Presses universitaires de Lyon, 2010.

Leiner, Jacqueline. "Entretien avec Aimé Césaire." In *Tropiques, 1941–45: Collection complète,* v–xxiv. Paris: Jean Michel Place, 1978.

Lévinas, Emmanuel. *Éthique et infini.* Paris: Fayard, 1982.

Liboiron, Max. "Why 'Discard Studies'? Why Not 'Waste Studies'?" *Discard Studies* (blog), September 4, 2014. https://discardstudies.com/2014/09/04/why-discard-studies-why-not-waste-studies-2.

Lispector, Clarice. "Report on the Thing." In *The Complete Stories,* edited by Benjamin Moser, translated by Katrina Dodson, 475–83. New York: New Directions, 2018.

Lorde, Audre. *Sister Outsider*. New York: Penguin Books, 2020.

Loret, Eric. "Anne F. Garréta, tambour béton." *Le Monde*, November 23, 2017.

Louar, Nadia. "Beckett's Bodies in the Trilogy, or Life as a Pensum." *Journal of Beckett Studies* 27, no. 1 (2018): 69–82.

Louette, Jean-François. "'L'enfance d'un chef ': La Fleur et le coin d'acier." *Revue d'histoire litteraire de la France* 109, no. 2 (2009): 365–84.

Lozier, Claire. *De l'abject au sublime: Georges Bataille, Jean Genet, Samuel Beckett* Oxford: Peter Lang, 2012.

Lucey, Michael. "Genet's *Notre-Dame-Des-Fleurs*: Fantasy and Sexual Identity." *Yale French Studies*, no. 91 (1997): 80–102.

Lucey, Michael. *Someone: The Pragmatics of Misfit Sexualities, from Colette to Hervé Guibert*. Chicago: University of Chicago Press, 2019.

Lukács, György. *Realism in Our Time: Literature and the Class Struggle*. Translated by John and Necke Mander. New York: Harper & Row, 1971.

Macaskill, Brian. "The Logic of Coprophilia: Mathematics and Beckett's 'Molloy.'" *SubStance* 17, no. 3 (1988): 13–21.

Magedera, Ian. "'Seing' Genet, Citation and Mourning; a propos *Glas* by Jacques Derrida." *Paragraph* 21, no. 1 (March 1998): 28–44.

Marin, Louis. *Food for Thought*. Translated by Mette Hjort. Baltimore: Johns Hopkins University Press, 1997.

Mathias, Manon, and Alison Moore, eds. *Gut Feeling and Digestive Health in Nineteenth-Century Literature, History, and Culture*. Cham: Palgrave Macmillan, 2018.

Maude, Ulrika. "'A Stirring beyond Coming and Going': Beckett and Tourette's." *Journal of Beckett Studies* 17, nos. 1–2 (September 2008): 153–68.

Mauriac, François. "L'Excrémentialisme." *Le Figaro*, August 15, 1950.

Mavrikakis, Catherine. "Le Sépulcre de merde ou le travail de la déjection chez Hervé Guibert." *ETC* 94 (December 2011): 30–32.

Mbembe, Achille. *Necropolitics*. Durham, N.C.: Duke University Press, 2019.

McSweeney, Joyelle. *The Necropastoral: Poetry, Media, Occults*. Ann Arbor: University of Michigan Press, 2014.

McSweeney, Joyelle. "What Is the Necropastoral?" *Poetry Foundation*, April 29, 2014. https://www.poetryfoundation.org/harriet/2014/04/what-is-the -necropastoral.

Mehlman, Jeffrey. "The Holocaust Comedies of 'Emile Ajar'." In *Genealogies of the Text: Literature, Psychoanalysis, and Politics in Modern France*, 154–73. Cambridge: Cambridge University Press, 1995.

Melcer-Padon, Nourit. "Romain Gary and the Aesthetics of Survival." *Partial Answers* 15, no. 1 (2017): 47–60.

Miller, Christopher. *Impostors: Literary Hoaxes and Cultural Authenticity.* Chicago: University of Chicago Press, 2018.

Miller, Ian, and Kay Souter. *Beckett and Bion: The (Im)Patient Voice in Psychotherapy and Literature.* London: Karnac Books, 2013.

Miroux, Pierre-Marie. *Matière et lumière: La Mort dans l'œuvre de Louis-Ferdinand Céline.* Paris: Société des études céliniennes, 2006.

Mole, Gary. "Scatology, Chopped Liver, and the Last Supper: Daniel Zimmermann's Holocaust Novel *L'Anus du monde*." *French Studies* 67, no. 1 (2013): 30–46.

Morin, Emilie. *Beckett's Political Imagination.* Cambridge: Cambridge University Press, 2017.

Morin, Marie-Eve. "Thinking Things: Heidegger, Sartre, Nancy." *Sartre Studies International* 15, no. 2 (2009): 35–53.

Morrison, Susan Signe. *Excrement in the Late Middle Ages: Sacred Filth and Chaucer's Fecopoetics.* New York: Palgrave Macmillan, 2008.

Morrison, Susan Signe. *The Literature of Waste: Material Ecopoetics and Ethical Matter.* New York: Palgrave Macmillan, 2015.

Morrison, Toni. *The Source of Self-Regard: Selected Essays, Speeches, and Meditations.* New York: Vintage Books, 2019.

Murat, Laure. "Un siècle de littérature lesbienne." *Le Magazine littéraire,* no. 426 (December 2003): 43–45.

Naulleau, Eric. "Le Coup de gueule de Naulleau: Pennac, à poil!" *Paris Match,* March 27, 2012. http://www.parismatch.com/Culture/Livres/Pennac-a-poil-la-critique-d-Eric-Naulleau-156059.

Noddings, Nel. *Caring: A Relational Approach to Ethics and Moral Education.* 2nd ed. Berkeley: University of California Press, 2013.

Noor, Poppy. "The Men Who Leave Their Spouses When They Have a Life-Threatening Illness." *The Guardian,* March 30, 2020. https://www.theguardian.com/lifeandstyle/2020/mar/30/the-men-who-give-up-on-their-spouses-when-they-have-cancer.

Noys, Benjamin. "Georges Bataille's Base Materialism." *Journal for Cultural Research* 2, no. 4 (1998): 499–517.

O'Hara, James Donald. *Samuel Beckett's Hidden Drives: Structural Uses of Depth Psychology.* Gainesville: University Press of Florida, 1997.

Okin, Susan. *Justice, Gender, and the Family.* New York: Basic Books, 1989.

O'Reilly, Edouard. "*Molloy*, Part II, Where the Shit Hits the Fan: Ballyba's

Economy and the Worth of the World." *Genetic Joyce Studies*, no. 6 (Spring 2006): http://www.geneticjoycestudies.org/articles/GJS6/GJS6OReilly.

Pachet, Yaël. "Casser des murs avec une masse." *En attendant Nadeau*, December 5, 2017.

Patry, Jacques. *L'Interdit, la transgression, Georges Bataille et nous*. Laval: Presses de l'Université Laval, 2012.

Penguin Random House. "This Is How Literary Fiction Teaches Us to Be Human." *Medium* (blog), October 10, 2016. https://medium.com/@penguinrandomus/this-is-how-literary-fiction-teaches-us-to-be-human-53d468dba179.

Pennac, Daniel. *Better Than Life*. Translated by David Homel. Toronto: Coach House Press, 1994.

Pennac, Daniel. *Comme un roman*. Paris: Gallimard, 1992.

Pennac, Daniel. *Diary of a Body*. Translated by Alyson Waters. London: MacLehose Press, 2016.

Pennac, Daniel. *Journal d'un corps*. Édition revue et augmentée. Folio. Paris: Gallimard, 2014.

Pépin, François. *Aspects du corps dans l'œuvre de Romain Gary*. Paris: L'Harmattan, 2003.

Persels, Jeff, and Russell Ganim, eds. *Fecal Matters in Early Modern Literature and Art: Studies in Scatology*. Burlington, Vt.: Ashgate, 2004.

Pitkin, Hanna. "Are Freedom and Liberty Twins?" *Political Theory* 16, no. 4 (1988): 523–52.

Plottel, Jeanine Parisier. "Memory, Fiction and History." *L'Esprit créateur* 30, no. 1 (1990): 47–55.

Plunka, Gene A. "Review of *The Body Abject: Self and Text in Jean Genet and Samuel Beckett*, by David Houston Jones." *French Forum* 28, no. 2 (2003): 124.

Prince, Gerald. "*La Nausée* and the Question of Closure." *Yale French Studies*, no. 67 (1984): 182–90.

Rabaté, Jean-Michel. *1913: The Cradle of Modernism*. Malden, Mass.: Blackwell Publishing, 2007.

Rabaté, Jean-Michel. "Beckett et la poésie de la zone: (Dante . . . Apollinaire. Céline . . . Lévi)." *Samuel Beckett Today/Aujourd'hui* 8, no. 1 (1999): 75–90.

Rabaté, Jean-Michel. *Think, Pig! Beckett at the Limit of the Human*. New York: Fordham University Press, 2016.

Raoul, Valerie. *The French Fictional Journal: Fictional Narcissism / Narcissistic Fiction*. Toronto: University of Toronto Press, 1980.

Renard, Jean-Claude. *Céline, les livres de la mère*. Paris: Buchet/Castel, 2004.

Robcis, Camille. *The Law of Kinship: Anthropology, Psychoanalysis, and the Family in Twentieth-Century France*. Ithaca, N.Y.: Cornell University Press, 2013.

Rockefeller, Abby A. "Civilization and Sludge: Notes on the History of the Management of Human Excreta." *Capitalism Nature Socialism* 9, no. 3 (September 1998): 3–18.

Rose, Sean James. "Zazie dans le BTP." *Livres Hebdo*, September 22, 2017.

Ross, Kristin. *Communal Luxury: The Political Imaginary of the Paris Commune*. Brooklyn: Verso, 2015.

Ross, Kristin. *Fast Cars, Clean Bodies: Decolonization and the Reordering of French Culture*. Cambridge, Mass.: MIT Press, 1994.

Rosse, Dominique. *Romain Gary et la modernité*. Ottawa: University of Ottawa Press, 1995.

Roumette, Julien. "'La hausse des cris': Romain Gary et l'irrespect carnivalesque." *Littératures* 65 (2011): 93–113.

Roussin, Philippe. "Tout dire: Pourquoi?" In Roussin, Schaffner, Tettamanzi, *Céline à l'épreuve*, 255–72.

Roussin, Philippe, Alain Schaffner, and Régis Tettamanzi, eds. *Céline à l'épreuve: Réceptions, critiques, influences*. Paris: Honoré Champion, 2016.

Rybalka, Michel. "Sartre: A Short Chronology." *French Review* 55, no. 7 (1982): 131–33.

Saada, Emmanuelle. "'Without Distinction of . . . Sex': The Constitutional Politics of Race and Sex in Contemporary France." Edgar L. Newman Memorial Lecture, Western Society for French History, Forty-Sixth Annual Meeting, November 3, 2018. https://youtu.be/uEnqPoN5qtM.

Samuels, Maurice. *The Right to Difference: French Universalism and the Jews*. Chicago: University of Chicago Press, 2016.

Sartre, Jean-Paul. *L'Enfance d'un Chef*. Folio. Paris: Gallimard, 2003.

Sartre, Jean-Paul. *La Nausée*. Folio. Paris: Gallimard, 1972.

Sartre, Jean-Paul. *Nausea*. Translated by Lloyd Alexander. New York: New Directions, 2007.

Sartre, Jean-Paul. *Œuvres romanesques*. Bibliothèque de la Pléiade. Paris: Gallimard, 1982.

Sartre, Jean-Paul. *Saint Genet: Actor and Martyr*. Translated by Bernard Frechtman. Minneapolis: University of Minnesota Press, 2012.

Sartre, Jean-Paul. *The Wall: (Intimacy) and Other Stories*. Translated by Lloyd Alexander. New York: New Directions, 1975. First published 1948.

Sartre, Jean-Paul. *The Words*. Translated by Bernard Frechtman. New York: George Braziller, 1964.

Schmidt, Christopher. *The Poetics of Waste: Queer Excess in Stein, Ashbery, Schuyler, and Goldsmith*. New York: Palgrave Macmillan, 2014.

Schor, Naomi. "The Crisis of French Universalism." *Yale French Studies* 100 (2001): 43–64.

Scott, Joan. *Parité! Sexual Equality and the Crisis of French Universalism*. Chicago: University of Chicago Press, 2007.

Serres, Michel. *The Natural Contract*. Translated by Elizabeth MacArthur and William Paulson. Ann Arbor: University of Michigan Press, 1995.

Sims, Alexandra. "Teenage Girl Dies from Heart Attack after Not Going to the Toilet for Eight Weeks." *Independent*, July 1, 2015. https://www.independent.co.uk/life-style/health-and-families/health-news/teenage-girl-dies-of-heart-attack-after-not-going-to-the-toilet-for-eight-weeks-10357533.html.

Sollers, Philippe. *Céline*. Paris: Éditions Écriture, 2009.

Spitzer, Anais. *Derrida, Myth and the Impossibility of Philosophy*. London: Continuum, 2011.

Stamatopoulou-Robbins, Sophia. *Waste Siege: The Life of Infrastructure in Palestine*. Stanford, Calif.: Stanford University Press, 2019.

Steiner, George, "Cry Havoc." *New Yorker*, January 13, 1968, 106.

Stewart, Paul. *Sex and Aesthetics in Samuel Beckett's Work*. New York: Palgrave Macmillan, 2011.

Stiegler, Bernard. *The Neganthropocene*. Translated by Daniel Ross. London: Open Humanities Press, 2018.

Stockton, Will. *Playing Dirty: Sexuality and Waste in Early Modern Comedy*. Minneapolis: University of Minnesota Press, 2011.

Sugiura, Yoriko. "Perte et deuil dans 'Mort à crédit.'" In Roussin, Schaffner, and Tettamanzi, *Céline à l'épreuve*, 199–213.

Surkis, Judith. "No Fun and Games until Someone Loses an Eye: Transgression and Masculinity in Bataille and Foucault." *Diacritics* 26, no. 2 (1996): 18–30.

Tajiri, Yoshiki. "Review of *Back to the Beckett Text* and *Beckett/Philosophy*." *Journal of Beckett Studies* 23, no. 2 (September 2014): 277–81.

Thompson, E. P. "Time, Work-Discipline, and Industrial Capitalism." *Past & Present* 38, no. 1 (1967): 56–97.

Thompson, Michael. *Rubbish Theory*. London: Pluto Press, 1979.

Tomès, Arnaud. "Petit lexique sartrien." *Cités* 22, no. 2 (2005): 185–96.

Tronto, Joan. *Moral Boundaries: A Political Argument for an Ethic of Care.* New York: Routledge, 1993.

Tronto, Joan. *Who Cares? How to Reshape a Democratic Politics.* Ithaca, N.Y.: Cornell University Press, 2015.

Tucker, David. *Samuel Beckett and Arnold Geulincx: Tracing "A Literary Fantasia."* New York: Bloomsbury Academic, 2014.

Van Hulle, Dirk. "Textual Scars: Beckett, Genetic Criticism and Textual Scholarship." In *The Edinburgh Companion to Samuel Beckett and the Arts,* edited by S. E. Gontarski, 306–19. Edinburgh: Edinburgh University Press, 2014.

Walker, David H. *Consumer Chronicles: Cultures of Consumptions in Modern French Literature.* Liverpool: Liverpool University Press, 2011.

Wasser, Audrey. *The Work of Difference: Modernism, Romanticism, and the Production of Literary Form.* New York: Fordham University Press, 2016.

Watts, Philip. "Postmodern Céline." In *Céline and the Politics of Difference,* edited by Rosemarie Scullion, Philip H. Solomon, and Thomas C. Spear, 203–15. Hanover, N.H.: University Press of New England, 1995.

Weisberg, David. *Chronicles of Disorder: Samuel Beckett and the Cultural Politics of the Modern Novel.* Albany: State University of New York Press, 2000.

White, Edmund. *Genet: A Biography.* New York: Alfred A. Knopf, 1993.

Whorton, James. *Inner Hygiene: Constipation and the Pursuit of Health in Modern Society.* New York: Oxford University Press, 2000.

Wilder, Gary. *Freedom Time: Negritude, Decolonization, and the Future of the World.* Durham, N.C.: Duke University Press, 2015.

Willging, Jennifer. "Partners in Slime: The Liquid and the Viscous in Sarraute and Sartre." *Romanic Review* 92, no. 3 (2001): 277–96.

Wilson, Elizabeth. *Gut Feminism.* Durham, N.C.: Duke University Press, 2015.

Winston, Jane. *Postcolonial Duras: Cultural Memory in Postwar France.* New York: Palgrave Macmillan, 2002.

Wittig, Monique. *Le Chantier littéraire.* Lyon: Presses universitaires de Lyon; Donnemarie-Dontilly: iXe, 2010.

Wittig, Monique. *L'Opoponax.* Paris: Minuit, 1964.

Wittig, Monique. *The Straight Mind.* Boston: Beacon Press, 1992.

Wolf, Nelly. *Le Peuple dans le roman français de Zola à Céline.* Paris: Presses universitaires de France, 1990.

Yorifuji, Bunpei, and Koichi Fujita. *Au cœur du caca: Pour une vie entière de beaux cacas.* Tokyo: Jitsugyo No Nihonsha, 2005.

INDEX

A and B (characters in Beckett's
Molloy), 98
abjection and the abject, 61, 101, 123,
228n32; Antelme and, 143, 148;
Beckett and, 84–85, 87, 97; fecality
and, 12–13, 23, 58; Genet and,
121–23, 241n41, 241n43; Kristeva
and, 41, 221n25
abstraction and the abstract, 9, 10,
25–27, 30, 43, 87, 109, 220n20,
231n56; Bataille and, 219n13,
219n16; shit and feces and, 12,
16, 18, 208. *See also* universalism:
abstract
absurdity and the absurd, 48, 53,
63, 65, 101, 111, 154, 171,
232–33n10
actant (Latour), 218n6
agency, 114, 118, 218n6
AIDS and HIV, 194–97, 246n26
alchemy, 85, 96, 102, 113. *See also* gold
and shit; philosopher's stone
Alexander, Lloyd, 240n31
alienation, 54
allegory, 61, 65
alterity, 15, 58
ambivalence, 32–33, 39, 49, 98, 141,
187; Genet's, 128–29

America, Americanization, 25, 180,
222n34, 245n17, 248n14
anality, 6, 33, 64, 116, 127; Beckett
and, 89, 235n24. *See also* anal sexuality and eroticism; anus
anal sexuality and eroticism, 12, 121,
242n49
anatomical dualism, 27, 223n55
Angélique (Poulette), in Garréta's
Dans l'béton, 172–75; covered in
concrete, 170–71, 178, 184
animalization/animals, 48, 144, 147,
150, 180; animal studies and,
77–78
Antelme, Robert: anus of, 137, 139,
151; Duras's care of, 144–50, 147;
L'Espèce humaine, 136; unhuman
shit of, 4, 137–43, 150, 244n4
Anthropocene period, 2, 21, 208;
necropolitics in, 22, 52–53, 223n44
anthropology/anthropologists, 217n4,
217n5, 218n7, 221n26
anti-gay marriage movement, 249n17
anti-Semitism: of Céline, 22, 39–40,
44, 79, 225n2, 225n3, 225n6,
228n29; in Sartre's *L'Enfance d'un
chef*, 109, 240n33
Antoine Roquentin (protagonist of

269

cowshit, in Garréta's *Dans l'béton*, 4, 175–77, 180

criminality/criminals, 122, 124, 125

crotte (solid excrement), 18, 51, 222n32. *See also* turd

Crowley, Martin, 244n2, 245n15, 245n16

cul (ass), as term, 15–16

Culafroy (child protagonist of Genet's *Notre-Dame-des-Fleurs*). *See* Lou Culafroy

culture, 17, 32, 97, 98, 222n34; art and, 39–40; language and, 185, 207, 251n4; shit and, 22, 102

Dachau, 4, 136

Dans l'béton (*In Concrete*) (Garréta), 248n15; concrete and family in, 168–73; grandmother in, 171–72, 175; narrator of, 164–65, 169, 172–73, 175, 178; political project of, 167, 182; political uses of shit in, 32, 163–84; prolegomenon of, 164–65; war against racism in, 173–81; word play in, 4, 164, 184

Darling (Mignon) (in Genet's *Notre-Dame-des-Fleurs*), 124, 126, 128, 243n58; final letter of, 130–32; shit of, 127–28

death, 68, 88, 194, 197; in Céline's *Mort à crédit*, 46, 51–52; Céline's project of writing, 50, 228n26; life and, 22, 52–53, 89, 97, 208, 223n44; of Madame Rosa in Gary's *La Vie devant soi*, 153–54; shit and, 51, 54, 58, 66–69, 89–90, 112, 139–42, 148; truth and, 42, 43; writing and, 80, 85, 193–94, 197–98

decay, 22, 195

déchet (shit, noun), 17, 141, 243n56

Declaration of the Rights of Man and the Citizen, 25–26

decolonization, 222n34

decomposition, 22, 53, 66, 84, 196, 209

defecation, 12, 15, 69–70, 114, 118–19, 135, 156, 197, 217n4, 230n43, 232n9, 237n48, 251n20; Céline and, 229n43, 230n45; euphemisms for, 59, 221n31; experienced by all, 26–27, 199, 204, 230n44; freedom of, 119–20; Gary and, 153–54; as inconvenience, 50, 102; new reality and, 65–66; verb *faire* and, 138–39. *See also* excrement; shit

déféquer (to defecate), as term, 16–17

degeneration, 20, 21

dehumanization, 23, 31, 147

déjection, as term, 17

Deleuze, Gilles, 77, 221n26, 238n5

Delphy, Christine, 248n14

dematerialization of shit, 11–12, 20

democracy and democratization, 15, 146; literature and, 32, 186, 200, 203, 209, 211; shit and, 32, 35, 211; universalism and, 4, 223n47

Democritus, 90

Denoël, 51

Derrida, Jacques, 35, 129, 243n58; *Glas*, 30, 133, 237n2, 238n5, 242–43n53

Descartes, René, 25, 120, 150; Beckett and, 78, 87, 90, 234–35n20

Despentes, Virginie, 164

destiny, 106; death as, 51, 53; of fecal matter, 11, 35, 211

Destouches, le docteur. *See* Céline, Louis-Ferdinand

determinism, 108, 123

deus ex machina, toilets as, 64, 75

erection/erections, 48–49. *See also*
 penis; phallus; prick
essentialism, 144, 145
Esty, Jed, 221n26
ethics, 3, 22, 160, 163, 245n16; fecality
 and shit and, 13–14, 21–24, 107–8,
 135
ethics of care, 146; fecal, 135–60; in
 Gary's *La Vie devant soi,* 155, 157;
 identity and, 135, 148
étron (turd; fecal matter), 18, 222n32
etymology of "shit" words, 16–17
Eugen Weidmann, in Genet's *Notre-
 Dame-des-Fleurs,* 124
euphemisms, 59, 96, 221n31
Europe and Eurocentrism, 17, 59, 93
exclusion: canon and, 207, 210;
 universalism and, 24–27, 209
excrement (*excrément*), 17, 19, 21, 69,
 132, 199, 218n9, 219n13, 219n17,
 222n34, 240n25, 245n11, 246n26;
 in Beckett's *Molloy,* 84–85, 232n9;
 in Céline's *Mort à crédit,* 45–46;
 excretion vs., 9–10; flatulence vs.,
 85–86; in Gary's *La Vie devant soi,*
 152, 153; Genet and, 237n4, 241–
 42n47; joy and, 98, 101; literature
 and, 31, 81, 83, 185; materiality
 of, 5, 10; as term, 16–18, 138–39;
 writing as, 191, 192, 196, 202–3.
 See also defecation; excremental,
 the; fecal matter and feces; shit;
 and "excremental" and "fecal" entries
excremental, the, 42, 124, 188,
 219n13, 229n41, 245n12, 247n35;
 Beckett and, 97, 236n34; care
 and, 148, 159; Céline and, 69,
 225n6, 227n20; Genet and,
 124–25; philosophy and, 90–96
excremental economy, excised from
 Beckett's *Molloy,* 90–92

excrementalism/excrementalists, 107;
 Sartre and, 105–6, 113, 132
excrementality, 6, 21, 23, 52, 154,
 226n12; Bataille and, 9, 10;
 Beckett and, 81, 94, 95, 102,
 232n9, 236n33; Céline and, 39, 41,
 46, 227n21; in French literature,
 207, 222n35; Genet and, 105, 108,
 121–23, 130; of prison, 124, 125;
 Sartre and, 105, 108; time and,
 47–48
excremental libertinism, of Sade,
 42–43
excremental literature and poetics,
 43, 185, 194, 199; excremental
 structure in, 65, 83; of Pennac,
 185–205; of Pennac's *Journal d'un
 corps,* 186, 197, 205; twentieth-
 century, 30–31
excremental sign, 57, 81, 83, 85, 188,
 194
excréter, as term, 17
excretion/excretions, 6; excrement
 vs., 9–10
existence, 111, 118, 122; contingency
 of, 106, 109–12
existentialism/existentialists, 106–7,
 115; problem of being of, 112,
 235n21; Sartre and, 108–9, 237n2
expectorating, 30. *See also* saliva; spit
exteriority/externality, 99, 118, 202,
 204

fabliaux, medieval, 1
fabulation, 147, 244n2
faire (to go), 17; materiality of shit
 and, 137–39
faith, 106, 108; good, 120, 132. *See also*
 bad faith
false universalism, 24
family/families, 167, 180; alternative,

shit and excrement as, 22, 33, 69,
84–85, 200, 234n19
fiction/fictions, 147, 194, 243–44n2;
diaries and, 197, 198
fiente (liquid excrement), 18
flatulence and flatus, 88, 89, 128–30,
188, 203; in Beckett's *Molloy*, 4,
82–83, 90, 95, 235n22; excrement
vs., 85–86. *See also* farting/farts
Flaubert, Gustave, 120; *Madame
Bovary*, 19, 80
floral/flowers, in Genet's works,
129–30
folklore, 12, 92
formalism, 12, 66, 188
formless (*l'informe*), 11
framing, narrative, 45, 89, 97
Frankfurt school, 221n26
Frechtman, Bernard, 224n59, 241n45
freedom, 106, 108, 127, 237n1,
243n59; to be oneself, 126–27;
contingency and, 109, 111, 118;
existentialist, 114, 132; fecality
and, 105, 115–16, 119–21; Genet
and, 107, 122, 132–33; literature
and, 121, 132, 208; Sartre and,
114, 118–19, 132–33, 238n9,
239n15; shit and, 31, 132, 135,
163. *See also* liberty
French identity and Frenchness, 3–4,
30
French language, 18, 71, 152, 209,
227n17, 251n4; Beckett and, 78,
79; fecal specificity of, 15–18. *See
also* French literature; translation/
translations
French literature, 15, 43, 62, 109, 136,
209, 226n12; Céline and, 39, 40;
excrementality and fecality of,
17–18, 23, 29, 44, 105; prizes in,
59, 152, 163, 173

French Resistance in World War II,
79
French Revolution, 24–25, 222n33
French studies, 2
Fresnes prison, Genet in, 120
Fressoz, Jean-Baptiste, 21
Freud, Sigmund, 12, 77, 113–16;
psychoanalysis and, 5, 92, 221n26.
See also Oedipal complex
friendship, of Sartre and Genet, 105,
132–33
Fujita, Kôchirô, 240n25

Gallimard, 243n1, 251n20
Gargantua (Rabelais), 1, 32–33
Garréta, Anne, 11, 221n28, 247n1;
Dans l'béton, 4, 32, 163–84; *Pas un
jour*, 163; *Sphinx*, 167; as Wittig's
spiritual heir, 181, 184, 249n21
Gary, Romain, 11, 152, 163, 243n1,
246n32; Holocaust and, 22–23; *La
Vie devant soi*, 4, 31, 135, 151–59,
247n36; *Les Racines du ciel*, 152
gastrointestinal tract, 66, 100, 166,
191, 204. *See also* digestion; digestive system
Gaullists, 136
Gautier, Théophile, 40
gay liberation movement, 174
gender, 27, 144, 172, 179, 181; human
rights and, 25–26; inequality of
care and, 31, 144–47; universalism
and, 24–25
Genet, Jean, 11, 163, 224n60, 238n5,
243n58; abjection and, 122,
241n41, 241n43; "Ce qui est resté
d'un Rembrandt . . . ," 29–30,
224n59; excrement and, 105–6,
120–33, 237n4; Genet material
and, 127–28, 132, 242n47, 242n50;
imprisonment of, 120–121; *Les*

Pompes funèbres, 242n49; *Miracle de
la rose,* 121; *Notre-Dame-des-Fleurs,* 4,
31, 107, 120, 124; as pariah, 105–6;
Sartre and, 105–6, 120, 132, 237n2,
238n6, 238n11
Germaine, in Sartre's *L'Enfance d'un
chef,* 116
Germans, 221n29. *See also* Nazis
Geulincx, Arnold, 90, 235n20
Gide, André, 30, 41, 122, 225n2
Gilligan, Carol, 144–46, 246n21
Giono, Jean: *Le Hussard sur le toit,* 30
Glaucon, 184, 249–50n27
Gobeil, Madeline, 238n6
God, 7, 122, 123
Godard, Henri, 41, 228n26, 229n37
gold and shit, 12, 44, 96, 102, 113. *See
also* alchemy; philosopher's stone
Goncourt prize, 152
Gorgui Seck, in Genet's *Notre-Dame-
des-Fleurs,* 126
Gouges, Olympe de, 26
Grainville, Patrick, 186
grandfathers, in Pennac's *Journal d'un
corps,* 188–89
Grégoire, in Pennac's *Journal d'un
corps,* 188–89
Grossman-Etoh, Amélie, 186
guano, 21
Guibert, Hervé, autofiction and
autobiography of, 194–98
gut, the, 2, 89, 217n3; emotions and,
229n41, 236n45; power of sight of,
100–101
Guthrie, Woody, 160
guts, in Céline's writings, 42

Haiti, 26
Hanrahan, Mairéad, 238n5, 242n50
Hartman, Geoffrey, 123
Hartman, Saidiya, 25

Harvey, C. J., 113
Harvey, Robert, 243n58
Haslanger, Sally, 248n13
Haussmannization, 222n34
Hawkins, Gay, 3
Hegel, Georg Wilhelm Friedrich, 30
Heidegger, Martin, 245n17
heterology, 9, 219n16
heterosexuality, 122, 164, 182, 183
hierarchy, 22, 167, 220n20, 221n28,
232n9; anti-, 35, 121; Beckett and,
96–98
HIV and AIDS, Guibert and, 194–97
Holocaust, 62, 78, 141, 159, 195,
221n26, 246n27; excrement and,
154, 245n11, 247n35; Gary and,
151–52; inhumanity of, 143, 147,
245n12; mass killings of, 22,
225n3. *See also* Nazis
homophobia, 228n29; in Garréta's
Dans l'béton, 167, 173, 247n9
homosexuality/homosexuals, 25, 121,
122, 248n11; in Sartre's *L'Enfance
d'un chef,* 113–16
horror/horrors, 12, 60, 62, 171,
197, 223n44, 229n37, 242n47; of
Holocaust, 139, 141
Huchet, Jean-Charles, 227n22
Hugo, Victor, 151; *Les Misérables,* 19,
20
human/humans, 54, 59, 111, 144, 150,
208; boundary of, 147–48; as fecal,
23, 125, 204
humanism, 65, 209; Gary's, 136, 152,
157, 158–59; nonhuman, 143,
245n15
humanitarianism, 173
humanity, 117, 130, 143, 208, 226n13;
shit and farts and, 4, 23–24, 160
human rights, 14–15; as exclusionary,
25–26

humor, 136, 163
Hunt, Lynn, 14
hybrid mode, of Genet, 124
hyperrealism, 62–63

ideas, 111
identitarianism, 13, 157, 221n28; anti-,
    14, 148
identity, 14, 22, 25, 27, 198, 204,
    224n60, 241–42n47
imaginary/imaginaries, 3, 74, 95, 211,
    222n34
immateriality, 8, 9, 71, 86, 90,
    242n50
imperialism, 207
impressionism, 71
impropre (the improper), 200–204
incarceration, 127
incest, 199
incontinence, 82, 114; in Gary's *La
    Vie devant soi,* 156, 247n36
inconvenience, defecation as, 50, 102
incrementalism, 51
inegalitarianism, 25, 28, 146, 181,
    208–11. *See also* egalitarianism;
    inequality
inequality, 50, 58, 146, 182, 210. *See
    also* hierarchy
inhumanity, 142, 143; of Holocaust,
    141, 245n12
inhumanness of Antelme's shit in
    Duras's "La Douleur," 137–41,
    143, 150
installment plan, 51
instinct, 143–44, 146, 246n22
intelligentsia, 136
interiority, 99, 202, 204
intersectionnalité (intersectionality), 174,
    248n14
ipseity, 159
Iser, Wolfgang, 198

James, Alison, 244n4
Jean, in Genet's *Les Pompes funèbres,*
    242n49
Jews, 24, 25, 151, 245n11. *See also*
    Holocaust
Joan of Arc, 188–89
Journal d'un corps (*Diary of a Body*)
    (Pennac), 32, 187, 204, 251n20; di-
    arrhea in, 4, 185, 251n20; fecal in,
    185, 203; narratives of, 187, 199;
    narrator of, 186–94, 198–99, 204;
    originary scene in, 185–86, 189,
    193–94, 201, 205, 250n1, 251n20
joy, 237n46; excrement and, 96, 98, 101
Joyce, James, 79
July, Miranda, 132
Jung, Carl, 77, 93

Kant, Immanuel, 77
Kaplan, Alice, 42, 68, 228n34
Kawa, Nicholas, 217n5
Kim, Annabel L.: *Unbecoming
    Language,* 221n28, 231n56, 247n1
King James Bible, 227n17
kinship, 174; heterosexual, 167, 183
Kristeva, Julia, 227n22; abjection and,
    148, 221n25; on Antelme's shit
    in in Duras's "La Douleur," 143,
    148; *Pouvoirs de l'horreur* (*Powers of
    Horror*), 12–13, 41–42, 143; psycho-
    analysis and, 5, 221n26, 225n6

Lacan, Jacques, 77, 249n17
Laclau, Ernesto, 223n47
La Douleur (*War*) (Duras), 4, 31,
    135–36, 142, 244n2; Bray's transla-
    tion of, 138–39, 244n5, 244n8
"La Douleur" ("War") (Duras):
    mistranslations in, 137–39; preface
    to, 136–37, 141, 244n2; shit in,
    137–43, 150